APR 0 9 2021

D0801522

Praise for
Overcoming Hate through Dialogue

"The bravest woman in Denmark goes on a beautiful
mission of bridge-building by sitting down for coffee
with those who are seething in anger."
—*Danske Kommuner*

"If you think this project and book title sound sentimental and
touchy-feely, keep reading. You'll soon be applauding the writer. The
writer's enormous emotional investment in humanity is made evident
by well-written passages which reveal the strength of the book and its
greatest accomplishment: giving a familiar face to those who hate."
—*Dagbladet Information*

"In this truly democratic and engaging book, the writer is
on a mission to inspire others to open dialogue with those
whom they disagree with—or maybe even despise."
—*Weekendavisen*

"This brilliant and well-researched book ought to be required
reading for anyone interested in conflict resolution; it
gives nuance to an otherwise stale-mated debate."
—*Journalisten*

"I was honestly inspired at how Cekic, all by herself,
faces down men who have lobbed threats at her."
—*Avisen*

"Cekic reports on the fringe elements of hatred, powerlessness
and anger. The result is a unique tour guide into the depths
of the darker sides of society, where the lack of empathy and
solidarity fosters racism, prejudice and fury. As a bridge-builder,
Cekic is refreshing; as a writer, she's surprisingly brilliant."
—*Politiken*

OVERCOMING
HATE
THROUGH
DIALOGUE

OVERCOMING HATE THROUGH DIALOGUE

Confronting Prejudice, Racism, and Bigotry
with **Conversation—and Coffee**

ÖZLEM SARA CEKIC
Translated by Logan Masterworks

Mango Publishing
CORAL GABLES

Cover Design: Roberto Nunez
Cover Photo: Robin Skjoldborg
Author Photo: Tina Rossing
Layout & Design: Carmen Fortunato

For permission requests, please contact the publisher at:
Mango Publishing Group
2850 S Douglas Road, 2nd Floor
Coral Gables, FL 33134 USA
info@mango.bz

For special orders, quantity sales, course adoptions and corporate sales, please email the publisher at sales@mango.bz. For trade and wholesale sales, please contact Ingram Publisher Services at customer.service@ingramcontent.com or +1.800.509.4887.

Overcoming Hate through Dialogue: Confronting Prejudice, Racism, and Bigotry with Conversation—and Coffee

Library of Congress Cataloging-in-Publication number: 2020940938
ISBN: (print) 978-1-64250-376-0, (ebook) 978-1-64250-377-7
BISAC category code SOC031000, SOCIAL SCIENCE / Discrimination & Race Relations

Printed in the United States of America

I dedicate this book to Finn Norgaard, who was attending an event celebrating freedom of expression at the Krudttonden Cultural Center on February 14, 2015, and to Dan Uzan, a volunteer guard who, on the same day, stood in front of the synagogue in Krystalgade, where a young Jewish girl was celebrating her bat mitzvah.

Both Finn and Dan fell victim to the lack of democratic dialogue in Denmark, losing their lives during the terrorist attack in Copenhagen.

I want to honor their memory.

TABLE OF CONTENTS

CHAPTER 1

WHY DO THEY HATE YOU?...10

CHAPTER 2

HOW I HATED THE DANES...20

CHAPTER 3

IT'S ALL THEIR FAULT...30

CHAPTER 4

GIVE THE DANES A TASTE OF THEIR OWN MEDICINE.................78

CHAPTER 5

THE SMELL OF HIZB UT-TAHRIR'S BAKERY.........................102

CHAPTER 6

BETWEEN EXTREMES...130

CHAPTER 7

CONSISTENT CHRISTIANITY...164

CHAPTER 8

WHERE DIALOGUE STOPS, VIOLENCE TAKES OVER.................198

CHAPTER 9

IS THERE A POINT?...250

ACKNOWLEDGMENTS...273

ABOUT THE AUTHOR...277

CHAPTER 1

WHY DO THEY HATE YOU?

"Learn from yesterday, live for today, hope for tomorrow. The important thing is not to stop questioning."

—Albert Einstein

As a Turkish immigrant born to Kurdish parents, I became one of the first ethnic minority women to win a seat in the Danish Parliament in 2007. It was also the year I began receiving hate mail. It's amazing how quickly I got used to finding my inbox full of hate.

"What's a Paki like you doing in our parliament?" they'd write. "You don't belong here!" Or simply, "Terrorist."

Delete. Delete. Delete. I never even considered replying. We had absolutely nothing in common; they didn't understand me, and I didn't understand them. As far as I was concerned, engaging with anyone so entrenched in their own ignorance would have been a complete waste of time and effort.

Then, one day, my colleague suggested I should save these messages. "If nothing else," she said, "they'll be useful to the police when something happens to you." I noted that she said "when" something happens, not "if."

Though I didn't really believe it would come to that, I took her advice and started saving every email that arrived. For a while, they were simply filed and forgotten. That is, until things took a more worrying turn. In 2008, I returned from my summer vacation to find a card in my mailbox. It was decorated with the Danish flag, and since, in Denmark, we use the flag to mark any festive occasion, my first thought was that it must be a party invitation.

But inside was something rather different. "Return tickets home. Go back to your terrorist brothers." These greetings had come from the Danish Association—an organization with deep roots in Denmark's extreme right. That they knew my address was frightening enough. But when I examined the envelope, I saw, to my horror, that there was no stamp. It hadn't arrived by post; it had been delivered by hand.

In my mind, that changed everything. The reassuring distance I thought I'd established between me and my abusers—between my kids and my abusers—had suddenly evaporated. Whoever these people were, they were too close for comfort now.

Immediately, I took steps to remove my address from public records. I made sure that the names of my children's daycare and schools were not publicly available either. But, at the same time, I knew that the more involved I became in parliamentary debates, the more I would attract this kind of attention, and the steadier the stream of threats and abuse would become.

These threats ranged from the vague ("We know where you live") to the terrifyingly specific ("The day you become a minister, we will cut your throat"). I received them; I read them; I passed them all on to the police. This became my new normal.

But in the spring of 2010, a neo-Nazi began to harass me. I couldn't dismiss his actions as an idle threat to my safety. This was a man who had previously attacked Muslim women in the street. For more than eight months, he called me day and night—sometimes upwards of forty times a day. I had become his obsession.

One day, while I visited the zoo with my kids, my phone rang. I ignored it, certain it was him. We had just arrived and had only gotten as far as the lions' den. I was determined not to allow him to ruin our day. But when I saw his text, I panicked.

Convinced that he was at the zoo—and that he was watching us—we got out of there fast.

When we were back at home, my son Furkan asked, "Mum, why does he hate you so much, when he doesn't even know you?"

I told him, "Some people are just stupid." At the time, I thought that was a pretty clever answer. "We're the good guys. They're the bad guys. That's all you need to know."

But how I wish it were that simple. The truth was this man had upended my life. He was the reason I parked my car in a different spot every night when I came home; the reason I constantly looked over my shoulder in the street; the reason I could no longer enjoy a day out with my children.

Several weeks after the incident at the zoo, I confided in my photographer friend, Jacob Holdt. Jacob had documented racism in the United States in his book *American Pictures,* so I was sure he was the right shoulder to cry on.

Tearfully, I told him my fears, and about the fury I felt over the restrictions this neo-Nazi idiot's behavior had created in my daily life. I waited for words of comfort and reassurance. Instead, his response knocked me sideways.

"You're just as judgmental of people like them as they are of people like you," he said.

I was stunned. I'm no racist! Is that what he was accusing me of? Sure, if I were to be totally honest, there had been times in my life when I had hated other people. Certain groups, who, I knew, hated me right back. But I had grown into an open-minded, liberal human being, right? I'd put it all behind me. Hadn't I?

"How many of your friends and family vote for right-wing parties?" he asked. "Do you even talk to people who do?"

I had to admit it: None. And no.

In fact, for a long time, this had been a source of pride for me. I often boasted to my friends that I never shook hands with MPs from the alt-right Danish People's Party. I was proud of the distance I had created between myself and them. I never questioned whether I was right in doing so, until Jacob suggested, "Go out and meet them. Your son deserves a better answer."

"Meet them?! They'd kill me!" I said.

"They don't kill MPs," Jacob said, before adding with a wry smile, "In any case, if they do, you'll be a martyr. Win-win."

I can't say that I found the prospect of martyrdom very reassuring at that point. But Jacob had planted the seed of an idea. So when, in the autumn of that year, the police tracked down the man who had been hounding me, I took a deep breath and suggested a mediation meeting. He refused, but I wasn't giving up.

It was clear to me that ignoring hate didn't simply make it disappear. I had to understand it better—I had to know why so many people hate Danish Muslims like me—and the obvious place to start was my inbox.

There were, by then, hundreds of emails. Several had come from the same handful of senders. Most began by addressing me as "Paki," "terrorist," "Muslim rat," or "whore." When it comes to insults, the Danish language is wonderfully diverse. I decided to contact a few of the people who'd emailed me.

My aim was not so much to get to know them, as Jacob had suggested, as it was to convert them to righteousness. I'm not sure what sort of miracle I imagined would occur when my haters finally came face-to-face with a Muslim. Perhaps I hoped that, by confronting them with their own prejudices, I could somehow cure them of making these baseless generalizations about us. I wanted to be a paragon of virtue: living proof that there are Muslims who work, abide by the law, and support democracy.

Today, I can see this as delusional. But back then, at the start of all this, I saw myself as a savior on a mission. Armed with a sense of justice, I sat down to type, and, before I knew it, I was inviting myself for a visit. And that's how the coffee dialogues began, and how, since the winter of 2010, I have sought out coffee and conversation with people I know harbor hatred toward me and people like me.

What began with that email has led to hundreds of encounters. Each one is another step toward understanding prejudice—my own, as well as theirs. Over time, I've given up on being a savior. I've learned not to try to convince people of anything, or to attempt to make them "good." Instead, I just listen—and try to discover where their feelings of impotence, fear, and hatred originate.

I've discovered that, no matter how abusive a person may be, they still serve cake with their coffee. And every time I begin a dialogue with coffee and cake on the table, I'm reminded of how right Jacob was when he told me I needed to confront my own racism.

The first of these meetings was with Ingolf, and I will never forget it. His email was brimming with bile. "All you care about is taking whatever you can for yourself and your kind," he wrote.

In my imagination, Ingolf was the embodiment of hatred: hard, nasty, and twisted. Before we met, I imagined the moment I would shake his hand, with its long, dirty fingernails, and enter his pigsty of a home. So imagine my disappointment when he opened his door and revealed himself to be a perfectly respectable-looking gentleman. He served coffee in the same coffee set that my parents have at home.

As expected, our conversation revealed that we disagreed on many things. Ingolf's views on Danish Muslims were extreme. Among other things, he had helped found Radio Holger, a radio station that caters to a neo-Nazi audience.

But we also had a lot in common. We shared the same type of working-class background, and even some of the same prejudices. I remember Ingolf telling me how angry he got whenever a "raghead" bus driver stopped ten meters away from where he was waiting at the bus stop. Immediately, I recognized that feeling. I told him that, when I was younger, if a bus didn't stop for me, I was sure that the driver was a racist. It struck me then that what we believe to be conscious acts of malice are often just innocent mistakes.

It was a shock to me that Ingolf could possibly feel as discriminated against as I did. But he did. Listening to him, I had to confront my own judgments. He was neither evil nor stupid. He was angry.

My meeting with him was the first of many meetings with racists, which turned into a reevaluation of my own preconceptions, interpretations, and generalizations. I have been surprised by how much I have found in common with the people I have visited—and the extent of my own racist prejudice.

I use the word "racist" in a broad sense. To me, a racist is someone with hateful prejudice against another demographic group, characterized by their race, religion, ethnicity, sexuality, gender, or age. In that sense, I know, I have been a racist.

As a child, I hated Jews. I never voiced the feeling, but when I saw pictures of murdered Palestinian children, I hated Jews—all Jews. Later, as a teenager, I was spat on in the street for wearing the hijab. In those moments, whenever I was on the receiving end of the hatred that one Dane felt toward all Muslims, I responded in kind, and began hating all Danes, believing them to be uniformly racist.

In the late 1990s—when the conflict between the Turks and the Kurds intensified—as an assimilated Kurd, ashamed by my inability to speak Kurdish, I was filled with loathing for the nationalist Turks. But meeting them, talking to them, and getting to know them personally helped this hatred melt away. I may still disagree with some of them politically, but the hatred is gone.

I confess that there was still one group for whom my hatred never waned, even as an adult: racists. Those who accused me and my family of being parasites, criminals, and fundamentalists; those who thought that, even though my children were born at the National Hospital and grew up in Denmark, they would never be Danes. For many years, I saw myself as superior to them, because I didn't judge them based on their religion, ethnicity, sexuality, gender, or age.

I was convinced that I was an open-minded person who treated everyone as an equal. That is, until I reached out to some racists, sought to understand them, and in doing so grew wiser about them, about myself, and most of all, about the things we share.

Building Bridges

This book tries to give my son's question—why do people hate people they don't know?—a more qualified answer than the one I offered him after our trip to the zoo. This book will take you with me into meetings with people who hate, fear, or feel threatened by other population groups; people whom many would shun; people whose arguments are ignored because they are difficult to accommodate and painful to countenance. And it asks: Is it possible to build a bridge over hate?

At all my coffee dialogues, there is one particular argument that emerges repeatedly, regardless of whether I am talking to a humanist or a racist. It is that someone else is always to blame for the divisiveness and discord, and that it is, therefore, their duty to rectify it: Parliament must do something; local government must do something; schools must do something; your neighbor must do something.

Only rarely do people say that they themselves must do something. But I feel that each and every one of us has to do something to support democracy. I believe we do this best by insisting on dialogue where there is disagreement, and history has shown that to be an effective means of building a better future.

Over one hundred years ago, women did not have the right to vote. Only forty-four years ago, abortion was illegal in Denmark. Only thirty-six years ago, many Danes believed that homosexuality was a disease. And it was only twenty years ago that corporal punishment of children became illegal.

Things have changed—because there were people who insisted that attitudes and legislation could be altered through debate. But the road to understanding is not paved by ignoring attitudes we dislike or by silencing others' points of view.

The distances between people seem to have grown wider. Extremists— both to the right and to the left—are increasingly influential. Abusive language is rampant on social media, and people readily label one another racists, traitors, or worse. Unfortunately, I get the impression that politicians exacerbate this situation all too often, with both wings competing to demonize their opponents.

Extremism must be opposed. But the solution isn't to meet hatred with more hatred or to imitate the hate speech of others. In order to understand the origins of other people's feelings of hopelessness, frustration, and sometimes seething hatred, we must listen to one another.

In this book, I invite you to join me as I visit people who loathe entire segments of the population. You'll meet Kim, a right-wing extremist, who lives in an allotment garden house on the island of Funen, and who—if he only had a gun—would take delight in killing the Muslims outside the local mosque. You'll meet Muslim adolescents with guns on Norrebro's Red Square, whose contempt for Danish society runs deep. I'll take you into the Hizb ut-Tahrir mosque, where the imam preaches against democracy and homosexuality. And along the way, I will also share my own history of hatred for Jews, Turks, Danes, and racists.

Finally, a small plea: Some of the people you will encounter, and some of the discussions you will read about in these pages, will put your fundamental values to the test. But I hope you will stay with me, even when you find it hard to bear.

CHAPTER 2

HOW I HATED THE DANES

"No one is born hating another person because of the color of his skin, or his background or his religion. People must learn to hate, and if they can learn to hate, they can be taught to love, for love comes more naturally to the human heart than its opposite."

–Nelson Mandela

Hatred of other ethnic groups is often ignited by personal experience. My own hatred of ethnic Danes began when I was twelve years old. It was summertime, and I had gone to town, wearing jeans and a hijab. Far from being a symbol of my oppression, as many non-Muslims are quick to assume, the hijab was, to me, a symbol of youthful rebellion.

My parents are devout, but when I suddenly started covering my hair with a hijab, my mother couldn't understand why. She wears a hijab herself and has been on pilgrimages—but if you ask her why she does it, she will simply say that it's part of her culture. In the Vesterbro district of Copenhagen, my upbringing was rather different from hers, culturally speaking. None of my friends wore the hijab which, I suspect, is why she could make no sense of my decision. But the truth was, I needed to shift people's focus away from my manner of speech. I had recently returned to Denmark after a two-year stay in Turkey and wanted my classmates to fixate on something other than the faults in my Danish grammar and pronunciation. I found the fact that the hijab irked my parents so much to be an amusing secondary benefit.

When my father attended a parents' meeting, my teacher gave him a long lecture about how he shouldn't force me to wear it. Since my father's Danish was not very good, I was asked to interpret—but he understood well enough to scold me all the way home for giving the impression he had forced me into covering up. I just thought it was funny. But when the other girls at school decided they thought it was cool to wear the hijab, I stopped wearing mine. Now that I was no longer the mysterious hijab girl, it had stopped being fun. But during the two years I wore it, I learned how many people see it as a provocation. The experience came at a cost.

At age twelve, as I walked alone into town, I saw a young man walking toward me. I remember he was tall, slim, and dressed in black. As we made eye contact, I saw that he was moving his mouth in an odd way.

I wondered if he might speak. Then, just as we were about to pass one another, he lunged and spat at me.

I froze. I couldn't even turn my head to say something, because there, hanging on the edge of my hijab, was a huge gob of spit threatening to swing toward my face.

So I stood there in the street, with my head bowed, hoping that gravity would eventually deal with the worst of it. With no tissues to hand, I waited and waited, and the gob of spit grew longer and longer—but stubbornly refused to drop to the ground. As I stood there, people walked past me as if I were invisible.

I could have taken the hijab off, but I didn't even contemplate it. I knew the hijab was the reason he'd spat at me in the first place. Removing it would mean capitulation, defeat.

I did, however, have to accept that the gob of spit was not going to fall of its own accord, so I flicked it off with my hand. As soon as I touched it, my lunch rose up my throat, my mouth filled with vomit. I threw up, then continued to retch for several minutes in the street. Strangely, it brought some kind of relief to purge myself like that. Before I turned around and began my walk back home, I took a bottle of water from my bag and washed my hands and mouth, then poured the rest over my hijab. For several years, I suppressed my memories of that day. The humiliation and degradation I felt, looking back, was too much to bear. Yet, in the moment, I remember feeling almost nothing—no anger, no vulnerability, no frustration. Nothing, except terrible nausea.

I guess I took my numbness as proof that he hadn't hurt me. I believed I was unaffected. But not long after, when an elderly man tried to pull off my hijab as I crossed the road at a crosswalk, I reacted with such fury that I don't doubt I had been bottling up my true feelings about the attack.

As I walked, again alone, across the intersection, I felt him take hold of my hijab from behind and yank me backward. I was about to fall on my back, when he pulled me upright again. Yelling and screaming at him, I stomped onto the traffic island—people must have thought I was having a hysterical fit—and began screaming at him, "Racist! Racist! Racist! Danish racist!"

Those were the words that flew out of my mouth, and from that moment on, I saw Danes differently. I began to notice all their small, everyday microaggressions. The more racist encounters I experienced, the more I became convinced that all Danes were racists.

In hindsight, I realize that some incidents reflected my own prejudices more than anyone else's. Like when some Danish guy at the supermarket checkout snapped at my mother for trying to buy twenty packs of sale-price butter when there was a five-packs-per-customer limit. Sure thing, I thought. Clearly, he was racist too.

But woven between incidents I perceived as racist were examples of genuine discrimination. Like when my mum was standing in a phone booth, calling her sister in Turkey, and a man in line screamed, "Speak Danish, dammit!" right in her face. They'd never met before, yet he still felt he had the right to yell at her, and even dictate the language she should speak.

The number of racists surrounding me grew. I started seeing them everywhere, and, at one point, I found it almost impossible to distinguish a tolerant Dane from a racist Dane. It became so difficult that I conflated one with the other. Both were my enemies. And so it was that I began to hate the Danes.

I hated them because they were xenophobic and full of generalizations. I hated them because they hated me, my family, and all Muslims. But I also hated them because they wanted to make us change. There was no satisfying them. Ever.

There was always something they felt they needed to criticize. Take Ramadan. I have always fasted during Ramadan and love the tranquility and contemplation that come with it. For me, Ramadan is the coziest, most comforting time of the year, and I look forward to it like a child anticipating Christmas.

But Ramadan isn't Christmas—and the teachers at my school rarely said anything positive about it. Instead, they asked a lot of critical questions like, "Isn't it tough?" "Isn't it very unhealthy?" "Do your parents force you to fast?" and "How can you stand it?" And when the month of Ramadan ended with a three-day feast, my teachers seldom asked what gifts I'd received, or complimented me on my new clothes. At school, we had to spend hours talking about Christmas, but Eid al-Fitr was sidelined.

"That's because they're racists," we Muslim students agreed at breaktime. "If we were Christians, they'd love us to talk about the food and the presents."

So, from very early on, I was convinced that this was how it was. We were different, and we were not a part of Danish society. To Danes, the community I belonged to was abnormal. But to me, it was the most natural thing in the world.

Even back then, I was aware of this pervasive notion of "normality," and I bristled at the idea of someone else deciding what was normal and abnormal. But my anger toward my teachers was essentially born of envy. I envied other children who could discuss Christmas with joy, without the fear of being accused of strangeness or otherness. For weeks, we counted down the days to Christmas Eve. There was an advent calendar in class, and stories about elves in our schoolbooks. It was fun! I always enjoyed December.

I used to long for Ramadan to coincide with Christmas, so that we Muslims could feel a part of all the festivities and the coziness. Ramadan moves ten days forward every year, and I remember sitting in the schoolyard with a calendar trying to figure out how many years would pass before Christmas and Ramadan overlapped: Fourteen! It is hopeless, I thought.

To hell with it all, I thought. They can stick their Christmas where the sun don't shine, and I can fast as I please. We don't have anything in common, and we never will. During my teens, I was proud that I wasn't a Dane, and I immediately corrected adults who referred to me as Danish. I was a Muslim, and I was a Kurd. My insistence on a strong Kurdish identity was difficult for my father, as he was never a nationalist. But I didn't want to be part of the racist, self-absorbed, infidel Danish community.

Back then, I lived with my parents in the Vesterbro district of Copenhagen. It was the 1990s, before urban renewal. At that time, rents in Vesterbro were reasonable, and students, workers, poor people, and academics lived side by side. I blended right in. My family and I were simply one more set of misfits in the misfit district. Many of my classmates' parents were ill, unemployed, or on welfare. Some received disability benefits, and others dreamed of getting it.

My mother was one of them. Physically worn out by her many unskilled jobs, she was in pain twenty-four hours a day. In class, we all kept abreast of our parents' applications for early retirement. When a Danish parent was given disability support, it was a topic of debate. "Wallah, my mum has been applying for that for ten years," one of the boys complained.

I said, "Social workers are racists!"

In class, we called each other the losers' kids. The probability of any of us ever putting "lawyer" or "scientist" on our résumé was small. "Pizza delivery guy" or "cleaner" was a safer bet. My mother and father both worked as cleaners.

My mother was a community-care cleaner. Sometimes the elderly people she was supposed to clean for wouldn't let her in, because they didn't want an "immigrant" or a "black pig" cleaning for them.

Afraid she would be fired, my mother would wait in front of their door for the allotted period, ringing the bell intermittently, so that she could report back to her boss that she had been refused entry despite repeated attempts. But there was no need for that, as the boss often called her, after receiving "black pig" complaints, to tell her she needn't wait, as they'd be sending a native Dane there in the future.

My mum was a really good cleaner, but her appearance, ethnicity, and skin color set her apart. I started to worry about what some of the elderly people might do to her and feared for her safety. In response, she stopped telling me about her experiences.

The feeling of being excluded from Danish society drove me toward a more radical interpretation of Islam. I began refusing to shake hands with men. My mum and dad were so annoyed about this that eventually my mum banned me from entering the living room when we had guests. My behavior was embarrassing, so they relegated me to the kitchen to make coffee and tea.

It was around that time that I began attending the Turkish mosque on Vesterbrogade more frequently. One day, a young man I met there handed me some books. Since I had few friends at school, and no hobbies to speak of, I had plenty of time to read. Over the course of a few evenings, I devoured the books he lent me, and soon went back for more. I felt as if every page I turned switched on a lightbulb in my mind. Ideas I had struggled my whole life to explain became suddenly clearer and simpler.

I began to reason this way: The Danes don't like us because we are Muslims. The Danes belong to the West, and the West hates Muslims. A real Muslim would not befriend these infidels; a real Muslim would fight them.

I didn't realize it at the time, but this was my crash course in jihad.

I read that the West had destroyed Afghanistan through repeated invasions—and all because the Afghans were Muslims. I read about my Muslim sisters and brothers who fought against the West, those who stood up against the pervasive objectification of women by lecherous Western men; those who fought against the influx of the drug trade which gave rise to violence and sexual abuse, destroying lives, families, and communities; those who fought against financial interests that wrecked social equity and enabled the rich to get richer as the poor grew poorer. It all seemed to add up.

I saw myself in a new, brighter light. My life was hard, and I was a victim—because I was a Muslim. It was time to take back control of my own life, and break the shackles I'd grown used to living in. These books described a free community, and I wanted, more than anything, to belong to it. Danish society had rejected me, but there were others—stronger and more powerful—waiting to embrace me.

A plan formed in my head. I began saving up for a flight to Afghanistan, where I'd join the fight against the West, alongside my Muslim brothers and sisters. I told no one about my plans until, one day, I chose to share them with my imam. He listened without interruption to my long rant against the West and the Danes. He nodded throughout, giving the impression of agreement, and so, feeling safe, I pulled no punches.

I told him I was sick of my parents thinking I was too extreme, sick of my mother refusing to segregate our guests by gender, and sick of my father watching half-naked belly dancers on tacky Turkish TV shows. Come to think of it, I was sick of half-naked women on the streets of Denmark. I was sick of racists, and sick of Danes. I wanted to leave, and fight for a better world with my Muslim brothers and sisters. I wanted to play my part in the holy war. I wanted to claim my freedom!

When I finished my speech, the imam took a deep breath. Then he asked me why I thought that Pakistan, Turkey, Saudi Arabia, Iran, and other Muslim countries did not help Afghanistan. I was completely speechless. He went on to ask, "Why are the Saudis cooperating with the United States, and why are Muslim countries constantly at war with each other, if the only enemy is the West?"

Over the following days, I had more conversations and discussions with the imam. He asked where I had gotten my ideas from, and I told him about the books I'd been given. He gave me new books. Books about how to become a good Muslim, why we must not kill innocent people, and why we must adapt to the country in which we live. "You must first and foremost be loyal to the country that feeds you," he said.

Shortly after this, I got a job in the shoe department of the Fotex supermarket. I started with a week's internship, but then I pulled myself together and asked my boss, Anne, if I could have a regular job. This is how I gave up my plans of martyrdom in Afghanistan and started working in Fotex, even though my Danish was terrible.

My boss and I spent many hours together, pairing shoes in the basement or putting new items on the shelves. Anne wasn't like the other Danes. She was friendly, cute, and very affectionate. So were the other bosses at Fotex. In fact, so were the other employees. There was a strong sense of fellowship, and I soon became part of it. I grew more fluent in Danish, and I made Danish friends. I even kissed a bottle boy once, because he said Muslim girls didn't dare kiss.

As I got to know the Danes, I discovered that they were as varied as the Kurds. Some believed in God, and others didn't. Some had a boyfriend, and others didn't. Some liked immigrant customers because they bought so much in the sales—while I was annoyed with them, because they never put the clothes back neatly. At Fotex, I discovered that some Danes were racists, but most were not.

The reason I didn't get stuck in my hatred of Danes was that I met people who upended my incoherent analyzes of who and what they were. These people gave me a more balanced viewpoint and invited me to join the democratic community. Together, Anne from Fotex, the imam from the mosque, and many other kindred spirits I encountered provided a strong antidote to my own racism.

Overcoming Hate Through Dialogue

Racism, hatred, impotence, and frustration exist in all ethnic groups, and in all social classes. But why and how and from whom do these emotions originate? And can we do anything about it, or is it naïve to believe that democratic conversation and friendships can build bridges?

CHAPTER 3

IT'S ALL THEIR FAULT

"Hate the sin, love the sinner."

–Mahatma Gandhi

I am on a train to Funen to visit three men, all of whom have sent me emails abusing Muslims. Kim believes that Muslims are the root of all evil, and that the answer to the problems they have caused is a machine gun. Angelo is convinced that Muslims will take over Denmark, and that their sick religion will destroy all that is good. Jimmy is more worried about all the special rules he believes Muslims insist on.

A tradesman is sitting opposite me. His big shoes are dusty, and his stained shirt is covered with holes. It's morning, and he's grasping a beer. He's fast asleep. Diagonally opposite me, a young couple is locked in an endless kiss. There are so many kinds of Danes. Imagine if everyone believed that Muslims were just as diverse.

Although we have our faith in common, Danish Muslims believe in Allah in a variety of ways. We have roots in many different cultures. Some of us are from the Middle East, others from Copenhagen. But the people I will be visiting today don't acknowledge this diversity. To them, I, and everyone who looks like me, belong in a single box.

Jimmy is the first person I'll be visiting. He agreed to meet with me on the condition that his wife Lone could be there too. This reminds me of my very first coffee meeting, when Ingolf wanted to make sure his wife Bente was present when I visited. It is interesting that the men, who write to me in such abusive and uncompromising language, only want to meet with me if their wives can be there too. The thought makes me smile. As much as I'm saddened by their offensive language, it's touching that they want our conversation to include their wives. It makes them more human.

My father uses abusive language too, at times. He is often convinced that he is right, and it is very difficult to change his views. But when he meets strangers or visits friends and acquaintances, his self-confidence often evaporates, and he wants my mother by his side—to provide him with a feeling of security, I think. So it's something I recognize: a hard exterior, which belies the soft interior; a human being with whom I strongly disagree, but who may not be so very different from my own father.

My cell phone vibrates. It is another text from Angelo. He is afraid that I might cancel our appointment.

"I'll text you back," I reply.

Angelo has sent me quite a few such messages. And I must admit that the idea of calling it off has crossed my mind a few times. I don't know if I'm wary of meeting him because he uses very sexual language and comes across as condescending and racist—or whether it's because his messages give the impression that he mistrusts me. It's probably a little of both. I look out the window. The landscape is idyllic—high skies, green fields, and small houses. It's easy to understand why many foreigners see Denmark as a fairytale country.

When my relatives from Turkey visit Denmark, they are surprised by how well everything functions—from orderly traffic and queueing to fundamental respect between people. As a politician, I receive fellow politicians from the Middle East, Eastern Europe, and Africa. Their eyes shine with hope when I tell them about our democracy and our collaborative parliamentary system, where we argue verbally, but eschew physical force. But at the same time, some of them say despairingly, "It is naively utopian to believe that our country could ever become such a wonderland."

In many ways, Denmark is a wonderland. We trust each other, which is probably why we confidently—and to the great surprise of foreigners—dare to leave our babies in their prams outside when we enter shops.

My old grandmother, a farmer's wife who left her Turkish village for the first time to visit us in Denmark, was excited by the amount of rain. "God must really love you very much, since it rains so much," she said.

I wasn't born in Denmark, but I will be buried here. All three of my children were born at the National Hospital, and Danish is their mother tongue. Sometimes, I remember to speak Turkish to them, but it's difficult since they speak Danish to each other, and my husband also favors Danish. I would love my children to speak Turkish, so they could talk to their grandparents—but at the same time, I am proud of them. When they use a typical Danish phrase with a Copenhagen accent, something inside me settles into place.

I love Denmark.

I love nature.

I love the sea, and I love democracy.

But I can't help thinking about why we Danes hate each other so much, despite the harmony. Or, rather, fear each other. This is perhaps both milder and more apt. I think that it makes a difference that we meet to discuss our differences, although it also is incredibly tough to listen to all the anger, hatred, and despair directed at Danish Muslims.

When I started my coffee project, my primary agenda was to meet with people who don't like Muslims, and to make them "good again." I sincerely thought that, if people were racist, it was because they hadn't met any Muslims. If they only met me, and heard all my good arguments, then they'd be reformed. I was the savior, and I was quite impressed with myself for meeting these people.

As I write these lines, I can't help laughing at myself. I must admit to having been pretty naïve. Today, I am just grateful that people who have such strong views about Muslims are willing to set aside the time to meet and talk. And I like listening—not in order to persuade, but more to examine and understand where their feelings of powerlessness, frustration, and anger originate.

Floating Voters

Jimmy and Lone live in a red-brick detached house with tulips by the entrance and a large, freshly-cut lawn. To the left of the house sits the family caravan.

I ring the bell.

When Lone opens the door, she reprimands the tiny dog jumping up at me, and invites me in. Jimmy sits in the living room. He is a large man. He tries to get up to shake hands, but he says that he has been injured and has trouble walking. The coffee table is laid out with a selection of white bread, cheese, and pastries.

Lone, like Jimmy, is on sick leave and at home after a fall that broke her shoulder. Jimmy has injured his back. The doctor has examined him and ordered a scan that will be performed in two months' time. We talk at length about health care, the lack of ambulance services in Southern Denmark, and the injustice of some people having private insurance, which enables them to jump to the head of the line for treatment. Jimmy gets angry when he talks about it. His face is serious, and his big hands give me the impression that I am sitting opposite a man who has worked tough jobs all his life.

Jimmy confirms my guess. Worn out at sixty, he has done just about every kind of manual work. "I have been a trash collector. I've worked as a carpenter and a mason. Farming, the lot. But I have never worked in the same place for long. Unlike Lone. She's worked the same job twenty-five years," says Jimmy. "Me and Lone, we've worked like slaves," he says, pride in his voice. They are homeowners, and virtually all of their savings have been used to pay the mortgage on the little red-brick house.

It is obvious that everyday life has sometimes been tough on them. But they are also proud to have managed on their own, and that they've taught their two children the importance of saving, rather than borrowing, when they want to buy something. We are very much in agreement when we talk about the deterioration of the welfare state, politicians, tax havens, and the folly of spending thirty billion kroner (four billion US dollars) on new fighter aircrafts. Suddenly he looks at me and says, "But I have respect for you. Because you stood firm when they tried to shake you from your position!"

He is talking about the tax reform, which gave enormous tax cuts to the billionaires by taking money from people on early retirement and cash assistance. When it was presented by the coalition government that included my former party, and later, when it came to the vote in parliament, I opposed it, despite the great personal and political consequences I would face. The party leadership deprived me of all my posts as political spokesman, and although some people believe that it was brave of me to defy the party line and the government, I was disappointed with the outcome. I could not prevent the tax reform from being adopted.

Not only that, I succumbed to stress as a result.

Jimmy is well acquainted with these events. I think he can see that it makes me unhappy. So he does exactly what my own father would do. He shows his sympathy by getting angry. He no longer believes in politicians. "They propose a hell of a lot of improvements in their manifestos and shove their fancy dreams down your throat! Then, once they're elected, they go straight to parliament, and do the opposite of what they promised. MPs should be fired if they renege on what they promised in their election campaigns. The same applies to politicians who switch parties," he says.

It dawns on me that I'm sitting across from someone who feels politically homeless. I am in his living room, on the leather couch, with the dog to my left and his wife Lone sitting opposite. And I feel the same. I feel just as homeless as Jimmy. After eight years of battling in parliament, I lost confidence in the system when my party agreed to a series of reforms which they knew would increase inequality and weaken democracy. When I spoke out against them, I was bullied and frozen out. It wasn't just my former political party that let me down. The worst disappointment came from seeing what many politicians were prepared to do for their own gain. Today, like Jimmy, I have no idea whom to vote for in the next election.

Although we have agreed on pretty much everything we've been talking about, I am conscious that it is not because of our like-mindedness that I am here. It seems hard for us to get started on what divides us. For my part, it has largely to do with wanting to hold onto the feeling that Jimmy and I are in sympathy. But I know our agreement will dissipate the moment I mention the word "Muslim." After almost two hours of beating around the bush, I finally summon the courage.

"But tax cuts for the rich aren't the reason I'm sitting in your living room—it's your attitude toward Muslims," I say.

"I believe that we should keep what is Danish, and what is Denmark. Because Denmark is a great country," Jimmy responds.

I nod. So far, I agree.

"I often think about why people come here and bring their bad stuff with them. If they don't want to change, why don't they just choose another country?" asks Jimmy.

I'm often asked this question, and I'm never sure if the questioner actually expects me to have an answer. "Who are *they*, and what is the bad stuff?" I ask in return.

Now Lone speaks. "We Danes are too stupid. I know full well why they do it. It's because we are so accepting and accommodating that they take advantage of us."

When I ask them whether they feel that Muslims have taken over Denmark, both Jimmy and Lone confirm that they do.

I sigh. I would like to add nuance to Jimmy and Lone's perspective on Muslims. I'd like our discussion to be based on their specific experiences with Muslims. I'd like examples. I know it will be a struggle, and I am not sure I'll succeed. But it is worth a try. I ask them to give examples that illustrate the Muslim takeover. I prepare myself for discussion of the individual topics that have preoccupied the media over the last six months.

The first topic is the waiting list for housing. Lone lays it out. "I know several people who are waiting for a home. But then some Muslims come along, they get it. Not always Muslims, maybe—but they make the most noise, so they're the ones we hear," she says. It is unfair, they say.

"Yes, I agree with you on that," I say. "But not all Muslims get a home because they are on a waiting list. Many from minority backgrounds have a much longer wait than ethnic Danes. You can see it in the recent survey the newspaper *Politiken* did. My mother is one of those who has spent almost thirty years on various waiting lists for public housing."

I tell Jimmy and Lone about my family, who came to Denmark in the 1980s. "When I was six, we lived in a top-floor apartment on Peter Faber Street in Norrebro. Back then, my mother dreamed of living in one of the apartments in Blaagarden, but after five years on the waiting list, she gave up. We moved to a larger apartment on Sigersteds Street, where we lived without a bath, hot water, or central heating. My mother would heat water on the stove and pour it over us in a large tub in the bedroom," I say, laughing at the thought.

Lone smiles back, and says her mother did the same.

"My mother tried her luck again and got on the waiting list for Mjolner Park," I go on. "But nothing came of that either, and our next home was an old cooperative apartment on South Boulevard in Vesterbro, with stucco ceilings and room for a washing machine and dishwasher. But my mother never gave up on the dream of living in public housing, so she continued to pay to be on the waiting list. When she was finally offered an apartment in a public housing area in a suburb of Copenhagen, she immediately sold the cooperative apartment. Today she lives with my father in an area that politicians describe as a ghetto. But all she sees are the good neighbors, the green spaces, and the big, beautiful apartments."

"We give in to them," Jimmy says.

"How do we give in?" I ask.

Again, it is Lone who provides the example. "I think our society is being organized according to Muslim requirements," she says. "For example, gender-segregated swimming."

When I ask whether she generally opposes all activities for women, Jimmy takes over. "I am opposed to a swimming pool that is open exclusively for Muslim women." I tell them that the gender-segregated swimming, which has been featured in the media, is for all women, both Muslim and non-Muslim. But Jimmy insists that he has read in the media that "it was only immigrants with veils, who are allowed entry."

I take a slow breath, and steel myself for confrontation. The facts, as I saw them, were these: The capital's swimming club, which has more than five thousand members, could see that girls were underrepresented among their ranks. So they consulted with local government and the housing association to find a way to entice more girls to swim. "Both pointed out that gender-segregated teams would be a good place to start," I say. "And this turned out to be correct, as more than two hundred girls started on the new team, both Muslim and non-Muslim. Some of them became so good that they continued as assistant coaches on the joint team."

I point out that all two hundred girls have learned to swim. "That's great, isn't it?" I ask.

Lone agrees with me, but before I can celebrate the bridging of a gap, Jimmy says, "When Muslims go into the showers, they want a shower curtain."

I tell him there may be several reasons why people prefer to shower in private. This can be anything from common modesty to physical or mental health problems. When I worked as a nurse, I witnessed it in cancer patients and girls with anorexia, among other people. Jimmy, however, is not convinced. In the old days, when Jimmy was a young lifeguard, there was a ladies' changing room and a men's changing room, and that was that.

I decide to share my own experience and tell them that I learned to swim on a team for retirees. My father had a very conservative approach to gender equality and was not fond of mixed swimming teams. He only said yes to my participation because I could join the senior team, which was women-only. A few years later, when we were on vacation in Turkey, he agreed that I could go in the water, even if there were men there. A few years later, my little sister was allowed to wear a bathing suit. In the school's swimming lessons, she was on equal footing with the other girls, and she went to the beach in the summer in Denmark.

"My father is living proof that it is possible to change parents' attitudes, and that we shouldn't punish the girls just because we disagree with their parents," I say.

Lone nods. "It's important that girls learn to swim too."

But Jimmy is still skeptical. "Sure, but you're unusual. There aren't many who think the same way," he says. He's probably unaware that there's no shortage of game-changers who rise from ethnic minority groups.

I tell him that most young people get an education and a job, and achieve economic stability. "The problem is that we rarely talk about what is going well." That sounds accusatory, and I see Jimmy's posture stiffen, so I quickly try to shift to a more positive tone. "Things are changing. My eight-year-old daughter goes to the swimming pool with her father, and changes into her swimsuit with him."

I don't know whether I was expecting a medal, but the response from Lone is not particularly uplifting. "But it still doesn't explain why. Why should we have to change things for the Muslim girls?" she asks.

This tires me. "Look, you don't complain when girls and boys train and compete separately in gymnastics or horseback riding or soccer. Are you suggesting we want to put an end to all of our female sports teams?"

Well, no. According to Jimmy, this is different, because that kind of segregation does not have religious undertones.

I lean forward in my chair. "In the past, how did you motivate women to join these sports clubs? Did you not create special teams for them, to make them feel safe and welcome and comfortable?" I ask. Then, without waiting for an answer, I add, "To some extent, I do agree with you. I want these Muslim girls to be as strong and independent as any other girl growing up in Denmark. But if they can begin that journey by learning to swim, maybe next year, they can insist on going to the beach." I'm straining to remain reasonable, but I'm exhausted.

Jimmy concedes this point. "But then they come swimming and they're wearing their turbans, or whatever they're called. That kind of thing's provocative. The way religion creeps into everything they do. I can't stand it."

I ask Jimmy if he agrees with me that equality is achieved one step at a time.

He does. "But," he says, "why should we accept that only the children of immigrants can adapt, and not their parents?"

I return to my own father. He has adapted, and I know many others like him. That's why we mustn't abandon the conversation with them. "Otherwise, we are failing the girls," I stress.

"But it doesn't always work," Jimmy says. "We've had several who've killed their daughters because they..."

I interrupt him. "Hardly any!" I don't say this to justify it, but to put the issue in proportion.

Jimmy does not agree. "It's happened a number of times."

I hear myself arguing that there are statistically far more family tragedies in Denmark among Danes, where the father kills both the children and the wife. I don't know why I feel the urge to pull out the "you lot are no better than us" card, but Jimmy has his own counterargument: "There are way more Danes than there are immigrants," he says.

So I'm back in a blind alley I have come to know well, in which we talk about percentages and statistics—selecting those that strengthen our arguments, and ultimately doing little to persuade each other of our own points of view.

I agree with Jimmy that some Danish Muslim families have gender equality problems, and that it is terrible when it leads to crime. But I find it hard to understand why we do not react in the same way to rape, sexual harassment, and jealousy killings among non-Muslims.

"Because Muslims have put themselves in the spotlight with all their ridiculous demands," he says. "They're drawing attention to themselves all the time. They make so much noise and, I'm afraid, Danish people don't want to be told what to do. That's why people are becoming aggressive," Jimmy says.

Jimmy's interpretation of things makes me frustrated. Is it the girls who go to swimming lessons who are drawing attention to themselves? Or could it be politicians, who take a local sports club's good, pragmatic initiative and turn it into an opportunity for political point-scoring? I think better of asking this aloud and decide to eat another cheese sandwich instead. The dog comes over. I'm trying to put on a smile, but Lone quickly sees that I don't feel safe. At least she shoos the dog off the couch.

It is their daughter's dog, which Jimmy and Lone are looking after, and she lends vitality to their small red-brick villa. Jimmy and Lone have two children, a boy and a girl. They grew up in a home with few resources, but strong values. Jimmy and Lone's parenting style strongly reminds me of the way I was brought up: Don't spend money you don't have; work, abide by the law, and support the welfare state.

We are beginning to bridge the gap again, Jimmy, Lone, and I. But as soon as we begin to discuss a new media story about Muslims, the gap widens back up, and the bridge has to be rebuilt from scratch. It's one step forward and two steps back.

"We have to keep making concessions for them. But why should we?" Lone repeats.

Now it's Jimmy who provides the example. "Why should they get special food in daycare?" he asks.

So I plunge back in. Jimmy and Lone listen while I explain that, as a mother of children in daycare, I have no wish to ban pork meatballs. And I'm not the only one. Not one single family has campaigned for a ban on pork meatballs. All they have done is to request an alternative for their children. I think daycare kids should be able to eat whatever they want. I just want a sandwich or a carrot on the plate too, for my kids. I pay daycare fees like everyone else. And besides, it is not the Muslims who draw up the menu guidelines, it's the parent board, which anyone can run for. And so forth.

I wonder what they are thinking. Do I come across as someone who is constantly defending Muslims? I hate that role, because Muslims are not a homogeneous group, and there are idiots among them too. But I find that many media stories are blown out of proportion, and I suspect that far fewer would have garnered attention at all, had Muslims not been involved. How many ministers, MPs, and local government politicians get worked up about the daycare centers that cater to vegetarian kids? Sure, there are problems, and some are created by Danish Muslims. But are they really such a big deal?

Now Lone mentions the TV2 documentary series *Behind the Veil*, where hidden cameras document imams who encourage welfare fraud and violence against women and children. "Oh no, not that story," I think. I haven't the strength. I feel helpless. I try to explain that I'm not here to defend the indefensible, but that not all Muslims are like that.

Lone speaks. "It seems to me that almost all *are* like that, actually. We have a mosque in this area, and on Fridays, when there's prayer, they park anywhere they want...and we can't help wondering what they're saying in there."

I can sympathize—even I find myself wondering that sometimes. "It frustrated me to watch the documentary, as it cast suspicion on all

Muslims," I say. "But, the fact is, without transparency in and around the mosques, there will be suspicion. We need transparency for all our sakes."

She is clearly pleased with my response, and we talk for a long time about the need to have religious training available for imams in Denmark, so they are not solely imported from countries unfamiliar with democracy, welfare society, and the right to freedom.

"If you leave one of those imams at the train station, he wouldn't even know how to get back to the mosque. They don't live here; they just come in from abroad. And they don't speak Danish. They do not know the Danish rules," I say. I can feel my anger rising. "I'm so sick and tired of the imams who give Muslims a bad name. But I am even more disappointed with the Muslims who don't take to the streets and demand that they leave. Those imams who learned everything they know from the internet? I call them Google-imams!"

We laugh together. Jimmy nods. "But it is not only Muslims. It's true of Danes, too. We've changed. In the past, we'd get together and fight for a cause. We can sit around and moan, but going out and demonstrating...no one does that anymore."

Lone backs him up. "I think it is because people are self-centered. If they can take care of themselves, then it doesn't really matter how their neighbor is doing."

We're talking about the possibilities of reforming Islam. I tell them about Islamists who lash out at me when I criticize them, and about the racists who lash out at me, because I'm just a "fucking Muslim."

Jimmy goes quiet. "You're caught between a rock and a hard place, so to speak," he finally says. "You need a strong spine to deal with that."

I appreciate this acknowledgment. It gives me hope for our conversation, and a new surge of energy.

"Just imagine how you'd have felt if the headlines had read: 200 MUSLIM SCHOOLGIRLS DEFY PARENTS AND LEARN TO SWIM. Wouldn't we all have said, 'That's amazing!'? Yet, that is, in fact, the reality. The girls have learned to swim, and they would never have done it without this opportunity. So why don't we see it *that* way? I feel sure that, if we insist on dialogue, rather than relying on headlines, our opinions can evolve to accommodate other points of view."

"You're absolutely right. If we'd all just talk to each other," Lone says.

"But I believe preventing us from talking is in some people's interests," I say, and I tell them I also encounter racists in Muslim homes.

Jimmy nods. "When it comes down to it, there are more extremist, 'hard-core' Muslims than there are moderates. Some of them are really bad," Jimmy says.

I can't help smiling. The old "they're far more racist than us" argument is a favorite among racists, I find. But, being fair, we all hold prejudices against each other. And we all take positions based on generalizations that can be very stigmatizing.

"I receive hate mail because I am a Muslim. But when I visit the people who send it, they are almost invariably nice, friendly, and open. I rarely feel uncomfortable," I tell them.

"It's often that the unknown is frightening," Lone says. "But when we face it, it's almost never as bad as we expect." She cites examples from the media, where young Muslims at risk seem to receive more help than their Danish counterparts, and it saddens me that Lone pits the two groups of vulnerable young people against each other. "But if they're treated differently, you can't help thinking that it's because one's a Muslim, and the other is a Dane. It's the logical conclusion," she says.

I cannot erase her doubt. It is too deeply ingrained. I see and hear the same suspicions when I talk to young first- and second-generation Danes who have applied repeatedly for internships. "It is because we are 'Pakis,' and you know that is true, Özlem," they say, with despair in their eyes. No matter how much I try to explain to them that many Danish young people do not get internships either, as many companies are not taking their social responsibility seriously, it is difficult to shake their suspicion. It reminds me of Lone's suspicions. Both groups share a feeling of injustice. But they don't focus their anger on those who create injustice—local area governments that do not interpret the law equally, or companies who do not create internships. Instead, they direct the anger and blame at one another.

While I sit with Jimmy and Lone, I am reaffirmed in my conviction that, if we are to build a bridge between ethnic groups, we must first ensure that living conditions are not in decline. When we take away their safety nets—welfare, education, and job opportunities—we only dig deeper ditches between those who are fighting for the same bread.

Both Jimmy and Lone are passionate about helping the weakest people in society. They want the conditions of vulnerable children and young people to improve. But they see the welfare system do nothing but shrink. Again, we've veered into territory on which we agree. Welfare fraud must be punished. The safety net for sick and vulnerable citizens must not deteriorate; tax havens are robbing the community; housing companies should not be allowed to renovate houses and then raise the rent; and we put the Danes' safety at risk every time Denmark joins a war. The list of problems that trouble Jimmy is long, and every item on it highlights his fundamental anger and powerlessness in the face of a system which isn't there for him when he needs it.

"But do you really think that the welfare system is bad because there are immigrants?" I ask.

"Yes! It's very expensive to integrate immigrants. And it never works anyway!" says Jimmy.

"Never?" I say with a smile. "Just look at me."

"Okay, there are a few who want to integrate," he concedes.

"Not just a few. Many!" I hear myself say.

By now, I'm beginning to feel like I'm having an out-of-body experience. From the outside, I can see myself sitting on the couch, slumping further and further as I argue as best I can, breathless and tired. I get the urge to stop altogether. Are my arguments having any impact? Are Jimmy and Lone just agreeing with me as long as we're not mentioning Muslims? Will my arguments have left any impression after I've said goodbye to them and gotten into the taxi? Both Jimmy and Lone know people who are Muslims, and they also have many positive experiences with some of them. Lone works with a Muslim, and they laugh together and help each other out. Her colleague even eats pork. Jimmy feels the same way about his Muslim friend, whom he has known for many years. "He's just like us. He eats pork, too," he says. But all the Muslims Jimmy doesn't know—they're not like him. Or is that those who don't eat pork are the problem?

Jimmy and Lone know that not all Muslims are the same. Jimmy also says quite spontaneously that, when terror strikes Europe, it is in retaliation for the actions of Denmark and other Western countries against the Muslim world. "If we bomb them, they'll want to bomb us. That's war," he says. We agree again!

This is how it is with most of the topics I discuss with Jimmy and Lone. We agree—but every time the conversation turns to Muslims, we are pulled apart again. If only the media's portrayal of immigrants were more balanced, I think. It too often focuses on differences between population groups. But we are not as different as the media portrays. I'm not saying that the media coverage of individual stories is wrong, but they are not being put in context. The pervasiveness of stories focused on cultural differences create a distorted narrative of first- and second-generation Danes.

The economist Hjarn V. Zernichow Borbjerg, who was previously employed as a civil servant in the Ministry of Integration, argues in his book *Nydansk* that it's misleading to portray immigrants as a group that chooses to huddle together in ghettos. The fact is nine out of ten immigrants choose to live outside these disadvantaged areas.

We are similarly misled when the media covers crime rates within immigrant populations. While it may be true that the crime rate is higher among immigrants than among ethnic Danes, it is also true that a higher proportion of immigrants have lower socioeconomic status, and it is this factor—not their immigration status—that makes them more likely to commit crime. According to some figures, 97 percent of immigrants are law-abiding citizens.

And while, yes, I would also like to see a higher proportion of the immigrant population find work, we must not forget that the majority are well-integrated and make a valuable contribution to Danish society. Why doesn't the media cover that story?

As I look up at the big flat-screen TV in the living room, I'm overcome with the urge to smash it. I have to do something to put some distance between Jimmy and Lone and the news they consume daily. I realize they have smartphones too, so in this brief fantasy, I'm denying them access to Facebook and the rest of the internet. And they cannot listen to the radio, either.

While I am transforming Denmark into a police state in my head, Lone says, "It was much better in the old days."

I don't know which "old days" Lone is referring to, but through the lens of childhood naïveté, as I remember my upbringing on Vesterbro in Copenhagen, I want to agree. In my memories, too, the old days were better.

My father-in-law once told me how, in the 1970s, when the Turks were welcomed into Aarhus harbor, an orchestra played for them. How happily they lived with the Danes, readily assisted and supported. "We immigrants have ruined it for ourselves," my father-in-law always says. "We have destroyed the confidence the Danes showed in us. We didn't behave properly. We committed crimes and social fraud, and we didn't treat the Danes fairly. We deserve all these austere measures. We deserve to be kicked out!" Of course, my father-in-law has not committed any crimes himself—just as many Danes do, he refers to immigrants, nonethnic Danes, and minorities in general terms.

I've had many heated conversations with my wonderful father-in-law. Of course, I understand his frustration. If everyone behaved properly, we'd be living in Utopia: no war, no corruption, no poverty. But let's be realistic! Having worked as a nurse, I've seen how people from minority backgrounds can be particularly vulnerable to mental illness, neglect, and abuse—some of them refugees suffering from post-traumatic stress disorder. I also know that not all children are raised to be good democratic citizens. And not every Muslim citizen is beyond reproach. But I believe that the mistakes made by Muslim families are made in Danish homes, too. And that most Muslims should not be held responsible for the misdeeds of the minority.

When I take my leave, I get a hug from both Lone and Jimmy. I tell him that I've noticed he's dragging his leg: my inner nurse is worried about his health. Jimmy promises me that he will send me the result of the scan. He appreciates my concern. The hug makes me happy.

I wave to Lone and Jimmy one last time before I get into the taxi. The driver can tell from my dialect that I'm from Copenhagen. When I say I want him to take me to one of Odense's allotment garden areas, he looks at me in puzzlement. I tell him the reason: I'm going to visit Kim. The driver thinks I'm crazy to be seeking out people who don't like Muslims.

In his eyes, I see both appreciation and wonder. "Why?" he asks. "Why do you want to visit them?"

It is the same question my husband, Devrim, asks me. He is a Kurdish Dane and works as a client advisor in a bank. No matter how much he agrees with me that we must bridge the gap between population groups, he doesn't understand why it has to be me entering the lions' den. He worries about my safety. And with good reason.

We've kept our address a secret ever since the neo-Nazi began harassing me. The police have taken out restraining orders on a number of other people, banning them from contacting me. I receive daily hate mail, and sadly, also death threats, which I report to the police. The vast majority come from right-wing nationalists, who either belong to the extreme right in Denmark or support Erdogan in Turkey. Their perception of democracy is very different from mine, and they will go to extreme lengths to limit my freedom and my rights, because they disagree with me.

I rarely tell my mum or dad about the hate mail and threats. My mother cannot take it. When I was a member of parliament, she wanted me to step down whenever I told her about the hate mail. She is afraid of "the racists."

"They will kill you one day," she says. For that reason, she'd prefer me to keep my head down and stay out of the debate. To her, "the racists" include people affiliated with the Grimhoj Mosque, known for its extremist views. When I get into verbal fights with Islamists, she is the first one to call me. "Watch out," she says. "Think of your kids. Think of yourself!"

I don't tell my kids about the hate mail I receive, either. I reason that what they don't know won't hurt them. But sometimes, when I receive threats so serious that I must involve the police, it is impossible not to inform them. I must tell them to be vigilant about locking the front door, that they cannot talk to strangers, and that we have to keep the curtains drawn. It frightens them, and it hurts me to see it. Although I try to appear brave, I know they see right through my act.

I will admit, I was especially afraid of the neo-Nazi. Police investigators told me that he had displayed pedophilic tendencies online, and, once I knew that, I became obsessively worried about what might happen to my children if he ever got his hands on them. I vividly remember one occasion when the abuse was at its most intense, and I was opening my mail in the parliament mailroom. I picked up an envelope, slightly thicker than the rest, and felt it carefully with my fingers. Feeling something soft inside, my anxiety went into overdrive. I struggled to breathe as I imagined he had gotten hold of my little girl and had sent me a lock of her hair in the post. Standing in the middle of the mailroom, I began to cry. Before I could bring myself to open the envelope, I called the daycare center. Was she there? Was she okay? Were they sure? Yes, they were sure. And the letter was just an ordinary letter.

I don't seek out those who send me actual death threats. Those go directly to the police. But sometimes, before a coffee dialogue, I start to worry. When I first held these discussions, I researched the people I planned to visit. But that offered a false sense of security. Even an upstanding family man, with no criminal record, could become so provoked by what I have to say that he'll want to attack me. So I don't research them up front anymore. I don't even Google them.

I do sometimes worry about my own safety. But when I look back at all the people I have met for a coffee dialogue since 2010, I can't recall a single person I felt unsafe with. They may well address me as "Paki shit" or "terrorist bitch" in their emails, but they still serve me cake on plates with floral decorations. None of them, I felt, would hurt me. It was all the other Muslims they disliked. As the Kurdish proverb says, "The fear of death should not prevent you from living."

"That's fine," the taxi driver says, when I tell him why I am going to the allotment gardens. "I'll hang around for a little while after we get there."

False security, I think, but it still feels good.

The "Real Viking"

Kim has been emailing me for a long time, often attaching articles
supporting his view that Muslims are a problem in Denmark and
should therefore be deported. He agrees straightaway when I ask
him if I can come by. He has warned me that his garden is a mess,
and I shouldn't be shocked by it. So I am surprised to find his lawn is
mowed, and his hedges newly trimmed. There is no trash or clutter
on the lawn. There is a narrow gravel path from the garden gate to the
house, which is painted white. Over the door it reads "FLA-U." Kim,
who has come outside to greet me, tells me that this means "relax" in
the local dialect on Funen Island. I think that this may be a sign from
the higher power, and I turn to wave at the taxi driver and signal it's
okay for him to leave.

I follow Kim into the house, and the first thing I notice are the many
knives hanging on a magnetic rack on the wall above the kitchen sink.
I start counting, but when I reach eight, I force myself to look away. I
look around, thinking of cakes on floral plates. I'm standing in a large
living room with an open kitchen. In the living room, there are two
doors: one for the bathroom, the other for the bedroom.

Danish flags hang from the ceiling and on the walls. Is Kim celebrating his birthday, or is the nationalistic decor for my benefit? Then I notice a throw pillow with embroidery depicting Elvis Presley—my mother's big idol. She doesn't speak English and can't understand his songs. But she has always thought he was good-looking and had a delicious voice. I contemplate mentioning my mother, but decide against it. I am not sure that Kim will appreciate the coincidence as much as I do.

On the coffee table is a homemade cake sitting next to a large blue porcelain teapot. Kim has put a white velvet tablecloth on the table. My mother's favorite fabric. The cake is obviously just out of the oven, as Kim has put a cutting board underneath it to protect the table, at the corner of which is a pile of newspaper clippings.

Kim bought his house a little more than twelve years ago. At the end of a long night at the Tin Soldier, a local dive bar, Kim struck up a conversation with a man who was leaving for Spain and wanted to sell his allotment garden. "I'll buy it," Kim promised—although it was undoubtedly the drink talking.

The next day, the man phoned Kim and invited him to come and see the house. It was in a bad state, almost falling apart, but Kim—a man of his word—ended up buying the house for five thousand kroner (or 740 US dollars). "I can't bear to fail someone," he tells me. "I hate to be let down, so I don't want to disappoint anyone else."

After the old allotment house burned to the ground, Kim proudly tells me, he designed the house we are standing in himself. I recognize that dream from my parents. It was the dream of buying a house and forty sheep that motivated my father to migrate from his village in Turkey to find work in a country he knew as "Europe." My parents did eventually earn the money to buy the house, but they never moved back. Their children were Danish and didn't share their dream of moving back to the village. Instead, they saved up for vacations in Thailand or Turkey.

I tell Kim that, when I agreed to the meeting, I imagined him living in a van on a lawn that was dug-up in most places. The van's door would be partly closed and wouldn't have a lock, and the lawn would be strewn with waste and old, broken Coke bottles. I shake my head at the expectations I have of people who dislike Muslims. In my head, they often live in a pigsty or in a muddy ditch. But every time, my prejudice turns out to be wrong. Kim laughs at my description of his home and says, "That's how it was before I rebuilt it."

Kim is forty-four and has been married for five years. He and his wife have been together for eleven years and have no children. Kim grew up with his mother, a social worker, and he never met his father, who he believes was "drunk all his life." Kim grew up believing that he was an only child, but when he was in his twenties, the police informed him that his father had died, and that he has six siblings. He was invited to the funeral, and to meet the family, but he said no.

In 1996, Kim suffered a work-related injury when he was pulled into a machine used to crush cardboard. The machine destroyed a large part of his face, and crushed his right shoulder, a number of ribs, and the upper part of his hip. Today, after eight years of rehabilitation and thirty-seven operations, there are no visible traces of the accident left on his face. He has been on subsidiary pay for the past twenty years and has been assessed as being capable of five to seven hours of work a week.

For the past ten years, he has volunteered in his parish, and has a small bike project with the elderly at the local nursing home. His headaches require him to nap halfway through the day, otherwise he "cannot function." I am surprised when he tells me that half of his jaw is made of steel. I get the urge to touch his face. He has a beard and is slightly round. He seems nice and friendly. I decide to resist my nursing instinct and focus on the purpose for my visit.

Like Jimmy, Kim mentions how much he respects me. He thinks it is a great honor that I am here. "Whether or not we agree or disagree,

I have respect for people who believe in their cause, and stand by it," Kim says.

"Then you must have a high level of respect for Hizb ut-Tahrir," I tease.

With a wry smile, Kim shakes his head, and says no, he doesn't. But his praise continues. "Your heart is in the right place, don't get me wrong. And you don't budge! You've been beaten up a lot for that. You believe in what you say, and you defend your position."

I am struggling to understand Kim's point.

"Imagine how much difference your passion, and enthusiasm, and your iron will could make to human rights in Turkey. Wouldn't it be great if you went back to your own country and fought for those things there?" he finishes, with a satisfied smile.

I tell him I'm not a Turk, but he insists I always will be to him. I shake my head. "I have Kurdish roots, but I am first and foremost a Dane," I say.

But Kim won't hear it. "That is where you must fight your fight. Couldn't you…?" he starts out, but I interrupt.

"Turkey is not my country, and I don't even have Turkish citizenship," I say calmly.

A light goes out in Kim's eyes. "It's difficult," he says quietly.

Kim tells me that he has been to Turkey with his wife and his mother. One evening, he ordered three glasses of beer to their hotel room. The next day, the room was cleaned, the bed made, and flowers scattered over the floor. But the glasses had not been removed, as the maids wouldn't touch alcohol. "In the seven days I was in Turkey, I saw what I don't want in my country," Kim says.

I remind him that Turkey has a population of seventy million people and ask him if his statement might be too broad. He disagrees emphatically. It is not only that experience, but also several other minor experiences that have confirmed his position.

We eat more cake. In contrast to my conversation with Jimmy and Lone, Kim and I only speak about Muslims. He says that he is a true Dane, a genuine "Viking." He eats pork and drinks alcohol. In his eyes, I am everything not Danish. I'm Muslim, I don't drink alcohol, and I eat only halal. He is convinced that most Danes think like him, and he will not accept that different Danes can have different perceptions of what it means to be Danish.

Kim has prepared himself thoroughly. He holds the pile of newspaper articles and repeats over and over that "it is important to be educated and enlightened." The difference between him and Muslims like myself is that he is educated and enlightened; we are not. To illustrate his point, he tells me a story about his ex-wife, who always cut off a slice at each end of the pork roast before she put it in the oven. One day, Kim asked her why she did this. She said it was what her mother had always done. Kim then asked his mother-in-law, who gave the same response. She had also watched her mother do it. When Kim asked her grandmother, he found an explanation. "Because the oven wasn't big enough for the entire joint," she told him.

"No one ever questioned it," Kim points out. "What one had witnessed and learned, the next one mimicked. That is the case with Muslims as well. They lack the knowledge to know that what they do is wrong."

I smile. His reasoning reminds me of my father-in-law's. My father-in-law is a communist, and very critical of religion. He believes that people, if they are enlightened, will stop believing in supernatural things. "Exactly," Kim says.

I don't appreciate debates with people who reduce disagreements to a lack of intelligence, I think. It's like me saying that all who vote for the far-right nationalist party are village idiots who've never opened a book and would turn their back on the party if only they got themselves an education. That's an arrogant and patronizing argument I don't care for. I don't share this thought with Kim.

There are Muslims living in several of the neighboring allotment garden houses, and it turns out that Kim likes one of them. "I was laying down pavement outside," he says. "We started at seven o'clock in the morning with the gravel and didn't finish until ten in the evening. At five o' clock, the neighbor brought delicious kebabs with onions and tomatoes to the backyard. It was halal of course, but I'm a sucker for good food, so I could not turn it down. He brought sodas and everything. I say that with the utmost respect," he says happily.

But, as for the other Muslims in the allotment garden association, they don't abide by the rules and regulations laid down by the garden association. Kim wants to kick them out of Denmark.

"Why not just settle for kicking them out of the allotment garden association?" I ask.

Kim replies that it takes an "unimaginably long time."

"Ah, yes," I say, struggling not to smile. "Such is democracy."

I say, sure, I understand his frustration with people who don't respect rules. But then, he says, it's not just the Muslims in the association he has issues with. It's the ones at the local mosque, too. "They park anywhere." Then he casually adds, "I'm thinking that a machine gun would fix that."

I'm shocked. "Do you really think violence is the way forward?" I ask, carefully.

"You can say I'm undemocratic—because they are..." Kim takes a breath. His indignation toward Muslims is evident. "I'd like to respect them, but they must respect me, too. Otherwise, they can't live in my country. Don't you see that?"

I pause, then ask, "What would it take for you and your good neighbor, who brings you grilled food, to establish a friendship?"

"That'll never happen," he says. "If I had a party, I'd like to invite him. I respect him; we get along; we help each other out from time to time. But if he came to my party, he wouldn't eat the food I cook or drink the beer that I serve. I'd have to make concessions for him, and that's not right," Kim says.

"But he could drink Coke, and I imagine that you don't serve pork as an appetizer, a main course, and a dessert?" I laugh.

But Kim insists that he might; that, if he wanted to, it would be his right. For Kim, it's not about the neighbor eating just his bread and salad. It's not about being a good, accommodating host. It's about the expectation that he should take his neighbor's diet into consideration at all. It's about conceding to a Muslim.

I continue to challenge him. "Your neighbor isn't obligated to offer you food when he has a barbecue. He does it because he's a good neighbor, just as you are when you help him fix something in his house. It's a bit ridiculous that you'd only want to serve him barbecued pork, just to prove that you're a true Dane. If he hosted a party, there would be many different dishes. When you hold a party, I assume there are many different dishes?"

"But will he serve me pork?" Kim asks.

I am so provoked by Kim's stubbornness that I want to be just as stubborn, but I restrict myself to replying, "No, he doesn't eat pork because of his faith. But couldn't you eat something other than pork? Just like you could make roast pork for your party, and still serve him a slice of bread with some salad?" I tell him that, in order to be a good guest, I would even eat meat that was not halal, if that were what Kim served me.

This makes him happy. "Then I would accept you opting out of the pork, and eating bread and salad instead," he says with a smile.

Kim is adept at maintaining a pleasant demeanor. It is quite impressive, I think more than once. His eyes seem to be always smiling. If I met him on the street, I would never guess that he is in favor of the death penalty and believes that homosexuality is abnormal, and that victims are to blame for rape.

"It is not right to prance around in miniskirts, showing off your breasts in a tiny top. I'm like a male lion, and when I see such a young calf, then obviously I want to hunt her. That, after all, is a male instinct. Iranian, Kurd, or Inuit, when a man sees a piece of juicy meat, he lusts after it. If not, he is almost abnormal. Will you agree with me on this?" he asks.

"No, I don't agree with you, as I don't believe it is the length of a woman's skirt that determines whether or not she deserves to be raped."

Kim concedes that he can understand why Muslim men want Muslim women to cover up, so they don't attract male attention.

"So you are in favor of covering women?" I ask indignantly.

"I'm just saying that it makes sense, if you understand how a man thinks," Kim says.

Suddenly, I'm glad that I'm always so cold that I'm wearing several layers of clothing.

To emphasize his point, Kim says, "If we were both sitting here naked, we would probably see things differently."

I don't like this conversation. My gaze falls upon the knives above the kitchen sink, and I decide to change the subject. I've heard Kim's point of view before. I have heard it from imams and from strongly conservative radical groups. I confront him with the fact that he shares his opinions with the very people he claims to oppose. "When you say rape is self-inflicted, you sound like a conservative Turk! When you say homosexuality is not normal, you sound like an imam!"

Kim does not care for my comparisons. He smiles through gritted teeth, and I brace myself—I don't know if this is the calm before the storm, or if he is truly giving thought to the things I'm saying. He pauses again. "You may well be right, but..." And then he returns to arguing his point of view on rape, homosexuals, and Muslims.

I respond by upping the stakes. "I'm more of a Dane than you are. Or at least much more of a democrat than you."

To lighten the confrontational mood, I tell him about a conversation between my husband and my son about homosexuality. "My son Yusuf is seven years old, and he asked my husband Devrim what a gay person is. Devrim explained that is when two men love each other. Yusuf responded, 'So are you and I gay? Because the two of us love each other.' "

We laugh together as we eat another piece of cake. We disagree, but at least we can talk about it. Sitting here, talking with Kim, I can see that this will be a long process, and we may need to meet halfway, but there is hope. This is what keeps me trying to find common ground. Kim also insists on conversation. His objective is not so much to understand what he loathes, but to enlighten the ignorant.

Kim says he's "born red," but is now considering shifting his support from the right-wing Danish People's Party to the ultra-right-wing party, the Danes' Party. In Kim's eyes, the Danish People's Party is no longer tough enough on Muslims. I point out that the chairman of the Danes' Party is a former Nazi who wants to deport all unassimilated residents with non-European backgrounds from Denmark. Our discussion goes back and forth, and in the end, I cannot help but laugh that I am using all my energy to insist that Kim should continue to vote for the Danish People's Party. Fortunately, Kim eventually agrees that the Danes' Party is too extreme for him, and he will stick with the Danish People's Party. My mission has been successful, I think triumphantly, before remembering that a vote for the Danish People's Party is not usually my idea of victory.

So, what is my mission, exactly? Is it to convince Kim and his like that the Danish People's Party is better than the Danes' Party? Or is it to, over time, help them reconsider their belief systems, become humanists, and vote for parties that embrace Muslims? It is not my goal to convert all the voters to one specific political party. That's not democracy. My mission then is to ensure that everyone feels welcome within the democratic community, where the right to freedom applies to everyone equally, no matter their name, religion, or skin color. This is paramount, because the alternative, violence, cannot replace conversation as a means of creating change. When I hear Kim talking about how a machine gun could solve the problems in front of the mosque, my resolve strengthens to keep dialogue open. No matter how extreme some positions seem, we must not demonize the people who hold them. Racists don't become less racist when we shout at them. But they also won't become more democratic if we just say what they want to hear. People like Kim must be met on equal terms, and with critical debate. The conversation with Kim has provoked me, and sorely tested my patience. I can sense that Kim feels the same way. But the way I see it, democracy is worth the extra dose of patience.

Before I leave, Kim asks to take a selfie with me. I also take a picture of him. He calls me a taxi, and we go out into the garden together. I tease him, and say now that I am leaving, he can take down all his Danish flags, and he laughs.

While we wait for the taxi, which will take me to Nyborg, and a meeting with Angelo, Kim tells me about his annoying Muslim neighbor on the other side of the gravel road. The neighbor often uses Kim's electricity, because he doesn't have any himself, but Kim doesn't mind. "Neighbors have to help each other out," he says. He doesn't want to be reimbursed. "But why not invite me for a glass of water or a cup of coffee?" he asks. "If there was a sense of community, then maybe I wouldn't want my hedges to be high enough to block their view."

Regardless of Kim's opinions about Muslims, he still wishes to share a sense of community with his neighbor. He wants to be treated with love and respect.

On one side, Kim has a sweet Muslim neighbor who shares grilled food, but whom Kim doesn't think he can befriend. On the other side, Kim has an annoying Muslim neighbor he'd like to share a sense of community with. I'm no longer solely angry at Kim, although it's his task to build any bridges he wants with his neighbors. Now I'm also annoyed at Muslims who fail to reach out and invite fellow Danish citizens into their homes.

I get an urge to jump the hedge for a talk with Kim's neighbor, but the taxi has arrived.

The Explosion at Nyborg Strand

In the taxi, I turn my phone back on, and it pings frantically with texts from Angelo. His messages are always so erratic, I'm not sure I have the energy to read them, but I do, and I'm unnerved.

Ping. "Sweet baby, are you on your way?" Ping. "You should know that I have kissed and hugged many immigrant girls." Ping. "Fuck the bloody Muslims. You should just be kicked out. You are all terrorists to me."

And so on.

At first, Angelo suggested we meet in his apartment, but, in this case, I feel safer in public. Usually, I reason that visiting someone at their home creates a more comfortable, relaxed atmosphere for what could potentially become a tense meeting. It helps foster honesty and sincerity. But I'm a little too wary of Angelo to take risks.

"How about a hotel?" he asked at one point. He also wanted to know what time I would arrive at the train station, but I didn't respond, in case he took it upon himself to pick me up. I said I'd rather meet at a café or restaurant of his choosing.

"Nyborg has a Turkish café," he says. "But we can't meet there. They're not good people. It can't be the Mexican place either—the seating is too crowded, and we don't want people listening in to our conversation."

"Perhaps Hotel Nyborg Strand," he wrote, eventually. And I agreed. Having been there several times before, I'm confident there will be plenty of people nearby, and I can yell for help if needed.

Angelo interests me, not just because he's an extremist, but because I suspect he advocates violence as a solution to Denmark's "immigration problem." People like him live in all communities, and they often end up ruining it, both for themselves and for others.

I arrive at the hotel before him. It's six thirty in the evening, and I am worn out. It's hard to deal with so much anger, powerlessness, prejudice, and hatred. I hope that I can maintain a positive conversation with Angelo, but I don't have much patience left. As soon as I see the view from the restaurant, I am convinced that it will be fine. The sun is shining, the sky is absolutely beautiful, and I can see the beach.

I decide to hold off on the food order until Angelo arrives. Then we can eat together. Where there is food, there is usually also peace, I think.

I text him. It's now past seven o'clock, and I wonder why he hasn't arrived. Will he stand me up?

"I am waiting for you at the entrance," he writes, and when he enters the restaurant, I cannot help but smile. He looks completely different from what I imagined. Angelo isn't sporting a hooded sweatshirt or a large Canada Goose jacket, nor does he have a shaved head. Instead, he is dressed in a dark blue Hugo Boss suit, a white shirt, and cufflinks. The shirt collar is plaid on the inside, and his shirt buttons match his blue jacket. He wears a thin gold chain with a small pendant around his neck.

"You must have Italian genes," I say when I shake his hand. He clearly accepts this as a compliment. His father is Italian, and his mother is Danish. He was born and raised in Denmark and has no siblings. Angelo speaks Italian, and sometimes he visits Italy. He is a Catholic but wears a small Buddha pendant on the chain around his neck. He practices meditation "because it is good for body and mind." He says, "It's like yoga. You become another person." He has practiced martial arts since he was ten years old and has competed in both the European and World Championships. He has a black belt in tae kwon do. He also has a fifteen-year-old son from his former marriage, and proudly tells me how well his boy is doing at school. "He speaks Spanish and is into martial arts."

Angelo's ex-wife is from the Philippines, and he immediately starts criticizing the Danish custody law, the Parental Responsibility Act. He suspects her of hitting their son but can't prove it. He is furious with the system. I struggle to figure out how to respond. "Imagine if we could mediate between the parents, early in the conflict, before it escalates," I say. We both agree that this would be a good idea, and I'm happy we have already found a topic upon which we agree. Dialogue is the way forward, I remind myself. But I'm barely able to order my food before Angelo starts in on Muslims.

"I'm well aware that some of the refugees here have been through trauma and torture," he says. "But many of them are refugees by convenience... I know them. We've got five hundred in Nyborg. They live in a place where people with disabilities used to live. There's always trouble. The police have to deal with brawls, stabbings, and other problems. I'm sick of it. And the gangs. And..."

I can barely keep up. Are we talking about refugees or gangs? "It's the gangs that are the problem, right?" I ask.

"Yes," he says. "They must be kicked out."

Of course, these immigrant gangs can't be compared to, say, the Danish Hell's Angels. Oh, no.

"Let me explain to you why Anders should stay, but Ahmet must be kicked out: Ahmet has a family in his home country, that he can go back to. He's an immigrant and not a Dane. And when we let people like Ahmet stay here, things only worsen for Denmark," Angelo says.

I tell him that, actually, Denmark is doing quite well. Crime is down; more young people are becoming educated; more people vote in elections, but I can tell that Angelo is no longer with me. The bridge between us is crumbling, almost before I started building it.

"You think that things are going well in Denmark? There is racism everywhere!"

I let that sink in.

He speaks nonstop about Muslims, refugees, sharia, insular communities, and war. He repeats several times that he is a good judge of character, implying that what he says about the Muslims he has met is the iron-clad truth. He begins to list one bad experience with Muslims after another. "Today, there were fifteen refugees crossing the road, and they gave me these evil stares," he insists. He experiences this a lot: evil stares, rudeness, dismissive attitudes. He says, years ago, he mixed with minority communities. He would go to the parties of Iranian friends, but was never allowed to talk to girls there, and struggled to understand why religion had to be central to everything. Today, he has no minority friends left. The old ones have scattered around the country, but the distance between them and Angelo is more than geographical. "I became more critical about immigrants and Muslims when I started reading about how terrible the situation is in Denmark," he says.

He barely pauses for breath as he talks. He is angry at Muslims; angry at all the fuss they make; angry about their complaints; angry that Muslim girls can't swim in public pools; angry that they keep demanding special treatment, and that they want to change Denmark.

I'm growing weary. I'm not sure I have enough energy left for another round of the same tired prejudices or a debate that offers the same old counterarguments. However, I also know this is an opportunity to have a positive impact on Angelo. And I asked for this. I'm angry, and I'm struggling not to let it show. Angelo, meanwhile, remains calm and measured. He leans back, resting his arm on the chair next to him. His voice and his body language are notably controlled. His anger is only apparent in his carefully chosen words.

"I was chatting with an elderly neighbor before coming to meet you today. He's worried that the Muslims will take over Europe in ten to twenty years, and I can see that happening. They're trying to get into Danish politics. They're saying we should enforce Muslim law, start stoning women...they want all sorts of things."

"What would it take to stop all this evil you're talking about?" I ask.

Angelo doesn't believe he can make a difference. "Only parliament has that power," he says.

"But hatred is created between ordinary people," I counter. "If we were better at talking with each other, then perhaps we wouldn't hate each other. We would be able to understand one another, and maybe even prevent discrimination and racism," I say, my voice so worn out from overuse I can barely hear myself speak. My words feel empty. It's been a long day.

Angelo ignores me. "In the end, the Muslims will win a majority in parliament, and with a majority, they can change laws. Before you know it, Danes will be under sharia law."

I've heard this prediction many times. Angelo believes the only solution is to shut down the mosques and close the borders. Muslims should be stripped of citizenship and kicked out of the country, and their freedom of expression should be limited. All to protect Denmark and democracy. I feel as if I'm in a gym, lying on my back, arms outstretched, holding a barbell, to which Angelo keeps adding weight. I know that, unless I maintain my position, the weight will drop on my chest, so I hold tight as long as possible, understanding that at some point, it will become more than I can bear, and I will buckle.

"Do you seriously think Muslims can get 51 percent of the vote in a parliamentary election? Not just Muslims, but fundamentalist Muslims, who want to introduce sharia law to Denmark?" I ask Angelo.

"Yes, the thought has crossed my mind," he says.

"You don't believe that!" I say, leaning forward across the table.

"I fear it," he says.

I try to explain that it would be impossible for an Islamist to win a parliament seat, in the same way no Nazi could. I assure him that my votes in parliament were guided by the rule of Danish law as a moral compass, not the Qur'an. But no matter what arguments I use, they bounce off him. He is genuinely worried, and I find it hard to take his fears seriously, as they seem utterly unrealistic and unjustified to me. "Where does this fear of Islamists taking over the Danish Parliament originate?" I ask.

Angelo responds, "I think many people in Denmark harbor that fear. And I think that many politicians share my view."

I feel ready to explode. The energy I had in conversation with Kim has dissipated completely. I become prickly too fast, and Angelo provokes me in a completely different way than Kim did, although his opinions are not so different from Kim's.

Food, I think. Where is the food? Angelo doesn't notice that I am fidgeting in my chair.

"Dear Özlem," he starts, but I cut him off.

"Don't patronize me," I say, surprising myself with my rudeness.

"How many Muslims in Denmark do you think are married to Danish citizens or have Danish boyfriends?" he asks. "Let's be honest."

I cannot stand him anymore. With more than a hint of sarcasm, I say there probably aren't any. Angelo doesn't quite agree, but he believes there are only a handful.

I take a deep breath and, in an icy voice, ask, "Can we turn that question around, and ask how many ethnic Danes are married to someone with minority roots?" I go on to argue that integration is everyone's responsibility. It's a two-way street. But I couldn't care less who marries whom. In this moment, the only question in my mind is: What is the point of meeting with Angelo?

He keeps talking. It all boils down to violence within the Muslim community, he says. "If a woman married a non-Muslim, there'd be murder!"

I shake my head. "More people are murdered out of secular jealousy than from religious honor, and thousands of people continue to marry each year," I say.

"I'm not a racist or anything, but I've met all..."

That's it. I don't let Angelo finish that sentence. I cannot bear the weight of this discussion any longer. I explode at him out of pain, frustration, and anger. I lean forward so there is less than a foot separating my face from his. Now's my chance, I think. Attack!

"All? You've met *all* 280,000 Danish Muslims? How many did you meet today? Ten, twenty, thirty?" I ask angrily.

Angelo says he doesn't know; he doesn't count people in the street.

"Do you know what wears me out?" I continue. "People like you, who constantly incite hatred, and never see the good side. People who hate Muslims. People who don't want dialogue, and constantly tell others to straighten up. Hateful people!"

"I want to talk to Muslims. It's not because I don't like them," he says.

I almost shout. "But you dislike Muslims. Don't try to hide it." Now I know that I've completely lost what little composure I began this discussion with.

Angelo just looks at me. He doesn't interrupt my tirade. I'm irritated at his lack of reaction. He's insulted me terribly, and I want him to feel how much that hurts.

"You keep bringing up the oppression of Muslim women. Do you know who fills the women's shelters? Women brought to Denmark by Danish husbands. Most of them imported from Thailand."

I know that my statement is not entirely true. I don't know whether most minority women in the shelters are from East Asia. But right now, I don't care about facts. It feels satisfying to give him a taste of his own medicine. It's obviously working. He's no longer calm and confident. I've gotten under his skin. Now he knows how I feel. But at the same time, I am torn. A voice inside me keeps saying, "Stop!" But I can't.

I continue to let him have it. "I came all the way to Nyborg on a Wednesday evening to meet you, and all I get is 'I'm not racist, but...' It happens everywhere I go, right before people pour their racist crap all over me. If these dialogues are to be fruitful, every segment of the population must take part in them. Everyone needs to get their act together, and that includes you! You've been complaining about Muslims for over an hour now, and I haven't once heard you acknowledge that I, a Muslim, paid out of my own pocket to come and meet you." I continue, "You've done nothing but trash people like me! Do you really expect me to just sit here and take it? You talk about how the refugees glare at you angrily. Well, if I met you on the street, I would, too! Have you ever considered that you might be the problem?"

"I don't hate Muslims," Angelo says quietly, and perhaps almost a little embarrassed.

I feel like I just left a brawl. My heart is pounding. I feel like I'm falling apart inside. I'm tired, but also a little embarrassed that I lost my composure. I'm sure Angelo sees me as confirmation of all his prejudices against Muslims.

The waiter brings my fish with potatoes and parsley sauce. We both smile at him, and act as if everything is fine. I start to eat. Fast. I want to go home. Angelo is starting to show some emotion. He tells me that he is sick of the daily news stories about feckless Muslims who don't even try to put their lives in order. "I won't say that I don't like Muslims. I'm just tired of what I'm seeing. Say what you like, I can see with my own eyes that 80 to 90 percent of all crimes are committed by people from non-Danish backgrounds."

I can't deny that there is a higher proportion of criminals amongst the migrant population. Only 1 percent of ethnic Danes have a criminal record, while the figure is 3 percent among Denmark's ethnic minorities. But the difference between those figures—especially when you consider socioeconomic factors—is really not so great.

Statistics can be ambiguous when it comes to defining "ethnic minority." Are we talking about people without permanent residency? First-generation legal immigrants, or their children too? You can slew the stats in every direction. But, right now, I don't have the energy.

Meanwhile, Angelo has moved on to Muslim ghettos, and how suburbs like Vollsmose are no-go areas for the police. He's complaining about Muslims who won't work, and Muslims who refuse to shake hands. "I'm just tired of seeing it on TV and reading about it in the news. Politicians aren't doing anything to fix these problems," he says.

I want to give a long speech about fake news, about politicians who inflame problems. Instead, I say, "I understand that you're tired of this. I am too."

He looks at me. "I really want to protect Denmark," he says.

"Me too!" I think. But I don't say it aloud. I understand his point of view. He is as deeply concerned about the discord as I am. We both want to keep Denmark safe. But we deeply disagree on a strategy. For one thing, Angelo, like Kim, supports the death penalty. Our perception of the scope of the problems, our preferred solutions, and our approaches to democracy are so fundamentally different that we will never be able to agree.

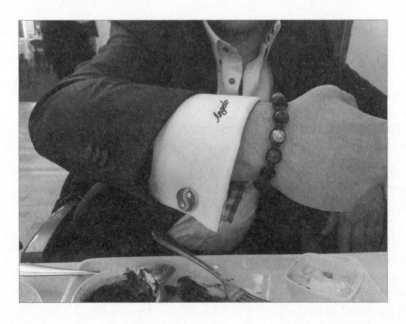

I look at Angelo. He's only a year older than I am. He's been married and divorced, just like me. He has ethnic roots, as I do: his from Italy, mine from Turkey. We both speak multiple languages, including fluent Danish, yet we're not speaking the same language on these issues. He looks at the sea filling the horizon outside the window, and suddenly it all seems so sad, I'm about to cry. I feel like a stranger in my own country, and then and there it dawns on me that, to Kim and Angelo, I will never be anything but "that Muslim woman." If they had the power to do so, they'd kick me out of my own country. And this rage is a heavy burden to carry. I shrink under the weight of it. My energy and my humor, which usually buffer me and allow me to not take it personally, are disintegrating. I'm only a "bloody Muslim." I remember Jacob Holdt, who said, "Racism is pain." When one is exposed to it, one feels the hurt of the other. Is Angelo in as much pain as I am?

"How can we be sitting so close, but have so much distance between us? How did we end up here?" I ask him.

"I don't know," he says.

"It's sad," I say. "It's very sad."

"I agree," he replies.

Then we go quiet. It's as if the silence says more than our quarreling.

We look out the window. The waves have subsided, and the sea is unbelievably large. Twilight is slowly replacing the gorgeous red shade that colors the sky. I think about my kids, to whom I'm reading a book about Norse mythology. Every time the sky turns red, they ask, "Which of the gods has won, Mum?"

I don't know who has won, but one thing's certain: both Angelo and I have lost.

Angelo finally breaks the silence. He begins talking about the time he was invited to the home of a Muslim family, how happy he was to be invited. He tells me how he rebuked his uncle when he talked trash about Muslims in the line at the bank. He talks about the Muslim dentist and the other assimilated Muslims he knows. "Some of them do well. I'll admit that much," he says.

"I'm drained," I say.

"You're drained?"

"I don't know how we can solve this," I say. I take a long pause. I can barely breathe. Everything is moving in slow motion, and I feel like a patient emerging from a long coma. I sigh. I want to say something that will make it all right. "I'm just wondering...if the media were more positive, and less fixated on all the problems, would that help?" I ask.

Angelo nods.

"But that won't happen, this will end badly. It'll turn into a war. Muslims will become the new Jews," I say. I've been infected by his pessimistic attitude. Hope is lost.

"Many Danes would leave to get away from Muslims," Angelo says. We're both scared of each other. It's surreal. I can't think of a response.

So, our conversation turns to karate. I'm only a beginner, but Angelo has been studying martial arts for years. He meditates too, and I tell him that I always fall asleep when I meditate.

"I'll teach you a trick for that one day," he says, but I don't know if that day will ever come.

Later, he'll reach out to me when he is in Copenhagen. "It was very interesting to talk to you," he'll say. I'll apologize for being hard on him, but Angelo won't feel that I was too harsh. "I've had discussions with guys who were a lot tougher," he'll say.

Now I wonder what experiences Angelo has had over the course of his life. What shaped him into the man he has become? He is silent as I pay the bill, and I wonder why he hasn't thanked me.

On the way out, he wants to pay the waiter his share of the bill, but I tell him that I've taken care of the bill.

"That was really sweet of you, and it wasn't necessary, but thank you very much," he says.

I'm embarrassed by how quickly I assumed he was being rude when he just hadn't realized I'd paid the bill. The distrust seems mutual.

As I find a seat on the train heading back to Copenhagen, I feel crushed. Good or bad, this is how I always feel after one of these discussions. They change me, the conversations, depending on whether I'm met with hatred or with love.

My phone pings. It's a text from Angelo. He writes that I need to feel inner calm to meditate. "You need to relax," he writes.

I can't help but laugh. He invites me to his birthday party. Unfortunately, I can't make it, but he wants to send a gift for my birthday, which is only a few days away. He also wants to teach me to meditate, buy me dinner, and practice martial arts with me. He is eager to keep in touch.

Part of me wants to meet with him, but another part doesn't feel up for it. He needs to recognize that his own hatred and prejudice against Muslims are part of the problem. At the same time, I understand that this is his way of trying. He's reaching out to me. I just hope another Muslim besides me can meet him halfway. I see the hypocrisy clearly. Wasn't this the exact thing I accused him of?

I write back. "Let me know when you are in my part of town. We'll have dinner."

But Angelo won't come to my side of town. "You have to come here," he writes.

My conversations with Jimmy and Lone, Kim, and Angelo have taught me one thing: As much as I don't want to be boxed, I can't put others in boxes either; I can't allow myself to judge them as nationalist extremists or racists. Being concerned about the influx of immigrants and refugees, or about the challenge of integration that we face in Denmark, doesn't make someone a racist or a right nationalist. So I can't really call Jimmy and Lone racists. Kim and Angelo, however, are different. Their views are deeply and unequivocally racist, undemocratic, and violent.

These four individuals are as different in their views as they are in their means of solution. But common among them are feelings of helplessness and anger toward Muslims. I have become better at recognizing these feelings in people, even if they are sometimes both irrational and deductive. Instead of trying to rationalize their concerns by citing social or cultural differences, I've become better at viewing the world from their vantage point and finding what common ground we share. I can say, "You're right; it's not fair that Muslim girls are treated differently than boys."

Some are critical of immigrants because of specific stories. Lone, for instance, had heard about a Muslim girl in foster care who received a hospital bed from the government in her municipality, while a non-Muslim Danish boy in another municipality had his claim rejected. I've noticed that, for many people, it only takes one story to jump to conclusions—in this case, about the preferential treatment of Muslims. But, for people like Angelo and Kim, it goes far beyond one or two examples. Any instances of perceived unfairness, discrimination, or erosion of the culture and morals they value have conflated and merged to become an all-encompassing, amorphous mass of anger and hatred. In situations like that, I feel it's necessary to try to correct their worldview and understanding of human nature.

We can't ignore our duty to have these conversations, even if they can be hard, exhausting, or painful. Sometimes I feel the heat, but at other times, I turn it back on them. Sometimes I can absorb their anger without taking it personally, other times I'm too sensitive. I'm only human. Sometimes these conversations are enlightening, even liberating. Whatever the outcome, I strongly believe we have to try to talk. What other choice do we have?

Rhetoric that implies we are sleepwalking our way to a Muslim invasion has become commonplace in Danish politics. Danish Muslims are routinely portrayed as terrorists, parasites, and criminals by politicians and the media. The call for a ban on Muslim immigration is now mainstream among opinion makers and those in power. Like Jimmy, Kim, and Angelo, I get infuriated when fanatic Muslims are given airtime to spread their hateful rhetoric because it's good for ratings. Above all, I'm angry that their voices are passed off as representative of average Muslims. How could that not create fear, outrage, and insecurity in people like Jimmy, Kim, and Angelo, who don't have regular contact with hard-working, law-abiding, tax-paying Danish Muslims? I would feel the same way they do. I did feel the same. I believed all Danes were racists, until I started working in the supermarket, and ordinary Danes became my friends and colleagues.

This is why it is so important to look your own prejudices in the eye; it can bring about miraculous change in our understanding of each other. I believe a democratic approach is better than imposing limits on freedom of expression. You can't ban opinions, and Jimmy, Kim, and Angelo are as entitled to theirs as I am to mine.

All religions, including Islam, should be subject to criticism in a democracy, which is why I'm a keen advocate for the abolition of the blasphemy clause. But when criticism continues beyond the bounds of religion and turns into racist stereotyping of its adherents, I cannot accept it, or ignore it. None of us should. Inequality breeds frustration and animosity. When people are placed under unbearable pressure, they turn, not on the politicians responsible, but on each other. The seeds for much of the racial hatred that exists globally are sown by inequality.

I'm reminded of my father-in-law, who always laments, "If only immigrants would behave themselves," and I decide that, if I am to truly understand the origins of this rancorous racial hatred, I should also meet with Muslims who hate all Danes in the same way they are despised by Danes like Kim and Angelo.

CHAPTER 4

GIVE THE DANES A TASTE OF THEIR OWN MEDICINE

"Always remember that others may hate you but those who hate you will never win unless you hate them. And then you destroy yourself."

–Richard Nixon

R ecently I posted an update on Facebook that reads like this: "Not all Danes are racist, alcoholic, or pedantic! I often come across these hateful generalizations, sometimes from people with minority roots. Although some of them are born and raised in Denmark, they are deeply racist toward the Danes. It's time I drink #dialoguecoffee with those who hate the Danes."

Soon after, I received an email from Mee:

Dear Özlem,

You hit a nerve with your FB post and its message about racism against the Danes. Normally, I'd agree with you, but not this time. You have some explaining and convincing to do.

I'm adopted from South Korea, and I believe that Danes fit the initial description in your post.

Sincerely,

Mee

We agreed to meet.

Lightning Chinese

It is one of the first summer days when the temperature reaches almost ninety degrees. Mee welcomes me in the yard in front of her yellow townhouse. She isn't very tall and suddenly my own height, five feet two, seems average—a feeling I don't often get in Denmark, where most people tower over me. We shake hands and walk through her garage to the patio. On one of the garage walls is a colorful drawing of Storm P.'s vagabonds.

The house consists of two small buildings, facing each other on either end of the cozy yellow courtyard. Mee lives on one side while her landlord lives on the other. The white garden chairs have white cushions with yellow stripes on them. The table is solid wood. The paint is starting to peel. The neighbor's garden consists of green hedges that match large potted plants in the courtyard.

The landlord is often away, in a cottage, and this arrangement pleases Mee. She likes the silence, and for this very reason she doesn't live with her wife, whom she married a few weeks ago. Her wife lives in Jutland, and neither she nor Mee have wanted to move. Mee's wife has a child, and they only see each other on holidays and on weekends.

"I also don't want to live so closely with another person," Mee says.

"Yes," I agree, without asking a follow-up question. I do want to know why, but I'm afraid of her answer. I know my anxiety is probably due to some of the other answers that I anticipate Mee will provide to my questions.

I already have some preconceptions about the kind of person Mee might be. Now, the question is whether she will fit in the box I created for her. I think she was probably sexually abused and had a difficult childhood, where she struggled with mental health issues. Maybe she's had to retire early. She's probably not on cash assistance, since after all, she lives in a city where the income is higher than average. I'm not proud of my biased attitude. In fact, I'm a little embarrassed by my own prejudices, and I'm relieved that Mee can't read my thoughts.

Mee is anything but Danish. She is highly educated, lives in North Zealand, shops in Irma, and does not buy "cheap bras."

We talk a little about the couples we each know, and have heard of, who live on the fringes. We quickly confirm that the much-touted "normal" does not exist. "Normal" certainly does not describe Mee's life. She was adopted when she was six months old. She calls herself a "cardboard kid."

"Are you familiar with that expression?" she asks, with a charming smile.

I am. I tell her about a trip to Ethiopia that I took with members of the Social Committee when I held a seat in parliament. There, a police chief told how they gathered all the "cardboard kids" in the morning. Unwanted children, who are often infants, are put in plastic bags or cardboard boxes and left in front of the police station. The police chief said that one to three children were surrendered daily, and that she had several cots in her office to accommodate the babies.

Then we stop talking about cardboard kids. At first I think it's probably because it's too painful, but the things Mee tells me afterward are no less painful. She was sexually abused by her adoptive father until she was twenty years old. It stopped when she moved away from home. When he visited her as an adult, she kicked him out of her new place. She can't remember when the assaults started exactly, but they go back as far as she can remember.

"He adopted us to abuse us," she says. She shows no feelings as she tells me how she and her sister were "rented out" to other men. She stoically states that she does not believe in the justice system and has therefore spent her energy trying to reform it, rather than wasting time by losing the case in court.

"Free" is a word that Mee uses again and again. "You're almost free to abuse children in Denmark; it only costs you if you take it too far."

I have great confidence in the Danish legal system myself, but I can feel Mee hitting a sore spot in me. When it comes to child abuse, our legislation is inadequate. And what meager laws we do have are underenforced.

I have chaired both the Social Committee and the Mayors' Council, and I've read full reports on the Tondersagen, Rebild, and Bronderslev cases, and on cases that have received less publicity, but were no less terrible. As Mee begins to talk about the abuse she has suffered, a series of children's wards runs through my memory, along with images of abused, broken children I cared for as a children's psychiatric nurse. I feel like hugging Mee. I want to hold her, and only let go once all her traumas are healed. But, as a nurse knows, physical contact can be difficult for people who have been sexually violated. And I don't know this woman sitting across from me at all. I don't want to delve into this too deeply. I don't want the conversation to hurt Mee. She must be able to read my mind after all, because Mee suddenly says, "You seem to know what I'm talking about." I nod and take a deep breath.

Mee drank away much of her pain. But for the past fifteen years, she has remained sober. As I praise her for it, she seems happy. "Your strength should be celebrated," I say.

"I celebrate my own strength when others seem unable to."

We laugh that off. The atmosphere is pleasant, and the cake from Lagkagehuset good. They probably have nothing else here where she lives, I think. Mee lives in the Whiskey Belt, and can name the best places to eat cake, drink coffee, or enjoy a delicious meal. "I may be a snob, but unlike others, I readily acknowledge it," she says as she blinks at me.

Mee was born two years before I was, speaks Danish with a North Zealand dialect, and belongs to the cultural elite. She is a specialist in historical clothing and knows people from the royal family. We go in to check out her wardrobe, where she shows me the beautiful suits she has sewn and embroidered. Some of them have been time-consuming, taking several years to create, and every outfit has a story, a memory, and a function attached to it. Mee tells me all about it with great vigor, and the almost expressionless face I sat across from on the patio earlier is now lit up so brightly that even her eyes glow. I try on some of the outfits, and we laugh together, like we've been friends for years.

As we return to the patio and sit under her white umbrella, Mee tells me about her experiences with Danes. How she is irritated by people speaking English to her because they assume she is a recent immigrant. How people treat her as an inferior because they assume she must be on cash assistance and have no education. "Haven't you experienced it yourself?" she asks.

It's my turn to share my experiences. I tell her how, when I was in parliament, during important negotiations, I was reprimanded for my use of language by political colleagues in front of a crowd of at least thirty people. It was a humiliating experience to be dressed down like that. So, yes, I can relate to this. But the difference between me and Mee is that, unlike the kneejerk reactions of my youth, I no longer call all Danes idiots just because I've met a few idiots along the way.

I ask Mee if she considers herself Danish. She points to the flag flying in the neighbor's garden. "No," she responds firmly. "I am not a Dane, and I will never consider myself Danish." Mee says she considers herself European. According to Mee, Danes are still living high on their reputation as Vikings and their history of conquest over large parts of Europe. She thinks that the conqueror's mentality still characterizes the Danes in their attitudes toward newly arrived citizens who immigrate into the country. Then Mee says something that makes me unable to hold back my smile. "I just don't get the Danes."

I try not to, because it's not funny, but I smile anyway. Because I'm recollecting my visit with Kim in the colonial house on Funen.

"Why are you smiling?" she asks. I talk about Kim, and how he constantly uses the same word—uninformed—when he talks about Muslims. It is interesting that human prejudices and deductive attitudes are very similar. When I confront Mee with that observation, her reaction is pretty much as I expect it to be. "But I'm right."

I suddenly want to put Kim and Mee in the same room. How would they debate their points of view? What would they say? Would they be able to hear each other at all?

"My loved ones call me 'Lightning Chinese,' " she laughs. Mee says she doesn't like the ugly manner in which some people talk to her, which is why she's not very diplomatic when she encounters racism. She is quickly angered when she's mistreated. She wants to give Danes a taste of what it feels like to be marginalized. I understand this instinct from my own youth, and it reinforces my view that what I have experienced is fairly universal, namely that hate often grows from very specific experiences. This is why I want to confront Mee about her hatred.

I ask her if her attitude toward the Danes is due to the experiences she had in childhood. I'm barely done formulating my question when she answers, "But you were never sexually abused, and you've had similar experiences with racists." I understand why her friends call her Lightning Chinese. For a moment, I lose my composure and spill cold water from my glass on her bare legs. She laughs as she wipes up the water and tells me she has an IQ of 141. I make a mental note to look that up when I get home, because I'm not sure if 141 is high or low. I think it must be high, but why even mention it?

I practice remaining neutral in this discussion to avoid presenting a defense for either the Danes or the immigrants. Again, as I have in all of these coffee dialogues, I start talking about how Mee can take personal responsibility for her biases, and maybe even try to work on eliminating her prejudice. How can I help her see that Danes are also a diverse group of people? Mee says she should try to contact some of the Danes who work with refugees. I have experienced miracles in face-to-face meetings between people who are firmly entrenched in a closed mindset, only to have it blown wide open when they see the humanity in their perceived enemies, and I think that if I can just get Mee to talk to some Danes who could at least balance her viewpoint, then my mission will have been a success.

I'm noticing something I haven't experienced in a coffee dialogue before. I'm starting to feel Mee's position is justified. Her frustration over her experiences triggers dormant feelings in me. Mee's reasoning is riddled with generalizations, but she is not unreasonable in her criticism. I'm afraid to admit she's right. But why? Maybe I'm afraid that, if I acknowledge her pain, it will absolve her of the responsibility to confront her own biases. I can't bring myself to confront her. It might ruin the camaraderie. I am anxious. I do not know if I have budged Mee's position at all, but we've forged a bond. We hug each other as I head out.

The question hangs in my head a few days after my meeting with Mee: How do I get her to meet the lovely Danes I've met? Then a text message from Mee pops up:

"I was out walking with the friendly residents yesterday. Again, the Danes showed me how prejudiced they can be. If you do keep Ramadan, then I wish you a good Ramadan."

My first reaction is to laugh over her text message. I can relate to the experience of trying to be helpful, only to have it all go badly. If your intentions are good, then most likely, good will come of it. But then, I think, it's also hard to satisfy Mee. When Danes are not open and inclusive, it's bad. And when they are open and inclusive, it's often no better. Is Mee's frustration because, as a humanist, she wants an inclusive society? Or is it just because she harbors prejudice? And how much does her feeling of powerlessness toward the Danes resemble what the boys at Norrebro feel?

The Battle of the Red Square

They could be young politicians with hearts burning for social justice and a passion for foreign policy. They could deliver speeches that would shape history. They could have the power to mobilize a contingent of thousands. But they settle for idling around the Red Square in the heart of Norrebro, smoking their cigarettes, while standing in a cloud of pretense.

From a distance, they all look the same: dark-haired, wearing sweatpants, sneakers, and white socks. They sit on chairs, and even though there are enough of them to form a circle, they sit in a straight row, backs to the wall, overlooking the square. It appears time has frozen, and they're gazing intently toward something unknown.

I pull out a chair and sit down to face them. It feels as if everything is happening in slow motion, as they straighten their backs and eye me with skepticism. Now that I can see their faces, I can see them as individuals. The boy sitting across from me is about the same height as I am. Next to him is Abdul. With full lips, long lashes, chocolate-brown eyes and a gentle smile, he is, without doubt, the most handsome among them.

The guy right next to him is quite his opposite. Thin, insecure, with a very strong local accent, Khalid seems to almost disappear in his baggy sweatpants and oversized hoodie. He is holding his cellphone, and as soon as I take my seat, he starts Googling me. He interrupts the conversation periodically to let the others know what he has discovered about me on the internet. Sometimes they laugh, because the information he relays interrupts our conversation awkwardly, but at other times he gets an appreciative nod as thanks for his good work.

One of them sits further apart from the others. His hood is pulled down over his face. He is slow to respond. The others chime in for him before he has time to open his mouth. Najib is a refugee from Afghanistan.

One of the boys stands out clearly from the rest. He is not taller or faster than the others, but there's something about him the others don't have, and he is aware of this and proud of it. It's a hat, but not just any ordinary hat. Naveed's cap is marked by the crescent and star. He just finished high school, and he is beaming underneath his student cap. He doesn't seem boastful, but sincerely happy.

"Congratulations," I say, before I sit down.

"Thank you," he replies, smiling back. It's clear the group is proud of him. The others pat him on the back, and he straightens up as he feels their recognition.

I introduce myself briefly. Some of them know I used to be a politician, some don't. Before I get a chance to say anything, Khalid reads from his cellphone: "Mental Health Advocate, 2007–2015."

"Yes," I nod.

"Comes from Vesterbro." New information. "She used to live in Norrebro," he continues.

In this moment, we connect. I give silent thanks to Wikipedia. Khalid tells me that he reads a lot. I ask him whether he reads books. "No." The only book he has read is the *Manual of Power*.

The others aren't convinced he's actually read the whole book; not even Naveed with the student cap did that. They ask me if I'm a writer, since I read so many books. I tell them that I am writing a book about the distance between groups in our society, and the anger and hatred between them.

"They hate us, and we hate them back," one of them says, as if he can't believe there would be more to say on the matter.

Most of them are in their early twenties, and they have lived most of their lives in Norrebro. They want to talk to me, but they have placed many conditions on our meeting. I can't write their names or show pictures of them in the book. When I'm talking with people from minority backgrounds, it's not unusual for them to express a distrust of journalists. I understand where it comes from. The media rarely portrays them in a positive light. But I get a sense that, with these guys, it must be because they have something to hide. I promise to change their names to protect their identities.

I've already silently judged them. They live up to all my prejudgments. They sit in a flock on Red Square, and they have dark skin. I am embarrassed at how much I blankly accepted the description of them as losers—especially considering that I used to be one of them. I stress repeatedly that I am not looking to expose them.

"You must promise!" they say.

"Wallah," I reply.

Wallah means that you swear by Allah's name; it means you are telling the truth. It is an Arabic word, and all Muslims use it. We reconnect through a common lexicon.

Suddenly, another guy comes over and sits in the chair across from me. An ethnic Danish man has also appeared. Everyone greets him, and so do I. One of the boys stands up and walks over to him, and together they leave the square. Though I'm surprised, I can see from their expressions that there's nothing unusual about this.

The young man who just sat down in front of me is called Hasan. The skin around his eyebrows is red, and I can't help but smile a little at his vanity. He wants to appear all macho, but at the same time, clearly, he has had his eyebrows plucked. He's wearing shorts that reveal a five-inch-long scar running down his leg. He has been stitched recently, and the small pieces of medical tape on his skin indicate that the wound has not yet healed. On his left upper arm, he has another scar, which is slightly longer than the one on his leg.

"She's a nurse," Khalid reads, looking up from his phone.

I am, I say. But you don't need to be a nurse to know he didn't get those scars climbing a tree.

As I look him up and down, Hasan discreetly lifts his t-shirt. Not much, just enough so that I can see he carries a gun. He fixes me with a cold stare, and, though I do my best to show no fear, my heart starts pounding. I might be uneasy, but I can't say I'm shocked. This is Norrebro, after all. (Though, of course, I shouldn't generalize.)

Without missing a beat, I keep talking. I ask Hasan if he has any siblings. But inside my head, thoughts are racing. I realize I'm not afraid of him. If the situation were to escalate, I'm confident that everything I learned as a psychiatric nurse would kick in, and I'd be able to talk him down. No, I'm more afraid of what I can't see; of what could happen behind my back. He is sitting with his back to the wall of the Norrebro Sports Hall, and I'm sitting in front of him. If someone wanted to shoot him from the Red Square, I would be his human shield. The bullet might pass through my heart or my shoulder.

Naveed gets up from his chair, clearly upset. "What are you thinking? What are you thinking?" he asks.

They all start talking among themselves. Everybody is angry with Hasan. They start speaking in Arabic to try to exclude me from their conversation. Though I recognize a couple of words, I can't tell if they're upset because Hasan is carrying a gun, or because he showed it to me. But Hasan seems quite satisfied with the drama he has created. He sits back and smiles defiantly. For my part, I try to appear just as unfazed. This is a test, I think. I need to hold firm. I grew up in Vesterbro, back in the days when it was as lawless as Norrebro is today. I recognize Hasan's little game because I've seen it played before. It's all about power. If I come too close, he'll try to scare me off. And, if he succeeds, it proves one of two things: either that he has all the power, or that I didn't really care about talking to him anyway.

But I do really want to talk to Hasan. And, once he starts, he talks nonstop. Two of his six siblings have university degrees, but he is training to become a tradesman. I catch myself thinking that the two siblings are probably girls.

"Don't you ever lie?" Abdul asks.

"No," I reply.

"That's probably why you were kicked out of parliament," Abdul says, despite his claim that he had never heard of me before.

I can't help but laugh. To them, all politicians are liars. If they don't lie, they're obviously not doing it right.

The situation is becoming a bit chaotic. People show up, others leave. The ethnic Danish man from earlier also returns. It turns out that he is a lawyer and, as he is signaling to a few of the boys in the group, he says—probably to me, as the other boys don't seem to listen—that it's more effective when he contacts his "clients" in person. It is much more convenient than when they forget their appointments at his office. And he also seems to enjoy running into his former clients while he's here. One of the boys mentions the name of a friend and asks the lawyer if he was able to help him.

"Yes, and he..."

I interrupt him. "I'm sure your lawyer can't answer this question, as he upholds lawyer-client confidentiality," I say, fixing the lawyer with a disapproving stare. "Asshole," I think. He is ready to break his secrecy. Professional protocol is clearly different on Red Square.

"It's okay, Özlem. He's one of our friends," one of the boys says as he takes a seat. Abdi has fair skin and bright bluish-green eyes. He is much taller and broader than the others and speaks with the traditional local Norrebro accent, where the "t" is pronounced as "tj." He is obviously experienced in rolling joints. He carefully breaks up a bud of marijuana, and soon, a sweet smell fills the air. I move away a little to avoid the smoke. It's the month of Ramadan, so I am fasting— and I'm light-headed enough already.

I stay with the boys for nearly two hours. The sun is shining, and children are playing in the square on their scooters, bikes, and roller skates. With my back to the square, I can only hear the sounds they make. I notice a lot of different languages being spoken around me. An ethnic Dane appears with a flyer and invites us all to watch the local acrobats later today. The boys stare at him as if he comes from another planet. No one says anything to him. I quickly take the flyer and thank him, before the situation becomes more awkward.

I don't judge the boys. Their lives are very different from that of the guy with the flyer, and maybe they don't even understand the word "acrobat." Many of them speak a kind of hybrid language that is half Danish, and half words from their mother tongue. They can't speak either language fluently.

I don't know these boys, but nevertheless, I feel a connection between us. Despite the gun in Hasan's belt, I feel safe with them. Perhaps I'm getting a little high from the marijuana, cigarettes, and aftershave, but it all feels pretty cozy. I feel I know them, and in a way, I do.

Many of the boys surrounding me are similar to boys I grew up with in Vesterbro. Maybe I even treated some of these boys' parents when I was a nurse in the psychiatric ward in Norrebro. I tell them that I am a Dane, just like them. They laugh a lot at my statement. One thing they're not is Danish! They don't hate the Danes, one of them states emphatically. They know a couple of them and are friendly with them.

"Who?" I ask. "What are the names of your friends?"

The whole group works together to answer my question. They are trying to remember some names. But it is not easy.

"We have many Danish friends, it's just hard to remember their names," Abdi says.

"Jimmi!" another boy shouts. They all nod.

"He also speaks like us. You know, with the accent and jargon," Abdi says.

Birds of a feather flock together, I think.

They keep searching for names. It's like a game of poker where everyone's waiting for someone to win the hand, so we can move on to something else.

"Brian!" someone shouts, and they heave a collective sigh of relief.

Brian is, according to Khalid with the cellphone, a "real" Dane. He is always cutting them down, calling them parasites and various other insults. I ask if they think it's funny.

"Sure!" Khalid says, and many of them nod.

The boys talk about themselves as immigrants. One by one, they tell me who has a criminal record, and who doesn't. About half do—that explains why the lawyer behaved as he did. Nevertheless, the mood is light, and I feel safe. The boys crack jokes at my expense. They take turns teasing me, and they laugh even louder when I tease them back. It almost feels like we're family.

But, as in all families, there are also taboo subjects, and when you touch upon these, the mood changes and conversation can almost escalate into violence. With this group, it happens as soon we start

discussing the Danes. They have nothing against the Danes, but—
and that "but" is a major caveat; the boys talk at the same time—it's
almost too much.

"Quiet!" I yell.

They stop. And then they take turns talking. They are outraged that
Danish forces are bombing Muslims in the Middle East. The wars in
Afghanistan, Iraq, Syria, and Libya take up the entire conversation.
They bombard me with the numbers of civilian casualties.

"In Afghanistan alone, Danes have killed 1.2 million innocent people,"
one of them says, and the others quickly confirm the outrageous
number. It reminds me of my meetings with people who hold many
prejudices toward Muslims. They also have an extremely distorted
picture of reality.

"The Taliban are good people," says Najib, who himself fled from
Afghanistan. "It is the Danes who are evil. They kill innocent people,
while the Taliban protects us." Several of the boys refer to the film
Armadillo, which is about Denmark's involvement in Afghanistan.

Abdi starts talking. He says that Danes are killing Muslims because of
oil, opium, and gas. Danes only go to war in the countries where they
stand to get something out of it, and, he concludes, this proves that
Danes don't care about Muslims.

I try to present counterarguments, but I can't keep up with all their
questions. "No, it's not the Danes, but the politicians who make
the choices," I repeat. "And sometimes it is necessary to go to war,
because there are no other solutions," I say, and I mention the Balkan
War as an example. "But then there are also wars where our efforts, in
hindsight, have helped to make the country more unstable," I admit.
"Like Afghanistan, Iraq, and Libya."

Even though I'm trying to present a balanced argument, I agree with
them in their claim that Danish foreign policy is riddled with double
standards. National interests have greater significance in the decision-

making process of going to war than the need to protect civilians from harm. For example, I can remember feeling wracked with doubt when, as an MP, I helped send F-16s to Libya. Parliament roared, "We Danes cannot just watch silently while Qaddafi butchers his people." I agreed with their position back then, but in hindsight, I'm not convinced we did the right thing. And I still don't understand why we remain passive while ISIL terrorists and Assad are slaughtering thousands of Kurds and Syrians. International politics are hard to figure out, and it's so easy for these boys to use headlines as the whole story.

As they talk, I'm thinking of Kim in his allotment, and his attitude toward Muslims. This conversation may be diametrically opposed to that one, but at the same time, it's strangely identical.

It feels as though we're never able to do more than scratch the surface of an issue before the focus shifts to a new topic of interest. And somehow, in my efforts to keep up and keep talking, I find myself defending the Danes. It is curious how I often end up playing devil's advocate when I encounter this level of hatred. I simply can't resist doing it. Maybe it's hatred of any kind I oppose. But, even if that's the case, I resent the role I'm cast in. Why should I be a spokesperson for an entire population group?

If I were sitting with my left-leaning friends, I would agree with them that Denmark's foreign policy has double standards. Western countries, on one hand, criticize oppressive regimes for not respecting human rights, but continue to trade with them. Take, for instance, Saudi Arabia, which has a reputation for human rights violations. We continue to sell them Danish products and purchase their oil in return. Turkey is as oppressive as China when it comes to human rights. Nevertheless, Denmark and the EU closely cooperate with Erdogan to prevent Syrian refugees from reaching Europe. And historically, many former dictators, such as Saddam Hussein, Muammar Qaddafi, and Bashar al-Assad, used to be Western allies.

Each nation-state makes many concessions in relation to its foreign policies. Friends and enemies change roles, depending on what is most lucrative. But why is it so hard for me to explain this foreign policy perspective to the boys from Norrebro? Why am I sitting across from them and defending Denmark's and the West's foreign policy when I agree with them that it is wrong?

I think it is because I am afraid that, if I agree with their oversimplified black-and-white views, they may think I also agree with their angry perception of Denmark and the Danes—and I don't. For me, there is a big difference between disagreeing on foreign policy issues and being angry with every Dane in the whole of Denmark.

While I'm slightly distracted by my own thoughts, the boys continue their lively discussion. Everyone's always on their case, because they are Muslims, because they are immigrants, because they don't want to be like the Danes. Because, because, because. It's always the fault of others, and never their own. I'm growing rather tired of victim mentality. They constantly complain about the Danes but, I wonder, how are they helping themselves?

"Do you vote in the elections?" I ask.

Some of them say yes, but Hasan says that it is "haram" (forbidden) to vote. The others get angry with him. Naveed, with the student cap, tells me not to include Hasan in my book. "He can't talk properly," he says, and adds angrily, "He's lying!"

Naveed is clearly as tired of him as I am of the victim mentality that seems to pervade every conversation with these boys. They keep saying they have nothing in common with the Danes.

"They want our women to go clubbing," Hasan says with a sneer, revealing his clear contempt for women who go clubbing. He's absolutely not going to vote for someone who wants Muslims to be like the Danes.

Naveed has had enough. He leans forward and raises his left hand. His gold watch shines in the sun. "Brother," he says to Hasan, managing to get Hasan to pipe down for a moment. "Brother, it is because we have not voted, and because thousands of Muslims don't vote, that conservative liberals are in power."

I notice that the fight is between Naveed and Hasan. Whoever wins, the rest of the group will follow. While the other boys are quietly paying attention to this debate, I'm thinking about the restless atmosphere our conversation is stirring up on the Red Square. I don't know whether any of the passers-by understand what we're saying—Danish, Arabic, and Turkish words are all mixed into this conversation. Arms are flailing and voices are raised. From the outside, it must look as if we're having a huge argument. But from the inside, it feels like the healthiest democratic discussion I've had in a long time.

I don't know who will win the fight in the long run, but right now the battle is intense. Hasan consistently refers to Muslim-ruled countries as "our country." For him, the Danish and European fear of terrorism is a fallacy, because the real terror is perpetrated on Muslim countries, where "our parents are being slaughtered and raped." He says, "There's nothing we can do. Voting in an evil system; it is the same as going to hell." Hasan is getting tired, overwhelmed by a sense of powerlessness. He smiles and repeats that, as a good Muslim, he will not vote.

I see an opening to reach him. I lean forward and look him directly in the eyes. "Let me tell you something, and I know it's something your mothers would tell you if they could see you right now." The seriousness of my voice grabs the boys' attention. They suddenly fall silent. "If you don't want to go to hell, then maybe you shouldn't be doing all the shit you're doing. It's Ramadan, but none of you are fasting. Instead, you're just sitting here, smoking weed and wasting your brains away. Don't you dare tell me you're a good Muslim, and that the Danes are pigs."

I'm still staring him down as I scold him like a small child. Hasan has suddenly become quiet and small, and I feel a pang of guilt. Am I coming down too harshly on him? I get up. There is just one small step between us, and I place myself directly in front of him. He remains sitting, the others are sitting still and listening. I lean down and put my arms around him. He reaches his hand up to my shoulder. I'm holding him, and he is not pushing me away.

As I sit back down in my chair, I notice the others are smiling. With peace restored, I take a deep breath, and attempt to explain again why a life of crime, weed, and deep-seated resentment for the country they live in may not be the most constructive use of their energies.

Naveed is leaning back comfortably. I have taken over his position in the group, at least temporarily. But Hasan is not finished. "Abdi's right, though. Danes take our gold, our oil, and our opium," he says. He often uses Abdi's arguments. Hasan agrees more with Abdi's arguments than he does with Naveed's.

"If it is 'our' oil and gold they are taking, why don't you go back to your country to look after it?" I ask.

He can't even hear what I'm asking him. He is no longer angry, but still determined in his line of argument. Without stopping, he explains how the Danes have slaughtered and plundered his people. They are the reason his parents fled to this country.

His words are triggering my fight instinct, and I repeat my question. "Why are you here, then? Why don't you go back to *your* country?" I say, knowing that it's not entirely fair.

Hasan was born in Denmark, and he is a Dane, even if he won't acknowledge it. He feels not a trace of pride in that fact. "Why should I go back there when I can 'flex' the state right from here?" he asks. While I'm wondering what he means by "flex," he continues, "As soon as I finish my training, I'll take all I can get from the welfare system, and I'll work under the table too. That's how to destroy the system!" he laughs.

As a Danish Muslim myself, I know that this attitude is wildly at odds with the teachings of Islam. One must first be loyal to the society in which one lives. You must comply with the laws, pay taxes, and not steal. I remind him of this. Some of the boys are quiet. Others back me up. My closest ally is Naveed. I look at him with admiration; he's a beacon of hope amid this darkness. His peers are jobless, uneducated, and flirting with crime. They are angry, frustrated, and full of resentment at the lack of options before them. Their resentment is aimed squarely at the Danes. Naveed has forged a different path—law-abiding, democratic—and he is eager to have his friends join him.

Hasan talks about the "kuffar," the infidels. In his mind, all Danes are infidels. He feels no gratitude for what Danish society provides. What he feels is anger, and he needs to express it. Benefits fraud is his revenge; he doesn't see a problem with stealing from the society he lives in. So, I ask him what's going to happen to the welfare system if we all take from it and pay nothing in through tax. "Who is going to pay for your education? Your mother's hospital treatments? Or for the maintenance of Norrebro Sports Hall, which you appear to frequent often?"

I continue my diatribe, telling him it's wrong to steal and cheat. The more I mention the Prophet Muhammad and the Qur'an, the more his friends seem to agree with me. I'm speaking their language. I'm succeeding in my mission, I think. Then I stop. Was it ever my mission to persuade Muslims to behave themselves? Is it my father-in-law's right to say how anyone should behave? Do Muslims just need to learn how to keep their noses clean and stay out of trouble? If so, is it possible that their religion could be a part of the solution, rather than the source of the problem? Would tensions exist if Muslims in Denmark were "good" Muslims?

Honestly, I don't know. I'm almost certain it's not that simple. But when I listen to Hasan, it's clear to me that some of these boys are twisting religion as a means to an end. Opposite him sits Naveed. While he is critical, like Hasan, to a point, he remains democratic in mindset. I look at his student cap with the crescent moon, which sparkles in the sun, and feel very proud on his behalf. He speaks again. "The Danes have bought combat aircraft for thirty billion kroner to bomb Muslims," he says, and it surprises me how much of his anger is rooted in foreign policy and is fed by events outside Denmark's borders.

I want to give the boys something to hope for. I want to show them how I started out in Norrebro and, despite that, I got an education and made something of my life. I tell them about my own experiences, how I, too, once hated the Danes as much as they do. I tell them about how I was elected to parliament, and I tell them about my children. I assure them I'm not so different from them. "You could very well have been my sons," I say. But the truth is, they couldn't. No son of mine would have been allowed to waste his time like this, watching his prospects go up in smoke.

I list all the addresses in Norrebro where I have lived. The more I talk, the heavier my Norrebro accent becomes, and the more closely they listen. They also begin to answer my questions more honestly. And when I tell them I seek out the people who send me hate mail, I sense their respect.

"Alone?!" one says. "Without security? Without a man to protect you? Without pepper spray?" They think I'm insane. You really don't have to scratch the surface too hard to see fear beneath their tough veneers.

But nothing changes the fact that Hasan, Abdi, Najib, Abdul, and Khalid do not trust the Danes, and certainly not the Danish political system. No matter what I say, they don't believe they enjoy the same privilege and freedoms as ethnic Danes, and they mention freedom of speech as an example. Why was it okay for Danes to draw the Prophet Muhammad, which in Islamic culture is akin to blasphemy, when there were attempts to restrict the freedom of expression of some imams? I'm a little surprised that they've followed the debate so closely, and I agree that we've seen a rise in double standards among Danish politicians. When a fundamental right like freedom of speech is reserved for people you agree with, but taken away from others, there is no equity.

When I went into politics here in Denmark, my father said, "No one has any right to complain if they haven't done everything in their power to make things better." Everyone has a measure of responsibility, he claimed. Having this as a fundamental principle from such a young age, it's almost instinctual for me to tell the boys that *they* must do something to build bridges between themselves and the Danes. They themselves must take initiative.

When Abdul asks, "But who is reaching out to us?" I feel his dilemma. I grew up as a "loser" child, I have experienced his despair, and to witness it now is just as painful. But, at the same time, I feel deep anger at his passivity, at his total lack of a sense of a responsibility. It would never have occurred to him to do something about his own problems, to build his own bridges. These conflicting emotions, my sympathy and my anger, are real and raw. Things are rarely black and white. Years of working with people have taught me this.

Worn out, Hasan looks to Abdi to take up the battle. Abdi, who is almost done smoking his joint, is calmer than Hasan. In reaching for a compromise, he looks back over the course of history and says cooperation between the West and the Muslim world has never worked. "It's their move," he says. "We can't do anything until they (the West) show us they are willing to cooperate with us."

For him, cooperation means an end to the senseless bombing of Muslim countries and no more investing in weapons of mass destruction. The money spent on killing civilians, or on arms and firepower, should instead be spent on rebuilding the countries that have been bombed to pieces. Hasan nods.

I slap my hand against my thigh and exclaim, "You should be in youth policy! You'd be so good at it!" I mean it sincerely.

They are excited that I am dreaming better futures for them on their behalf. "Yeeeeah!" they cry in unison. But Abdi has lost his steam, and, with an air of resignation, he says he may know a lot, but he can't do much. Hasan, on the other hand, has caught hold of the idea. He asks if I really believe they could build a career in politics. This is the first time I've heard sincere happiness in his voice. We talk at length about youth parties and memberships, and different ways to be active in politics.

I'm about to get up when Abdul asks me whether the meeting with them has been the highlight of my life. I laugh out loud and say no, they are not as exciting as some of my haters. "And it takes more than a gun to impress me," I say. They all laugh. "But I won't forget you," I add.

The boys tell me I now have friends for life on Red Square, and to be sure to let them know if anyone hassles me. They hug me, and I hug them back. One takes a selfie with me, but then quickly deletes the image when he remembers they're supposed to remain anonymous. This meeting has never taken place.

When I get into my car, I find myself pondering the impact of foreign policy agendas on us as individuals, as human beings. Even the boys at the Red Square in Norrebro have an opinion about war, weapons, and peace. These boys need to be part of the community and, if this doesn't happen because of their background, they are at high risk of being pulled toward sinister fundamentalist forces that offer an alternative sense of community—a community that pits them against the Danes and against democracy. Several times during our conversation, I noticed the parallels between the boys' arguments and arguments expounded by certain imams who take a more vocal role in opposition to democracy. It's clear to me whose door I need to knock on next: I must seek out radical imams to find out if it's possible to have a democratic conversation with someone bent on weakening democracy, if not eliminating it altogether.

CHAPTER 5

THE SMELL OF HIZB UT-TAHRIR'S BAKERY

"Evil can only be overcome by goodness between people. Goodness requires courage."

–Sergeot Uzan, father of Dan Uzan

I have been outspoken about Hizb ut-Tahrir for more than a decade. I have criticized the organization in interviews, and I have quarreled with its members for inciting hatred against Jews and homosexuals and for urging Danish Muslims not to vote. When they invited foreign imams known for preaching hatred to deliver sermons in gender-segregated meetings, I was vocal in my opposition to the message. I've argued against their claim to be the voice of all Muslims—a platform which the media has unfortunately given them. The association's spokesman, Junes Kock, as I see him, is the epitome of a converted Muslim who doesn't just embrace a new religion, but also blindly accepts a fundamentalist interpretation as truth.

Despite the number of times I've criticized the organization, I have never met with anyone from Hizb ut-Tahrir. This is due to two factors: First, I was afraid that someone would accuse me of legitimizing their attitudes—or worse, that people would think I shared their fanatical attitudes. Because my own background is Muslim, I've always been concerned about being lumped in with the extremists. Secondly, I didn't think a conversation with them could make a difference. I simply could not imagine that one could shake extremist positions through conversation, and I didn't think I'd learn anything new by meeting with them. I already knew everything I thought I needed to know through the media.

In many ways, Hizb ut-Tahrir is difficult to compare with other parties in a Danish context. Their rabid attitudes are closest to the Danes' Party, even though they are at an opposite extreme on the political spectrum. The Danes' Party was formed by a former neo-Nazi and supports the forced expulsion of all citizens of Denmark who come from non-Western countries. If they had their way, they would strip me of my Danish citizenship. In the last municipal elections, the Danes' Party received a thousand votes. This is roughly the same number of people Hizb ut-Tahrir has been able to gather at a couple of high-profile meetings and demonstrations. On Wikipedia you can read, among other things, that in 2014 the organization managed to gather a thousand people in Norrebrohallen for a gathering called

"Proud of Sharia." The same year, Assistant Professor Kirstine Sinclair at the University of Southern Denmark estimated that there were 100 to 150 full-fledged members nationwide, most of them in the Copenhagen area.

The party was founded in Jerusalem in 1953, and its name means the "liberation party." Today, Hizb ut-Tahrir is an international Islamic political party working to create an Islamic state governed by Islamic law, the sharia. They call this transnational empire the Caliphate. In Denmark, we regularly discuss how far Hizb ut-Tahrir's influence has spread. In 2003, the American think tank Heritage Foundation estimated that Hizb ut-Tahrir was active in forty countries and had between five and ten thousand core members and tens of thousands of sympathizers.

Hizb ut-Tahrir calls for Muslims to overthrow their governments and advocates armed struggle against Israel and the West. Their hatred of Jews is well known, and the party has been declared illegal in most Arab countries. In England, Hizb ut-Tahrir has been banned from a number of universities and educational institutions following conflicts with other religious minorities.

Hizb ut-Tahrir is best known in Denmark for its opposition to democracy. Its members believe that Islamic law and democracy are opposites, and they therefore support the boycotting of democratic elections.

Unfortunately, in Denmark, ethnic minority citizens are less likely to vote than other Danes. This is most clearly seen in the municipal elections, where all citizens who have lived in Denmark for more than three years have the right to vote, but turnout remains low among new Danes.

During the 2013 municipal elections, I contacted the religious leadership of large Muslim organizations to engage in dialogue. Although the Muslim organizations disagree on many issues, they agreed on one thing: They wanted to participate in a comprehensive call for Muslim citizens with minority backgrounds to take an active part in the political process by exercising their right to vote. Many imams used a Friday prayer leading up to the municipal elections to preach democracy and urge Muslims to seize the opportunity to influence Danish society. In addition, a large contingent of Muslims joined me in a supplemental section in the weekend newspaper which emphasized that participation in democracy is both a right and a duty. The message of the religious leaders was clear: there is no contradiction between being a Muslim and being part of the democratic community.

This attitude was in sharp contrast to Hizb ut-Tahrir's, and a few days after the newspaper ran our call to vote, they countered with a press release that proclaimed Muslims should not participate in democratic elections, because the process is in opposition to Islamic law—and thus, it is sinful to vote. There were no signatories to the message other than Hizb ut-Tahir. The municipal elections in 2013 showed how isolated Hizb ut-Tahrir remains in their rejection of democracy.

Although I know that very few Muslims support Hizb ut-Tahrir, I also know that the organization is very active in its engagement with young people. For example, they hand out flyers in front of colleges, and deliberately speak to the undefined anger of vulnerable youth from the lower echelons of the community. I recognized their influence when I talked to the boys at Red Square. That energetic young people engage emotionally with the world around them is nothing new. Hizb ut-Tahrir is adept at channeling the energy of the young and redirecting it toward an enemy of their choosing: the Danes, the West, and democracy.

But now, on my way to Norrebro to visit the mosque where Hizb ut-Tahrir meets, I don't want to talk about them anymore, but with them. Many years of seeking out the people who send me hate emails have bolstered my courage and sparked within me a sincere curiosity. I want to get to the root of why they are so set on creating division instead of unity, chaos instead of consensus.

In 2003, Hizb-ut-Tahrir's spokesman at the time, Fadi Abdullatif, was convicted of hate speech after encouraging violence against Jews. But Hizb ut-Tahrir doesn't just attack other religious groups, they also create friction within their own faith group when they try to define how Muslims should behave.

There are many interpretations of Islam. How do they reach the conclusion that Islam justifies hatred?

In 2004, I attended a wedding in Indonesia. The bride was Muslim, and the groom was Buddhist. "This is Islam," I thought back then. Accommodating and nonjudgmental. But in the years that have passed since then, terrible things have happened all over the world in the name of religion. I do not believe there is anything antithetical about Islam and democracy. I'm both a supporter of representative democracy and a Muslim. Many Muslims in Denmark agree with me.

Religion can be, and historically has been, used as a weapon of hatred by extremists of all faiths. In the newspapers we don't read about interfaith weddings like the one I attended in Indonesia. Instead, we read about how terribly wrong things go when religions mix. And while I understand that the media should be more balanced in how they report stories about Muslims, at the same time, I carry some resentment against Muslim groups who are bent on creating active hostility. I don't want to live in a community with these people. This feeling, which is more powerlessness than anger, is reminiscent of how I once felt toward the Danes. If I had to eat pork and drink beer to become Danish, well, I wouldn't be Danish.

But if Hizb ut-Tahrir represents Islam, then I'm not a Muslim either, I think. (I immediately regret that thought.) In fact, I wonder why they hold their meetings in a mosque. They describe themselves as "a political party whose ideology is Islam," so why don't they have political offices like other parties? I wouldn't expect the Christian Democrats to hold their meetings in a church.

I park my car on Heimdalsgade and enter the mosque through an open gate. I'm standing in a yard that seems very empty and not reminiscent of the park-like environments I associate with Norrebro. There is no playground or sandbox for children to play in, and other than a few trees and a hedge there is not much greenery. A black sign catches my attention. The sign hangs next to an open door and says "Masjid al-Faruq." Masjid means mosque in Arabic, so I must be in the right place.

I stand close to the hedge and my head begins spinning. I can't figure out if it's because I'm scared or if I'm just excited about the meeting. I feel out of place, and it feels like people are staring at me. A bunch of women with baby carriages spot me and smile, while others are busy talking to their children. Two young women with blond hair come into the yard. "It smells so good," one says, and I notice the smell of freshly baked bread and a large sign that reads "Ali Bakery." Is there a bakery under Hizb ut-Tahrir's mosque? The building looks more industrial than a traditional mosque. It has two floors, so the mosque must be upstairs.

There is some foot traffic in and out of the bakery, but it seems like the mosque is empty. Under normal circumstances, I would just knock. But I hesitate. In the time I've been arranging coffee dialogues, I haven't felt this level of trepidation. Something is holding me back. Maybe it's the articles I've read in the newspapers about the segregation of women within the community. Maybe it's the images of angry Hizb ut-Tahrir men. Perhaps it's the fear of a journalist writing that I have been seen in Hizb ut-Tahrir's mosque. Maybe it's a combination of it all.

While all these thoughts are racing through my mind, a tall young man emerges from the entrance to the mosque. I walk toward him, and as he catches my eye, he smiles. "Aren't you Özlem?" he asks.

I confirm my identity, tell him that I have come to talk to someone from Hizb ut-Tahrir, and ask if he is one of them.

"Who?" he asks. His eyes are vacant. When I tell him that Hizb ut-Tahrir utilizes the mosque, he turns and looks at the sign, and says he just needed a place to rest and pray. I wonder why such a young man needs rest so early in the afternoon. He is at least five feet nine and dressed in black jogging pants, a black hoodie, and a black cap. His dark beard has been trimmed, and he has been careful to shave high up on his cheekbones, so his beard appears to be drawn on his face. There is something in his gaze that makes me think of the patients I cared for when I worked in psychiatry. His eyes seem blurry, maybe drugged. I choose to be direct and ask him if he needs rest because he is sick. "I'm tired of my head," he replies.

I ask him if he can check in the mosque for me and see if there is anyone I can talk to inside. He agrees to help, but is sure there is no one. I find some courage and offer to go in with him.

As we enter the staircase, I see a bulletin board with a note that reads "Love our Prophet." On the floor is a blue Ikea bag filled with CDs, free for the taking.

On the first floor, we enter a hallway. To the left is a large shelf with a sign asking visitors to remove their shoes before entering the mosque.

To the right, six taps hang over a large sink equipped with soap for ritual cleansing before prayer. Next to the sink, white towels are stacked on top of one another in a clear plastic bin. Above the bin, there's a sign written in red ink that reads "CLEAN," and next to it a large bag with a sign that reads "DIRTY." I take off my sandals and enter the mosque. It saddens me that I forgot my scarf, because I do want to show respect for the religious spaces I enter. But there is not much I can do about that now. I want to go into the mosque.

I don't know what I expected, but I'm disappointed in a way. There are no angry imams waiting to kidnap me, nor any of the angry young men I see in the media. The mosque appears to be empty and peaceful. It is similar to hundreds of mosques I have visited in Denmark and abroad. The floor is covered with red wall-to-wall carpeting, on the walls are a few quotations from the Qur'an in stylized calligraphy, and in the corner stands the imam's pulpit. The only thing I haven't seen before is a large piece of black fabric with Arabic writing hanging on the wall. At first glance it looks like ISIL's flag, but since I can read a little Arabic, I quickly realize that it is the "Shahadah" creed. I read the text to myself: *Lä íláha íllá iláhu wa muhammadun rasúlu ilái*," which means, "There is no god except Allah, and Muhammad is Allah's Prophet."

"If you come back in an hour, when the dinner prayer starts, someone should be able to help you," the young man who escorted me says. We continue to chat on our way out of the mosque. He lives in Norrebro, has no education, and does not attend school. His parents come from the Kurdish part of Turkey. "I'm twenty-four years old and tired of life," he says.

I ask why. He tells me he has been sentenced to psychiatric treatment, and that his lawyer is working to get his sentence lifted.

I ask what he has done.

"It's a long story," he replies. He wants to know if I know his lawyer, who is also Kurdish.

Yes, I do know him. This isn't surprising. In Norrebro, the world always seems so small. Suddenly his empty eyes make sense. He's in the mood to talk, and I try to convince him not to visit this mosque. I talk about all the hatred that Hizb ut-Tahrir preaches. He promises he won't return, but I don't know if he'll keep his promise. He seems to be in his own world.

I walk out into the street, sit in my car and wait for the hour to pass.

I see people entering the yard who, I gather, must be on their way to prayer. I know that a dinner prayer takes about fifteen minutes, so I lock my car and go back into the yard. While I wait for the prayer to end, I can't help but think of Omar El-Hussein, who visited this mosque just before he murdered film director Finn Norgaard in front of Krudttonden and then killed a volunteer guard, Dan Uzan, in front of the synagogue at Krystalgade. Did Omar hear anything at the mosque that inspired his attacks, or was the mosque just a stop on the road?

I can't be certain, but I'm filled with anger at the thought, and that bolsters my courage. As the first men step out of the mosque, I approach them. They refer me to another man standing in front of Ali Bakery. He agrees to talk with me, and we negotiate how long our conversation will last. He says I can have twenty minutes, but I know this is going to take longer.

As we enter the mosque again, I hear someone shout, "Özlem, wait!" I turn around and see a man in his fifties cycling toward me. He is dressed in traditional Pakistani clothing and has a long white beard. At first glance, I think he looks angry, so I step back, but he is anything but angry. "I heard you on Radio 24/7. You need to know, I'm proud of you. My kids are proud of you. My daughters are proud of you. You are one of the few people who defend us Muslims. I will pray to Allah that all goes well for you," he says. I thank him and smile back at him. I'm a little embarrassed by my initial reaction. The man was just trying to be kind, and I thought he might knock me down. But can anyone blame me for being afraid?

We walk up the stairs, put our shoes on the shelf in the hallway, and enter the mosque. "*Assalamu alaikum*," I say to the men in the room. It means "Peace be with you," and is a greeting that Muslims use when they meet. The men return my greeting.

One of them is clearly different from the others. He has a light gray coat, and long hair and beard. As I pass him, I think he might be Said Mansour, better known as the "Bronshoj Bookseller," who was recently stripped of his Danish citizenship and expelled from the country in response to calls he made for terrorist attacks. But then I recall that Mansour's hair and beard were black in the pictures I've seen of him. The man who greets me is gray-haired, and based on his attire, I think he must be a Salafist. I have had previous encounters with Salafists, especially during election campaigns. Once, several young Salafists surrounded me on the street and harassed me because they believed I was a disbeliever, a kafir. Like this man, they wore long robes, and kept their hair and beards long and untrimmed.

Anti-Democrats

As we leave the mosque, another man joins us. We walk into a café in a back room. I smile as I see the menu hanging on the wall. Hot dogs, milkshakes, and energy drinks are some of the things they serve. This café could belong to any association. I am offered a Coca-Cola.

The two men I talk with wish their names to remain confidential. I'll call the man I met in front of the mosque Ahmed. He volunteers for the mosque and manages Ali Bakery.

"Is the bakery connected to the mosque?" I ask.

"No, no, no, no," he repeats. "It's independent...but it's a family-run business for the association." I interpret that to mean that the bakery raises funds for the Hizb ut-Tahrir. But I don't ask him directly and don't receive a direct response from him. The naïve Danes who come into the yard because "it smells so good" are unaware that they may be helping to fund something that smells particularly ugly: the hatred of Jews, gays, and democracy.

Ahmed is skinny and maybe three or four inches taller than me. He is forty-four years old and wears a pair of jeans fastened tightly at the waist with a belt. His army-green polo shirt highlights his smiling brown eyes. He seems kind and polite. He recently moved from Norrebro to Rodovre and has four children. He is originally from Palestine and is a stateless refugee. "I came in September 1986, when I was fourteen," he says.

I'll call the other man Hamza. Ahmed's daughter is married to Hamza's son. Hamza is a little taller than Ahmed, fifty years old, with thinning hair, and a little stocky. His face seems familiar, but I can't place where I might have seen him. He is also a stateless Palestinian, who emigrated to Denmark thirty years ago from Lebanon, where he was born and raised. His parents fled Palestine in 1948. "Away from the Israelis," he says. He speaks Danish fluently, but repeatedly tells me that he isn't so good with the language. Like Ahmet, he volunteers in the mosque, and when needed, he also acts as the mosque's imam. "You could say I'm a company imam," he says. He adds that, unfortunately, he has no education, but then proudly tells me about his children and their accomplishments.

I notice happy surprise in the two men's faces when I tell them about my sons and mention them by name. My elder son's name, Furkan, is written in the Qur'an. Yusuf is my youngest son.

"Nice name," says Ahmed. This is the same reaction I am often met with from Jews, because the name Yusuf is also written in the Torah.

I tell them my children's names for a good reason. I need to build a bridge with Ahmed and Hamza, so that they feel more comfortable opening up and honestly answering my questions. It has been my experience that a tough conversation has a better chance of reaching accord when it starts off on common ground. Everyday life, children, and family are usually good places to find a connection, no matter how tenuous it seems at first.

I tell them how uncomfortable I felt when I stood in front of the mosque. "You always seem so angry when I see you on television. I wasn't sure how this meeting would pan out," I say with a smile.

"I think you might have some prejudice there," Ahmed says dryly.

Hamza has four daughters and two sons. "I'll soon become a grandfather," he says, smiling. His three eldest children are married. They are twenty-six, twenty-four, and twenty-two years old.

I also married when I was twenty-two, I note.

"*Alhamdulillah* (Thanks to Allah), they all go to university," Hamza continues. The twenty-six-year-old has completed pharmacy education, while the next three are still pursuing their degrees in mechanical engineering, civil engineering, and pharmacy training. The two youngest are in fourth and ninth grade.

"I didn't get the opportunity to go to college myself," he says, with a crack in his voice. He has a high school education from Lebanon. His initial plan was also to continue his education in Denmark, but being a refugee while trying to support a family left back in Lebanon was not as easy as he anticipated.

Instead, Hamza became one of the "best-known produce traders in Norrebro," Ahmed says. But life as a greengrocer was tough. Eventually, Hamza sold his shop, and right now he is unemployed. His face also seems very familiar, but again, I'm not sure where to place it.

Both Ahmed and Hamza are members of Hizb ut-Tahrir, but they stress several times that the mosque is not affiliated with Hizb ut-Tahrir. "We needed a place to meet. Many kinds of people come here, and we're probably the smallest group," says Ahmed with a smile.

While we drink the Coke, I look around the room. We sit on chairs that resemble copies of Mies van der Rohe's Barcelona chairs. They are burgundy and face each other. A horizontal line divides the wall into two, and mosques and crowds are drawn on that line, and in the middle of it all is a black banner painted with sacred text.

But I'm not in the mosque to drink cola or analyze the decor. After our initial polite talk about children and families, I decide to address my questions. Why did they join Hizb ut-Tahrir? Why are they so adamantly opposed to democratic government? What do they think about ISIL, about Jews, about homosexuals? It's a long list. I decide to start by asking about Jews and homosexuality.

People from Hizb ut-Tahrir have on several occasions voiced condemnation toward the two minority groups, and since I have both Jewish and gay friends, I know that I can have a hard time managing my anger when the conversation is heated with homophobia and anti-Semitism. There is no need to start a quarrel, I think.

"What distinguishes Hizb ut-Tahrir's members?" I ask.

"We are Muslims," Ahmed and Hamza say almost in chorus.

"So am I. But I am not a member of Hizb ut-Tahrir," I say.

"Islam is an ideology, a way of life that has the solution to humanity. The best solution. That's why I work to convince people to support an Islamic system of government," Ahmed says. He is an active proselytizer, building a citizenry for the future Islamic state he dreams of. "Of course, not in Denmark," he emphasizes. "We are not working for an Islamic state in Denmark."

Instead, he longs for an Islamic government in "our homeland." For Ahmed, this is Algeria, Pakistan, and the Middle East, including Turkey. It's a vast region of land, encompassing many cultures, from which a large contingent of Muslims have been displaced by political upheaval and power struggles stretching back over a millennium.

The political upheaval is ongoing, and I can relate to his concerns. I've been paying close attention to a crisis in the country of my birth. "Are you happy about what happened in Turkey after the military coup attempt?" I ask him.

"Both yes and no," Ahmed replies. He is glad the military lost. "The military are secularists," he says. "They would have opposed Islamism." But he is also not happy with Turkish President Recep Tayyip Erdogan. "Some people hate Islam, and some people merely tolerate it. Erdogan can tolerate Islam," he says. Thus, in Ahmed's eyes, Erdogan is the lesser of two evils, but not an ideal. To my surprise, he also regards Erdogan as a secularist.

I have a hard time hiding my wonder. "Do you really think Erdogan is a secularist?" I ask.

Without hesitation, Ahmed answers yes. He justifies it with the president's words from a speech given after the failed coup attempt, in which he said, "Democracy won over military forces." According to Ahmed, because Erdogan supports democracy, he is a secularist. I can feel myself biting my tongue as I try to find the logic in his analysis. I follow news coverage from Turkish, Danish, English, and Nordic sources, but I have never heard this argument before. Virtually all domestic and foreign media believe that Erdogan rose to power through tyranny and has a vision for the future of Islamic rule in Turkey. This is the first time I've heard anyone call Erdogan secular.

Now is the time to ask my big question. "Is Hizb ut-Tahrir opposed to democracy?" I already know the answer, but I am excited about whether I can understand the argument.

Ahmed, of course, affirms that he and Hizb ut-Tahrir are against democracy. Neither Ahmed nor Hamza votes in Danish elections, nor do they intend to do so as long as the law is determined by constitution and not the Qur'an. This matter is not open for debate, they emphasize. "People cannot find solutions to human problems through legislation. The only answer to suffering is through submission to the rule of the Creator. People have their own vested interests; they are not objective and neutral. And mankind cannot even control itself, how is it supposed to legislate for others?" Ahmed asks rhetorically. He cites problems such as suicide, substance abuse, and illness as examples of societal ills that cannot be resolved with legislation. His best solution is to follow the law of Allah as described in the Qur'an. He says, "Allah knows most and knows best."

He tells me that, although man is commanded to follow the laws contained in the Qur'an, we are given freedom by Allah to administer the law. So even in the utopian society Ahmed dreams of, ruled by the mandate of God, speed limits must be set to prevent traffic fatalities. I ask him who determines the speed limit. "We find the most qualified person for the job," he replies.

I point out to them, "In Denmark we have discussions about how fast traffic can flow on the highways. In Hizb ut-Tahrir's world, who is going to decide these things, and how should they be chosen?" I ask.

"Professional people," Ahmed replies.

"But who chooses them?" I ask again.

Ahmed avoids giving a direct reply. "Say, for example, you'd like to build a high-rise building. You wouldn't ask an imam how to build it, right? You'd find the best architect."

We reach agreement that different professionals may have different opinions. For example, some doctors believe that back injuries can be healed with surgical intervention, while others would relieve the pain through medication or physical therapy.

I've reached a new understanding that brings tears to my eyes. Hizb ut-Tahrir does not mind the electoral process itself, but the fact that legislation is based on something other than Qur'anic law. I don't agree completely, but I am glad that the nuance is clearly evident.

It's Hamza's turn. He says that, as long as legislation in Denmark is not based on the Qur'an, he cannot support democracy. "Islam clearly states that Allah has already written the laws. It's not a choice. One day, when we have an Islamic state, we'll also need to figure out a voting system."

Although he speaks fervently in support of an Islamic regime, Hamza admits that Muslims have also quarreled amongst themselves. "We have never lived as miserably as today!" Hamza says.

Ahmed agrees. He believes that what is happening in the Middle East is happening because of democratic processes. He cites the Iraq War as an example of how Western countries, led by the United States, have used democracy as an excuse to take over other countries by force. I remember my conversation with the boys at the Red Square, where the Iraq War also came up.

I concede to Ahmed that the Iraq War has worsened rather than improved the situation in Iraq. The question, however, is whether the Iraqis were doing well before. I point out that the Kurds were poisoned by Iraq's dictatorial leader Saddam Hussein, and hundreds of thousands more were killed.

"The West said that they wanted to spread democracy, but Iraq didn't gain anything except more death," Ahmed says in a serious voice. In his and Hamza's eyes, the West—especially the United States—is the enemy, constantly causing turmoil in the Muslim countries.

In orthodox Muslim circles, the analysis that Muslims are being killed by the West is spreading like wildfire. But the truth is not that the West kills most Muslims, but that Muslims are killing each other. I don't know how so many people reach the conclusion that the West is opposed to Islam. Perhaps it is because it can be difficult to direct anger at an untenable situation toward one's own people. Perhaps it is a lack of knowledge of what is happening. And maybe it also ties into the disappointment of the democratic powers watching passively while people are suffering.

I can't argue against the logic that the West has had a role in the destabilization of Iraq, Libya, and Afghanistan, but for me, the picture is complicated by other problems, like the mixing of politics and religion. In addition, there is widespread poverty, inequality, and lack of educational opportunities that keep many Muslims in the region in misery, while kings, presidents, and governments profit from corruption and from the natural resources they have sold to the outside world.

I think it is much too simplistic to blame the West for all the atrocities in the Middle East; the regimes have a good deal of responsibility for their own problems. Syria's president, Bashar al-Assad, has killed hundreds of thousands of civilians in Syria. Saddam did the same in Iraq, as did Libya's leader, Muammar Qaddafi. As I think about all those despots, it gnaws at me. They were all supported by the US and the West. Is Hizb ut-Tahrir right in their criticism of the foreign policy of Denmark and the West? Do we listen too little to Hizb ut-Tahrir about their views on foreign policy because their approach to democracy is different? I can agree up to a point, but their reasoning becomes too conspiratorial; fault always seems to lie outside the border. There doesn't seem to be much self-reflection on the role of civic responsibility, and hardly any self-criticism. There must be a better solution than what they propose. If these are Islamist countries, why do Turkey, Saudi Arabia, and Qatar assist ISIL, the organization that kidnaps children from their beds and lops off the heads of its enemies in graphic displays of brutality? And why does Iran help Assad, a leader who has been open in his intent to kill off ethnic minorities by bombing their homes and hospitals? How could that be ordained by Allah?

Foreign policy is not as clear-cut as Hamza and Ahmed make it out to be. They believe the West is at war with Islam itself. Unfortunately, this appears to be confirmed by reports from high-ranking nationalist politicians who say exactly the same thing: we are at war with Islam.

I can feel myself getting tired again. "What's the solution?" I ask. "Is ISIL the solution?"

"No," Hamza replies confidently.

We launch into a discussion of ISIL, which Ahmed and Hamza consistently call "Daesh," reminiscent of the Arabic word for "trampling on." Hamza mentions the Iraqi city of Mosul, which Daesh occupied in 2014. Five to six thousand soldiers from Daesh conquered the city in one day. The forty thousand soldiers who were guarding the city left behind all their weapons when they turned tail and ran.

"How can that be possible?" Hamza asks.

I do not know. I don't know the numbers either. But I know power. How can Daesh be so strong and yet so destructive?

Ahmed believes that Daesh was formed with the intent to destroy Islam, and it sounds like he thinks the West is behind it. "The West uses Daesh as an excuse to crack down on Muslims." He points out that when countries from the West and Russia drop bombs in the fight against Daesh and terror, it is primarily civilians who die. He doesn't understand how leaders in the United States and the rest of the world can justify the estimate that it will take thirty to forty years to fight the movement. "It's illogical."

Hamza agrees. According to him, the only thing creating instability is outside interference. Hamza says, "They said they were going to Syria to fight Daesh, but they kill 90 percent civilians."

I think it sounds farfetched that the West should have created Daesh, but I have to admit that I've wondered how an army that appeared over a summer is now so powerful that even the world's mightiest forces can't stop it. But I've also heard Western experts argue that Daesh was spawned as a result of the invasion of Iraq. It's pretty hard to navigate.

I return to the misery of the Middle East. Is the solution democracy, or is it better with the war, internal conflicts, instability, and poverty that characterize the area now?

Ahmed points out I'm the one who's being too simplistic, "It's not just a matter of choosing between tyranny and democracy. We have other options. We have Islam."

I ask how Islam can be the solution when Daesh justifies their brutality with the same faith, claiming to be faithful Muslims.

"We are not saying that they are not Muslims," Ahmed says, reminding me that the profession of faith is unquestionable in Islam. "But their behavior is not Islamic."

Both Ahmed and Hamza say that they actively recruit new members for Hizb ut-Tahrir. They proudly tell me they specifically target young people with criminal backgrounds or mental illness. They say that young people who are lost and vulnerable especially need to know that there is a righteous path of liberation through the rule of Islam.

Besides, he adds, every other political group is looking to fill ranks from the same demographic.

In all fairness, Hizb ut-Tahrir is only one group among the many passing out literature in front of schools and universities or ringing doorbells in hopes of converting people to their mission. An integral part of democratic culture involves respect for differing opinions and a process of open debate. Then, war is safely waged using words, not violence. But there's something about Hizb ut-Tahrir that sparks outrage.

My own opinion of the group is impacted by an understanding I gained while working directly with immigrants and traumatized refugees as a psychiatric nurse. I know how vulnerable that population is. I met parents who were psychotic, violent, and traumatized, and treated their children with terrible neglect. The problems for the children and adolescents who grew up in those homes were rooted in crime, mental illness, and drug abuse; Hizb ut-Tahrir didn't create the problem, but they also don't offer a comprehensive solution.

We're just going around in circles now, it seems, taking up the same issues again and again. I move on to questions about welfare, equal access to health, education, and care for the elderly. "You have access to so many resources! Your kids get free university educations. What are you missing, Hamza? Why live in Denmark when you despise Denmark and the democratic system so much?" I ask him. I know there's no real answer to this question, and that it can bring the whole conversation to a screeching halt.

Hamza breathes deeply and relaxes his voice. He says the question should be asked in reverse. "What brought us here?" he asks. "The West has taken our land and taken our natural resources. They dragged us out of our homeland."

He tells me it was wealthy Jews from the United States and West who broke international law in an effort supported by Israel to drive

Palestinians out of the West Bank and Gaza strip. When Hamza talks about Jews, his voice is full of hatred and contempt.

I tell him that I personally oppose the settlements and am in favor of a two-state solution. I also tell him that I have Jewish friends who agree with me that Palestine should be recognized. "I don't understand how you can stereotype all Jews," I tell him.

Hamza doesn't believe he is speaking of all Jews. "I hate the Jews who stole our land from us. It's not something I hide. But I don't mind Jews living outside the region, like the ones in Denmark," Hamza says.

I receive Hizb ut-Tahrir's newsletters, and some of the statements they've made in it are pure anti-Semitism. In 2003, the spokesperson for Hizb ut-Tahrir was convicted of hate speech. According to Hamza, the spokesperson was found guilty based on anti-Semitic statements that were directed at Jews themselves, instead of at the state of Israel.

Why not make a distinction between Jewish people and the state of Israel? Hamza's response is simply, "Because we do not recognize Israel." Then, why not call Israeli Jews something else? "They call themselves Jews," Hamza says "And anytime we've seen Jews in Palestine, they are from Israel."

Ahmed backs him up. "We don't mind Jews living in Denmark. Islam doesn't call us to do battle with them. The people who live here have nothing to do with the war being waged against Islam and its followers."

I find it deeply problematic that Hizb ut-Tahrir doesn't clarify when they are directing statements toward a state and when they are talking about its citizens. I'd like to see this enter public debate using clear language to establish the distinction between the two. I'd also like it made clear that Hizb ut-Tahrir doesn't represent all of Islam, especially since they are creating a schism in Denmark with their hate speech that is tearing the country apart. It will take more time, trust, and patience to close the divide than Ahmed, Hamza, and I have to offer.

It feels like we are reaching the end of a long discussion, but there is one final topic I need to bring up. "Can a homosexual worship in your mosque?" I ask.

Hamza's body language changes when I ask this. His face tightens up, and he begins to stammer for Danish words to express what he's feeling. He's too angry to maintain the peace he held onto earlier during our conversation. "Is he a Muslim?" Hamza asks.

"Yes," I reply calmly. I enjoy watching Hamza lose a measure of his self-control.

"Can he be both Muslim and gay?" Hamza asks.

"Many people identify as both," I point out.

"None that I know!" Hamza replies angrily.

I remind Hamza that we just agreed that, according to Islam, only an adherent to the faith can make a self-determination of their own status as a Muslim. Ahmed wants to know if I have direct knowledge that a gay Muslim has actually entered the mosque.

I have to laugh a little at how fired up he's getting over this. "No, that's a hypothetical question, but I do want to know if they would be allowed to pray here," I say.

For Hamza, this is absolutely unacceptable. "We can't forbid him to pray...but...never!" Hamza shouts, rolls his eyes, shrugs, looks at Ahmed, looks at me. "Islam forbids that!" He thunders. The angrier he gets, the calmer I become. His eyes radiate hatred for homosexuals, even deeper than the disdain they conveyed toward Jews in Israel. "It's inhuman...abnormal." The attacks fly through the air as he spits them from his mouth at me. I know I've seen Hamza before, but where?

Then I say something I know might be completely lost on Hamza and Ahmed. "I believe that Allah created everything and every individual, even those with disabilities, men, women, and gay people. And only Allah can punish or reward. Human beings play at being the creator when they pass judgment on others. If Allah hated homosexuals, how could He have created them?" I ask.

Hamza doesn't bite. "Allah created everything," he repeats. "He also gave us the right to make choices. Why didn't you choose to be gay? Allah created me. Why didn't I choose to be gay?" In their thinking, the issue is black and white, two options only. For Hamza and Ahmed, homosexuality is something you choose. And if you choose incorrectly, it comes with a consequence.

What are we really getting at here? I wonder. Do I really need to pull their arguments apart? I've learned at least one thing from our discussion. I can see now how important it is to include moderate imams in discussions with more reactionary imams like Hamza, rather than trying to counter his position on my own. I can argue so much, but another imam will lend more credibility to the conversation.

The issue with low voter turnout among new immigrants must be addressed. I have a hard time understanding why anyone would neglect to exercise their right to vote. It may be that people just aren't aware that they have the right to vote in municipal and other local elections, even before they receive Danish citizenship—everyone who has lived in Denmark for more than three years is granted the right to vote locally. Others don't cast their ballots because they feel unheard by the candidates who seek to represent their interests, or because they feel separated from their community. Many Muslims also come from countries where there is electoral corruption, or where making their way to the polling places is too dangerous.

There are young people going in and out of the café. They all greet each other and seem friendly. It is far from the image I had of the mosque before today. There are no angry young men. No one is shouting. No one seems threatening. There was nothing to be afraid of, I think.

I look at my watch. The twenty minutes that Ahmed put aside for our meeting have turned into almost two hours. Over the course of those two hours, we disagreed bitterly on some issues, reached partial consensus on some matters, and laughed about a lot of little things. Hamza gets up from his seat and tells me, "You have to bring some bread from the bakery to your children." Ahmed agrees.

Three hours ago, I stood in front of the mosque and didn't dare go up, and now they are sending me home with bread.

The Hypocrisy Card

We're heading out of the café when Hamza says, "We are here for Muslims. We defend them when there is a ban on scarves, burkas, or prayer in schools. Or when democratic hypocrites want to restrict the freedom of speech of the imams."

I'm thinking he is referring to the newly proposed Imam Law, where the majority of the parliament wants to decide that "with respect to section sixty-seven of the Constitution on religious freedom, criminal statements that undermine Danish law can be criminalized." At this very point, I share Hamza's skepticism. Let's say my friend Bent Melchior, who is a rabbi, decides he wants to say something that contradicts Danish law. I've probably never heard him do that, but let's just say that one day he was in the synagogue and said, for example, that he was in favor of polygamy. Under the Imam Law, he would be punished for undermining Danish law. But if I were in the room with him, and he whispered this in my ear and I then repeated it out loud, I could do so without being punished.

I am fundamentally opposed to criminalizing opinions, whether they come from imams like Hamza, rabbis like Bent, or former politicians like myself. Statements calling for violence are already punishable under Danish law. Of course, actions must be punishable if they do not conform to the laws of society, but attitudes don't disappear if we ban them. On the contrary, they grow when left to fester in the darkness of silence and misunderstanding, in even darker rooms, where they glide around each other like small, poisonous snakes that bite all those who come into contact with them, spreading the venomous poison of fear throughout society. Instead of prohibition, we must insist on democratic conversation and critical debate. We must believe in the strength of democracy. If we take away anyone's fundamental rights, we don't gain a stronger democracy, we simply hand over a weaker one to those who are fighting to destroy it—people like Hamza and Ahmed.

The hypocrisy card Hamza just played is a trump card of sorts. Freedom of speech, which we claim to value for everyone, doesn't apply to everyone anyway. Hamza thinks this is hypocritical, and I agree with him. It is undeniably annoying to me that in a democracy, we have started to operate under the control of the thought police, regulating consensus by placing the expression of ideas in a punitive frame.

A few years ago, there was a huge controversy in Denmark when a series of cartoons depicting the Prophet Muhammad in a satirical manner were printed. It led to tremendous uproar and violence, because some Muslims believe the Prophet's image—any art that depicts human beings—is blasphemous. Since the Muhammad drawings were printed, I have defended the artists, Flemming Rose and Kurt Westergaard, and the *Jyllands-Posten* newspaper that published the cartoons, and their freedom of expression, even though I did not agree with what they expressed. In the years that have gone by, I have repeatedly seen that politicians are willing to fight for freedom of expression only when it represents a majority viewpoint, which leaves the minority unprotected. Each time this happened, I expressed my indignation, because of course freedom of speech applies to everyone in Denmark. It applies to Loki as well as to Thor. But now, I've faced two members of Hizb ut-Tahrir who say that

Danish politicians are operating under a double standard. And I have to admit, they are right in their criticism.

I don't think that Hizb ut-Tahrir should be banned as long as the organization does not encourage violence. They should get equal protection under the law to the Danes' Party, which, as mentioned, was formed by a former neo-Nazi, has about as much support as Hizb ut-Tahrir, and in my eyes is also a venomous organization that wants to undermine democracy.

In a democracy, you don't shut down the speech of those you disagree with—you argue against them so that the opposition is apparent to vulnerable people who go to them seeking refuge from an unfair society. That is the difference between a democracy and a dictatorship.

Tying legality to an organization's right to meet will only drive them underground. For organizations in Denmark, there has long been an issue around which organizations are considered legitimate, and which are forbidden from operating in public. For example, lawful organizations can rent municipal premises as long as there are no illegal activities. Illegal organizations cannot. If the Imam Law passes, municipalities will have the power to assess and assign privileges based on what is said in meetings. This could mean, for example, that a legal association such as Hizb ut-Tahrir could no longer rent premises from the City of Copenhagen if the assessor doesn't agree with them, arbitrarily.

I understand the impulse to restrict freedom of speech for groups that seem so threatening. It infuriates me when groups like Hizb ut-Tahrir and the Grimhoj Mosque speak as though they represent all Danish Muslims, or when they try to define Islam for all Muslims. In my rage, I have even gone so far as to express my outrage on social media by saying we should just shut down the Grimhoj Mosque, even though they haven't violated any laws. But I'm not infallible. My good friend, author Carsten Jensen, expressed it best, in words I often turn to when anger gets the best of me: "Democracy cannot be protected through censorship and prohibition. In a democracy, your opponent has as much right to express himself as you do, so long as he does not call for violence." He reminds me that democracy is always inclusive and seeks solutions.

The one thing that gives Hizb ut-Tahrir any power is the energy that exclusion provides. With it, it mobilizes young people to seek undemocratic communities. We must hold that liberties apply to everyone—even the most venomous.

My thoughts are interrupted by Hamza, who asks with a smile if I will attend Friday prayer the following day. That feeling of recognition comes back to me. Where do I know him from? I ask him why his face looks so familiar.

"I'm the imam who was in the news for speaking out about gays," he says proudly. Now I remember him clearly. I remember what he said. I can barely breathe, and just want to leave.

We walk out of the café and into the mosque again. I gather a few propaganda leaflets from Hizb ut-Tahrir. While standing in front of the bookshelf, I hear my name being called. When I turn, I see the man I thought might be the bookseller from Bronshoj earlier, the one I think is a Salafist, come toward me. He asks if I have time to talk to him. "Tomorrow, after the Friday prayer," I say.

"*Inshallah*," he replies. If Allah wills. His name is Mahmud.

In the bakery, I take the men up on their offer of food. I get a bag with four piping hot pieces of pizza. I also take some cookies for my kids. Ahmed gives me his business card and thanks me for the conversation, while Hamza shows me the women's entrance for Friday prayer.

"Remember to wear a scarf," Hamza says.

"*Inshallah*," I reply.

CHAPTER 6

BETWEEN EXTREMES

*"We can easily forgive a child who is afraid of darkness;
the real tragedy of life is when men are afraid of the light."*

—Socrates

On Friday, the August sun is shining hot in the sky as I make my way to the mosque on my bicycle. By the time I arrive, my skin feels like it is cooking under the long-sleeved jersey I'm wearing, so I barely cover my head with the scarf I was instructed to wear, and leave my neck uncovered before entering the mosque for Friday prayer via the women's entrance. The congregation in Hizb ut-Tahrir's women's section consists of a total of four women, a child, and a near-silence, which is unfamiliar to me from the other mosques I have visited. After the prayer, I leave through the terrace and enter the men's wing. To my great disappointment, I am told that Mahmud is not there. "Try at Titangade 15," says a young guy. He tells me that's where the Salafists gather.

No one is waiting for me when I reach Titangade. Just as I begin to get annoyed at being stood up, my phone rings. It's Mahmud. He is back at the mosque and apologizes for being late for our meeting. I agree to ride my bike back to him. I channel all of my energy into the ride back over. It helps to calm my nervousness.

My husband was also anxious this morning. I could hear it in the worried tone of his voice as he said goodbye and gave me an extra hug.

I rarely tell anyone who I'm planning to meet for a dialogue coffee. I don't want the added stress of carrying their worry with me into those meetings. People pick up on anxiety, and it is harder to find commonalities if I walk into such a meeting cowering in fear. I believe that anxiety and fear are the main culprits in the huge impasses we find between different ideological groups.

However, the one person I always make sure knows where I am headed is my husband. The first few times I visited someone who had sent me hate emails, he was very concerned. Over time, the anxiety lessened, and he stopped objecting. Maybe it's because he knows that in the end I always do what I think is best anyway, but it probably also helps that I always return to him unscathed when the meeting is over. But I can still tell that he worries. The day of a meeting, he gives me a special hug in the morning, sends an extra text message—"Take care of yourself, honey"—and kisses me with relief when I return home. I tell him what was discussed in these meetings, and I make sure he has a clear picture of the person I met in his head. I start by describing their human side. I tell him about their house, how I was greeted at the front door. I show him pictures of the cups with tea and coffee. I want him to feel he's there with me.

But today my husband was more worried than usual. Not because I was going to Hizb ut-Tahrir, but because I was going to meet a Salafist. Many ISIL members are Salafists, and many of them advocate violence. The few Salafists I've met on the street have been criminals, mentally ill, or both, and most of the imams I've talked to have warned me not to meet Salafists alone, encouraging me to meet them only in public.

Despite their reputation, what exactly makes a Salafist is a little complicated. Salafism belongs to the Sunni branch of Islam, in which there are four schools: Maliki, Shafi, Hanbali, and Hanafi. It may vary from Salafist to Salafist which of the Sunni schools one follows, but common to the Salafists is the belief that the Qur'an should be read and followed literally. The word "Salaf" carries a connotation of "old," but also of "the original." It is indicative of the desire Salafists have to return to the source of knowledge and worship a very fundamental

Islam. The Salafists advocate a strict interpretation of sharia and religious laws, which means, among other things, that social and family life must be led under a range of obligations and prohibitions, which can cover everything from marriage and sex life to child-rearing and much more. They reject Western ideologies such as socialism and capitalism and do not engage in many Western activities. Instead, they spend their time spreading knowledge about Islam and trying to convert people to their faith.

It is not just in relation to the Sunni schools that the Salafists are divided into different groups. They are further divided by widely differing attitudes on how to relate to society. For example, certain Salafists encourage believers to support the state in which they live and propagate Salafism through nonviolent missionary activities, social work, and political organizing. Other Salafists, known as jihadist Salafists, believe that it is not only permissible, but also necessary, to use violence against those who do not comply with sharia law. It is this group in particular that we hear about in the media in Denmark. For example, the terrorist group al-Qaeda is a Salafist group, as is ISIL. What they have in common is that they have an extremist interpretation of Islam, advocate for religious violence, and consider those who disagree with their interpretations unbelievers.

I do not know which Sunni school Mahmud professes. Nor do I know if he is a jihadist Salafist or whether he is abstaining from the use of violence. I just know that the Salafists and their interpretations of the religious texts are so central in public debate in Denmark that I have to talk to him. The war being waged among Muslims in the Middle East makes me sleepless. Why does ISIL so barbarously oppose Muslims in the Middle East? How does a Salafist argue? My curiosity takes over for my anxiety as I again park my bike in the yard on Heimdalsgade.

I climb back up the stairs to the mosque. I pass some men on the stairs, but have no trouble passing into the main entrance. I cannot help but think of all the drama the press creates around Hizb ut-Tahrir, about their views on keeping genders segregated. Where are the angry men now who seem so insistent on keeping people so separated?

The Heart in the Freezer

I spot Mahmud. We greet without a handshake and he shows me into the little room next to the pulpit. I can't tell whether it is Arabic or Kurdish, but Mahmud speaks to a young man in the mosque and he follows us into the room. Mahmud opens the door and we enter a small, elongated room. At the end of the room there is a windowed wall. To the left and right of the door, there are bookshelves filled with books written in Arabic. In the middle of the floor is a large mahogany desk and behind it an office chair. There is a red carpet on the floor, just like in the mosque. Mahmud sits at the desk. The young man picks up a chair for me and himself, and I sit across the desk from Mahmud. The heavy furniture makes the room feel dark and compact.

I will be served Coca-Cola again, even though it's American.

"American, Turkish, Kurdish, it's all the same," Mahmud says. "If it's halal, we'll drink it." Halal means "allowed" in Arabic. Haram means "forbidden."

"But I'm not from Hizb ut-Tahrir," Mahmud hastens to say.

The young man is seated to my left, about three feet away. He also faces Mahmud. He does not introduce himself. So I ask him who he is. He tells me he is twenty-five years old. He is dressed in black, is balding, and wears a long, thin beard.

"Where do you live?" I ask him.

"In Osterbro," he says in such a low voice that I can hardly hear it.

"How long have you been in Hizb ut-Tahrir?" I ask.

"A couple of years."

Mahmud says to me in Kurdish, "He is also Kurdish. His job is to sit with us. Because it is haram for me to be alone with you," Mahmud explains.

I say hello in Kurdish. At least we have ethnic ties in common, I think. I am very familiar with the strict religious adage that, if a woman is alone in a confined space with a strange man, the third presence in the room is the devil. In other words, the young man has to stay in the room to make sure we behave with decorum. I turn around and look at the open door.

"You can sit in a room with me if the door is open, can't you?" I ask teasingly.

Mahmud is obviously surprised that I am aware of what the rule is technically in Islam, because it is rarely argued.

"He has to sit there, even if the door is open," Mahmud says, closing that part of the conversation. Admittedly, I know people who belong to an Islamic sect in Turkey who would think that having an open door is enough. But that is not enough for Mahmud. He goes one step further. I interpret this as an extreme way of practicing the religion. Extremists often think better Muslims do more than Allah expects.

I let it go. I turn to the young man again and ask where his Kurdish roots originated.

"Muş," he says.

"A real Kurd." I smile. Muş is one of the poorest Kurdish cities in eastern Turkey, where the standard of living and education is very low.

I don't know if Mahmud can read my thoughts, but he says, "He was born in Denmark. You might know his father. But we're not here to talk about him today. Today I need your attention, Özlem."

The young man accepts this. His keeps his gaze steady on Mahmud. No feedback. No reaction. Only a silent acceptance.

Mahmud wears an ankle-length, light gray robe. Before settling in the office chair, he lifted it slightly so that it would be loose under him. I noticed that under the robe he is wearing a pair of dark green trousers with big pockets. Over his robe, he wears a light green military vest with a pocket on the left side, with a small notepad and a pen poking out. He has long gray hair that curls at the ends and cascades into his beard, which is also long and gray.

"How old do you think I am?" he asks. I'd guess he's about sixty-five, but out of courtesy, I lie and say sixty.

"Thank you. You are generous," he replies with a smile. "I'm exactly fifty-five years old. Physically, you're right, I feel older than I am, but mentally I'm even older than you gathered."

He's only fifty-five? It doesn't seem possible. He looks older than my father, who has retired. What has he been through in life that wore him out so completely?

Then Mahmud goes on to tell his story. "Physically, I have been in Denmark since 1992, but mentally I only arrived in 2005," he says. "I've been in jail in Diyarbakir."

I get goose bumps. When I was younger, I read some of the book *Diyarbakir Sorgu Ve 5 Nolu* by F. Welat. The author used a pseudonym to protect his identity, and the book's title refers to Turkey's most notorious prison for Kurdish political prisoners. The memoir was written from the prison, but reminisces on the author's time as a college student between 1982 and 1987. The 196-plus-page book describes in detail the torture the author suffered in the prison. I struggled to get through the first 130 pages and then had to admit I had neither the psyche nor the strength to read more about what the author had gone through. When Mahmud tells that he has been to Diyarbakir, the descriptions of torture come back to me. How the prisoners receive hour-long electric shocks through their penises. How they are waterboarded until they feel they might drown. How in January the guards take them outside naked and toss them around on the ice until their skin is numb from the cold, and then set guard dogs on them to bite and snap at their bare skin.

"I have so much I want to say to you," Mahmud says. "You should not interrupt me with questions. Then I lose concentration." He takes a piece of paper. "I wrote down my questions so I wouldn't forget them," he says. "I have been on hunger strikes so many times, it has ruined my memory." Mahmud's gaze is intense. He leans forward and looks me in the eye. "I did not bow to Turkish racism. I was one of the leaders in the fight," he says. His voice sounds calm, but also tired.

"So you were tortured a lot?" I ask.

"Not more than the others. We all got the same thing." Mahmud's voice is fragile and his eyes are on the table. The room is silent. I don't want to put pressure on him. He must tell me only what he wants to let me know. I feel myself stepping back into my role as a nurse. I have experience as a contact nurse for PTSD patients.

"What I learned in prison is similar to what is taught at most universities. You learn psychology, sociology, religion, atheism, and all the other isms. But everything, especially fascism, is taught through experience. You learn about people and your sixth sense is sharpened. Everything becomes important to survival." Mahmud stops. He looks at me intensely. "Do you know what a basin is?" he asks.

"Something with water in it," I reply.

"Yes, but what kind of basin, and what kind of water?" He doesn't wait for my answer. He starts talking. "Prison guards opened the sewer pipes, so that urine and lumps of shit flooded our cells. When the sewage got to be knee-deep the guards officers entered. They told us to say we were Turks, and if we refused, they would grab our heads and push them under the sewage, until we felt like we'd drown. They'd pull our heads up for air and ask us, 'What are you now? Kurds or Turks?' Kurds, we'd say, and then they'd push our heads back into the shit. That is what a basin is."

And the more he tells me, the worse it gets. "Then there were the baths. We took our baths as a group, and the guards blew whistles to force us to act in unison. We had two seconds to soap our hair. Then they whistled at us again. They took us into the hallways, covered with lather head to toe, and then they made us crawl naked in front of them, while fifty to sixty guards watched us. If we crawled with our asses too high, they'd tease us, so our bodies hit the floor, and were covered in filth again." Mahmud laughs at the bizarre tale of the buttocks. I'm shocked.

"One evening, the prison guards called us out of our cells. Two hundred prisoners were gathered in the hallway. We were ordered to strip naked, and afterward we were crammed, twenty people in each cell, which normally could only accommodate five prisoners. Before the doors were locked, one of us was removed from the crowded cell. I stood in the back of the cell. We heard screams and cries on the other side of the door. Powerful shouting. We even started shouting out, 'What's happening?!' 'Nothing,' they said. Then we heard screams again." Mahmud mimics the screams. "When the door opened, I could see they had taken my friend." Mahmud pauses.

"Was he raped?" I ask.

"Later, they had to stitch him up," Mahmud says. He breathes slowly. His eyes are wet and his voice cracks. He cries, and I have a hard time holding back my tears. "The torture was terrible, but the worst injuries were what they did to our psyches." He says that even before he went to jail, he knew someone who had been through the same thing as the man who required stitching up. That man had been engaged when he was attacked, and he had such a hard time after the assault that he had committed suicide.

Occasionally, Mahmud looks at me; other times, he is completely absent. "I don't remember many details from the prison. If I open up the box, and let my memories out, it will be a book in itself," he adds earnestly.

Mahmud was imprisoned and originally sentenced to death for being a conspirator. He was part of an illegal group called KAWA. The group was communist, inspired by Mao, and advocated armed struggle. Mahmud was nineteen years old when he was jailed, but his lawyer "did something" with his papers, making it appear he was a minor. It was the only reason he escaped the death penalty.

In the ten years he spent in prison, there were only a few visits from the family. Mahmud describes one in the present tense: "Hands are tied behind our backs, and only when the prison guard whistles can we turn around and see our family members on the other side of the iron bars. If you try to speak in Kurdish, both prisoners and visitors are given a blow. And then your visit is also cut short. But if you don't speak Kurdish, you only have two minutes to talk before the whistle sounds again. Then the visit is over."

Mahmud decided to spend his time in prison reading books and educating the prisoners in the hope that they would rebel together against the oppression. He went on periodic hunger strikes; the longest lasted four months. He was twenty-nine years old when he was released. "My heart wasn't broken. It was as if it had been in a freezer. But my body was broken," Mahmud says.

Mahmud comes from a Kurdish Muslim family in the Kurdish part of Turkey. His father owned a cement store and his mother was a homemaker. The parents were both conservative Muslims without education, but Mahmud's brothers are academics.

In his youth, Mahmud was more Kurdish than he was Muslim. "Even when I was seven, it hurt my heart when my family sometimes spoke Turkish to their guests." At a young age, he began to take an interest in the injustices and oppression experienced by the Kurds. As a nine-year-old, he encountered the word "Kurdistan" in a magazine for the first time, and it excited him. "I knew it. I knew we had a country. I knew the Kurds had a country!" Mahmud says. He raises his arms with enthusiasm as he tells me this, and his whole face lights up in a smile. But even as a boy, he knew that "Kurdistan" was a word he mustn't say out loud. The older boys who went to universities in Istanbul, Ankara, and Izmir brought him magazines, newspapers, and books. He read them in secrecy and kept them hidden from his parents. His father didn't know what his son was reading. "As long as I helped in his cement shop, whatever I wanted to read was fine," Mahmud says.

In the 1970s, a military coup took place in Turkey that changed everything in Mahmud's city. Many young people were imprisoned and executed, and many Kurdish groups began to revolt. So-called Peshmerga militias gathered in the mountains, where their families smuggled food to them. "The great Kurdish national leader, Massoud Barzani, needed our support. My father sold his television and sent the money to Barzani. We were some of the first in the city to have a television," Mahmud says. Then he becomes silent. His eyes are distant, and I can see that he is deeply unhappy. Mahmud is crying again. I look over at the young man. He has not moved an inch. I ask Mahmud why he is upset. He takes some deep breaths. Wipes his eyes. Drinks some water. "People were losing their identity. They didn't have to teach their children Kurdish. They had no reason to say they were Kurds. Children would go through seven years in school and never speak a word of Kurdish." Mahmud sighs.

I'm going to reconsider my thinking in the debate over who should call himself a Dane. How it affects the individual's identity when others question one's connections to an ethnic identity. And what it means when someone brands a nationality. I have Kurdish roots myself, and it is important to me that my roots are recognized by those around me. Insisting I have Kurdish roots has burned many bridges I could have been building. It happened when I talked to Turkish journalists, Turkish rulers, and Turkish opinion makers.

But I also experienced it in conversations with ordinary Turks, who I thought were my friends, but who couldn't come to terms with my insistence that I be seen for my Kurdish heritage.

I've also had the feeling that others were trying to brand a nationality in relation to my identity as a Dane. I am Danish. I have Danish citizenship. I feel Danish. Nevertheless, in a radio program, Danish People's Party spokesman Martin Henriksen could not say he considered me a Dane. I've also received messages from nationalist Danes, provoked that I'd dare to call myself a Dane, who wrote me things like, "A pig does not become a cow just because it eats a specific diet from birth." I live in Denmark, but to them, it's not enough to make me Danish.

I am conscious of who I am. No one can take that from me, even though sometimes I get tired of fighting for my identity and want to abandon the fight. I can understand when young people who feel powerless shout, "Fuck your Danish!" We often underestimate how much it means to be allowed to be recognized as you want to be. It can lead some people to turn their backs on society and shout back at that rejection, "Fuck you!" But another option is to do as Mahmud did, and fight for his national identity.

Mahmud talks about his time in primary school in Turkey. There, he had a classmate who got into trouble because he couldn't speak Turkish. "I remember that the teacher struck him, first on the left cheek, and then on the right cheek, because my classmate couldn't speak a word in Turkish." Each morning, Mahmud stood in the schoolyard with the other Kurdish children and read the student pact aloud: "I am Turkish. I'm real. I am diligent. I am happy to be Turkish." The covenant was written in 1933 and was read collectively by all students in Turkish schools at the beginning of each school day. Fortunately, this humiliating and racist mandate was abolished in 2013, but Mahmud can't let it go.

The more Mahmud experienced the oppression, the more courageous he became. But any courage came at the cost of the Islamic faith his parents professed. He didn't understand why the Kurds did not revolt. How could they remain under the oppression of Turkish rule? He could find only one reason why the Kurds did not go to war with the Turks: "Because of Islam, they would not fight against the Turks, the Iranians, the Iraqis, and the Syrians. Because they are Muslims, and Islam forbids them to go to war with people who share their faith." He started reading books on Marxist philosophy at the age of thirteen or fourteen. "It helped me to reject Islam," Mahmud says. His family was deeply concerned about his revolutionary thoughts. "My father was tolerant of his sons, and he didn't know much about politics. But my mother started to oppose my thinking. She cursed me, saying things like, 'May Allah be against you. I hope you are buried under your ideas.' "

In eastern Turkey, many Kurds smuggled goods from Iran, Iraq, or Syria, which were then sold in Turkey. "I knew someone who had such a business, and he talked about what was happening in Kurdish areas on the other side of the border," Mahmud says. He heard about the Kurdish Party, which at that time was a movement called the Kurdistan Democratic Party (KDP). In connection with an internal struggle, one of the movement's great leaders, Dr. Swan, was killed, and Barzani fled to the Iranian side of Kurdistan. As I write, he is President of Kurdistan in northern Iraq. The KDP is no longer a movement, but still functions as a political party. "The split between the Kurds during that period created many movements, groups, and parties. The Turkish left wing and the intelligence service in Turkey took advantage of the situation. The Kurds were no longer a united group," Mahmud says.

When Mahmud was seventeen and attending high school, his Kurdish teacher was sent into exile. "I couldn't accept it. We boycotted school." It was the start of a high school revolt in which Mahmud engaged. He helped organize the boycott, and when the police made mass arrests at the school, Mahmud was lucky to escape. As an eighteen-year-old, he declared himself a communist and became active in a number of Kurdish movements. But he felt disappointed that most Kurdish organizations and movements didn't have greater aspirations of autonomy. He found hope in a new movement, the PKK, the Kurdish workers' party, because it was more action-oriented. He wasn't a member of the PKK but, as I mentioned, belonged to KAWA, a Kurdish rebel group that emerged in the wake of the worldwide youth revolt in 1968, and was named for the rebel Kawa, who, according to ancient legends, led the Kurds' freedom struggle against Syrian tyrant Zahak.

Mahmud spent much of his time talking to farmers about oppression and class struggle. He learned through these discussions that he could only sway them if he did not openly criticize Islam, so he stopped doing so. He also cut his long hair, which all leftists had done at the time. "I could not be stupid and criticize Islam aloud. I had to pretend to follow the same beliefs to get them to listen to me." While trying to sway the peasants' attitudes, he also helped to organize the guerrilla war in the mountains with the Peshmerga militia—that is, with Barzani.

Mahmud was detained and jailed on several occasions. In the ten years he spent in prison, he had the opportunity to choose which political identity he would retain. He opted out of the Communist Party, for which he had already gained notoriety. He would rather be unaffiliated, so that he could recruit more from the prison to the communist struggle.

When he was released as a twenty-nine-year-old, after ten years of a frozen heart and tortured body, he found Kurdish identity weakened even further than it had been before his imprisonment, as was the communist movement following a new military coup in the 1980s. The common consciousness among the Kurds was gone, and there was more internal fighting among the groups that remained.

On the other side of the desk, I can see Mahmud gathering his strength. He continues his story with a voice heavy with disappointment. "Özlem, I thought everyone knew what was happening in the prisons." It became important for him to mobilize more people to speak out against oppression. Many in his group were killed or broken in prison, so Mahmud decided to start his own Marxist-Leninist Kurdish organization. Meanwhile, the Turkish State Attorney had filed a new case against Mahmud, this time for his activities in prison. The sentence looming over him was sixty-nine years in prison, and it became clear to Mahmud that he needed to escape. "The police were after me. I had to flee. All my friends and enemies advised me to flee." Mahmud did not want to leave Kurdistan, so he went to South Kurdistan, located in northern Iraq. "I was well received by Jalal Talabani's group, who is also leftist." Talabani later became president of Iraq.

I am impressed by Mahmud's very detailed knowledge of all the Kurdish groups, organizations, and parties. It is clear that he is deeply invested in the cause and knows the movements' internal conflicts, similarities, and differences. His language skills are also quite well developed. Mahmud speaks Kurdish, Arabic, Turkish, and English fluently. And Danish.

When one of Mahmud's friends from KAWA was killed in northern Iraq, Mahmud was warned that the KAWA Central Committee was behind the killing. "I was told to take care of myself." After that, Mahmud was on guard all the time, and traveled to Iran to seek asylum there. In Tehran, he heard that in Denmark he could find asylum and treatment for the damage the torture had caused. His dream of reaching Denmark was put on hold for a few years, so he waited out the time in Kurdistan. "The Danish embassy refused me asylum, but said I should go to the UN refugee center." Here, documentation was obtained from Amnesty International that Mahmud had been fighting to get for the previous thirteen years, of which he had spent ten in the prison. "The secret ballot report said that I was under persecution and that there were cases pending against me." On February 29, 1992, Mahmud landed at Kastrup Airport.

The room is warm and I sweat under my scarf. I look again at the young man. He still sits with his hands on his knees, looking straight ahead. Do you look like this when you are brainwashed? Are you never influenced by the things you hear? I wonder.

Mahmud's story is extreme in every way. How could a former communist become a Salafist? How could he go from one extreme to another? Or is it easier to choose a new radical position when you are already on an outer wing? The few people I've known who have swung so polemically, I met through politics. Ole Sohn, who started as a communist and ended up with the Social Democrats. Karen Jespersen, who started on the far left, quit the left, and today publishes the *Short Newspaper*, which is known for writing extremely negative and, in some cases, even false stories about immigrants and Muslims. Soren Espersen also belonged to the far left and today plays a leading role with the Danish People's Party. There is also Ahmed Akkari, "the Imam," who started the Muhammad crisis when he toured around with fake Muhammad drawings and set the Middle East on fire, but today appears to have abandoned everything he stood for. All are examples of the possibility of radical evolution of thought. At the same time, I also know that for many communists and people on the left in Turkey, a void occurred after the military coups in the 1970s and 1980s. Some of them were also horribly traumatized, which destroyed them for life. They were isolated, their friends killed, and some were labeled as traitors by their own movements because they could not resist the torture and ended up passing on information and names to Turkish authorities. Some moved to the right and ended up with the Turkish social democrats. Others were completely isolated on the far left. Others sought answers through religion.

In Denmark, Mahmud quickly found other Kurds. "In Denmark, I would not interfere in politics. I wanted to lie low until I could go back to Kurdistan. But the rumor quickly spread that I was in Denmark for KAWA. Many were unhappy that the chairman of the organization in Denmark was very passive. On rare occasions he wrote an article in a magazine, and otherwise he did nothing." Mahmud increasingly felt that he needed to get involved anyway. "But then I was approached by someone who told me to stay away from KAWA, or I would end up taking over the entire organization. And that's why the Central Committee had asked him to 'solve the problem.' "

Mahmud asks me if I know what it means to "solve the problem." When I don't answer, he explains. "They would kill me. So I asked the man who had visited me if he would kill me himself. But he couldn't do it." Mahmud was now convinced that it was not only the Turkish authorities, but also people in Kurdish movements, or rather his own organization, who wanted him killed. He immediately stopped his involvement with KAWA. "The organization no longer existed for me," he says.

Mahmud's story gets more and more messy as he opens up his time in Denmark. I want him to tell me why he became a Salafist and what exactly made him do it. But there is nothing concrete. There are many episodes, experiences, and situations that helped shape Mahmud into the man he has become.

1999 was the year in which Mahmud began reading the Qur'an. But it was different from when he was a child, when Mahmud's parents forced him to read it. "I wanted to find contradictions so that I could travel to Kurdistan and build my own Kurdish organization—but I couldn't find contradictions in the Qur'an," Mahmud says. "Then, in 1999, there was a solar eclipse, and a teacher told me about Nostradamus, who could predict the future." Although Mahmud knew logically that no one could predict the future, he was nevertheless caught up in these predictions. Mahmud takes out a book of Nostradamus's prophecies and shows it to me. He has highlighted much of the text and eagerly tells us about the predictions. It is not just Nostradamus who has been able to predict the future, says Mahmud. "I knew the Qur'an very well. I also knew of Prophet Muhammad's predictions of the future. Information about the future existed," Mahmud says enthusiastically. He is both lively and clear in voice. The frailty and sadness he displayed when telling about the torture are completely gone. It is clear that learning about Nostradamus was a turning point for him. "It gave me energy to read on in the Qur'an. I had read the most important verses and hoped I could find contradictions. But I found no contradictions," Mahmud says. "Instead, I began to look at things that were missing in the Qur'an. Why was there nothing about women's rights? Why should one cut off the hand of thieves?" Later, Mahmud encountered the verse in the Qur'an which says that those who do not believe in the Prophet and in Allah will die as unbelievers. He has a hard time putting that thought away.

Mahmud wants to tell me more, but time is running out. I have to pick up my kids and we agree to meet in the same place after the weekend. As Mahmud gets up, the young man gets up too. I am amazed at how he has been able to sit for almost two hours without moving in the chair—and without interfering in the debate. Not even once!

The True Muslim

On Monday, I'm back in the mosque again. The room is new, and the third man has also been changed out. But Mahmud is wearing the same clothes, and it feels as if we haven't had a two-day break at all. He continues his story, as if it was five minutes since we said goodbye to each other.

Mahmud talks about his first time in Denmark. He joined the International Forum and joined the Youth House in Norrebro. "I had no contact with anyone in the community other than the left." Although his long hair and beard scared some people around him, he felt more secure there. It got harder when he moved outside that environment. "Whether it was at the library, the pharmacy or elsewhere, I always got in trouble," he says, sighing.

"Why?" I ask.

"Good question," he replies, but then refers to his appearance. "You should see pictures of me from that time," he smiles.

The more he tells me, the more I understand that Mahmud at that time was dealing with many problems and conflicts. One day, he was hit by a bus as it pulled out of a stop. He became convinced that the driver had done it intentionally and ran after the bus. He caught it at an intersection, made it stop, and demanded an apology from the driver. The incident escalated so quickly that the driver called the police. Mahmud ended up on the ground with his hands tied behind his back. He didn't understand how he had gotten in that position, because in his thinking, it wasn't him but the driver who was at fault. He was given a mandatory treatment sentence and was forced into the psychiatric ward. He was not discharged until a month and a half later. It was the only time he was hospitalized, but several more violent episodes followed. It culminated in 2005 at Copenhagen Central Station, where he got into a fight with a group of neo-Nazis. Mahmud says he was attacked by the neo-Nazis while they were rallying. "They thought I was a Jew," he says. He pulled out a boxcutter and cut one of them in the face. In court he could not prove that the act occurred in self-defense.

Overcoming Hate Through Dialogue

I have a hard time figuring out Mahmud. Is the man sick from all the torture he has been subjected to, or does he just have venomous attitudes? Is the episode with the bus driver real or a hallucination? I do not know. Mahmud denies that he is mentally ill. I ask him if he is on any medication. "No," he replies, "I've never been given medicine." I try to put the pieces together. To me, here sits a man who has been subjected to extreme torture and who experienced a great emptiness when he came to Denmark and could not be part of the Kurdish environment. The Kurdish movement he believed in was divisive and the political theory he lived by had collapsed with the fall of the Soviet Union. He could not find the contradictions that he had been looking for in the Qur'an. Maybe all of this helped the Qur'an make sense to him? I do not know. But I still can't see what drove him to become a Salafist.

"I am a Muslim and I also have to die as a Muslim. I want to be sincere in my faith to Allah and I do not want to die sinful. I am very, very afraid that I will die with the responsibility of all the Danes on my shoulders who have not seen the truth of Islam. Allah might ask me, 'Why did you not pass on the knowledge you have gained from me?' "

When I ask him what he is afraid of, he says, "The worst are not the unbelievers. The worst are those who dress up as Muslims, but who are not righteous Muslims."

I still have doubts about what Mahmud is talking about. Is this about his doubt in relation to me, whether I am a real Muslim or simply dressed as one? Or is Mahmud really scared on his own behalf? Afraid that Allah does not think he is a real Muslim because he does not spread the message of Islam enough among the Danes, or perhaps, because, many years ago, he pretended to be a Muslim when he tried to win over Kurdish peasants to communism to incite them to revolt? Is it ultimately the fear of not being a real Muslim in the eyes of Allah that is his driving force?

I notice that our conversation has changed character. It has become more burdened by religious arguments and narratives. Some of it doesn't make sense. He's saying things I haven't heard before. Other things I've heard repeatedly. But Mahmud also interpreted the Qur'an and the religious scriptures in such a way that his conclusions surprise me. He is hard-line in the profession of his faith and there is no doubt in his eyes. "Muslims must keep their own rules. They must be sincere in the profession of faith and keep the agreements laid out in the Qur'an. But Muslims lost power because they did not abide by the basic rules," Mahmud says. He proudly explains how Muslims once ruled over many parts of the world. "It was not with war and weapons, but through good deeds that the Muslims had taken over the lands all the way to Indonesia."

I do not fully agree with his analysis. The Ottoman Empire, to which Mahmud refers, was known for using brutal methods as they conquered one country after another. "Do you advocate the introduction of Islam by force?" I ask.

Mahmud pauses and thinks. His voice becomes gentle. "Self-defense is not violence, Özlem. The Prophet also defended himself in Mecca, until Allah's commands came to him and gave the Muslims the right to keep their land under Islam." Mahmud seems insecure and not very happy about the issue. "This topic doesn't interest me," he says. He explains that he is not learned, and therefore cannot go into detail about it. He knows where this conversation is headed. "I know what your question is," he says, as if reading my thoughts.

I choose to be more direct. "Do you believe ISIL represents Islam?" I ask.

"I don't want to comment on that," he replies. For the first time, I've hit a wall with Mahmud. Why? Is it because he is afraid that I might use his answer against him, or is it because he would rather not tell his honest opinion?

I'm biased. I assume he supports ISIL. The vast majority of young people who join ISIL are Salafists, so I assume that the same applies to Mahmud. I admit this is a gross and unfair generalization, but I choose to hold on to it to see if my prejudice holds true. I look him directly in the eye. "I want to know if you sympathize with ISIL."

Mahmud, who up to this point gushed out answers like a waterfall, claps shut like an oyster. The man is suddenly silent. "That's not my business," he finally says.

"Why?" I ask again.

Mahmud is annoyed. "You don't focus on anything I tell you at all," he says. Then Mahmud says something that is ambiguous. "I am a grateful person who was protected in Denmark," he says. "But if Abdullah Ocalan (PKK's leader) contradicted the Qur'an, I would also go to battle against him."

Does that mean he thinks that ISIL is right to open war on unbelievers because they contradict ISIL's interpretation of the Qur'an? What is Mahmud trying to tell me? "What is battle, Mahmud?" I ask him.

Mahmud answers me in a different way. "Rights of Muslims and the laws of Allah must be observed. I'm not saying you should wear a scarf, Özlem. That's Allah's commandment. It is not mine, but Allah also commands that he who has committed adultery should be stoned," he says.

"Do you favor stoning?" I ask.

"I agree with what Allah commands us," says Mahmud. "You must do the same and you must not falter."

I interrupt him. "Aren't there many interpretations of Islam?"

Mahmud's facial expression becomes serious. "What kind of interpretations?" he asks.

I talk about the different interpretations in which some Muslims have an extreme approach to religion, while others are more pragmatic. I cite, for example, that the majority of Muslims vote in democratic elections, while the few who follow Hizb ut-Tahrir believe that Muslims should not vote.

Mahmud takes out his Qur'an. He browses the pages and finds Surah al-Hashr, Chapter 59, verse number 7. He emphasizes the last sentence, "And whatever the Messenger has given you—take; and what he has forbidden you—refrain from. And fear Allah; indeed, Allah is severe in penalty." Mahmud says that is very crucial to him and central to why he is a Salafist. I'm leaning forward in the chair, because maybe here's an important piece of the puzzle. "We must receive everything that Allah gives us," he says.

But will Mahmud really follow the Qur'an literally? I try to explain to him that in the Qur'an there are many surahs (Arabic for chapters) and that they can be interpreted in many ways.

"You must not," he objects.

I continue, "There are passages in the Qur'an that can be translated in a thousand ways."

I am familiar with this line of argument, for I have heard it from several moderate imams preaching that Muslims should be aware that the Qur'an can be viewed from different angles. The question of interpretation is significant because the most fervent radicals interpret Islam in an extreme, black-and-white way when they use the Qur'an to justify the abuses they commit in the name of Allah. It is in many ways a focal point for the entire conflict between Muslims.

"No," says Mahmud.

I reply, "But that's what I mean."

And then Mahmud says something that shows me what he really thinks of me. "That is the argument of the unbelievers and the Islamic hostilities."

I protest, "Then justify the differences between Sunni and Shia Muslims..."

Mahmud interrupts me with a raised voice. "Shias are not Muslims."

That comment shocks me. I can understand how Mahmud might see me as an infidel. But with that argument, I have to lump him in with the ISIL supporters and other jihadist Salafists. ISIL terrorists, namely, argue that Shia Muslims are unrighteous and therefore the archenemy. "Can only Sunnis be real Muslims?" I ask in amazement.

"Who else?" he replies. "Only those who follow the Qur'an."

I don't believe my own ears. Does he really mean that? This is equivalent to saying that only Catholics are Christians, while Protestants, Orthodox, and others who believe in different movements within Christianity are not.

As upset as I am that Mahmud will not recognize millions of Muslims, he can't get past my claim that anyone other than Sunnis can be Muslims. "The Prophet said that his congregation was divided into seventy-three sects. And beyond one sect, all the rest will end up in hell," Mahmud says with his index finger lifted.

"But isn't the definition of who is a Muslim that, if you yourself feel like a Muslim, then another person cannot believe you are not?" I ask.

"Yes," Mahmud admits.

I love this rule again, even though I had a hard time advocating it when the Hizb ut-Tahrir people argued that I couldn't believe the ISIL terrorists were not Muslims when they themselves professed the faith.

"But," Mahmud continues, "it is not enough to say that you are a Muslim. One's actions must also show it."

I agree with him, I think. And that's why I mean, the ISIL terrorists can never be Muslims.

"It takes three things to be a Muslim," says Mahmud. "You must say you are a Muslim. You have to feel in your heart that you are a Muslim. And…"

"...you have to show that you are a Muslim," I finish. I can tell that again I surprise him with my knowledge of Islam. "What about Alevites?" I ask. The Alevites do not usually go to mosques, but pray at their own places of worship. Men and women pray together, and music plays a major role in their faith practice. They regard the universe and Allah as a unit. Their goal for man is to reach the highest stage of human development—that is, to be the perfect man. Humans, nature, environment, and animals matter a lot to the Alevites, as they believe that Allah is equal to the universe itself. For many years, under many different regimes, Alevites have been persecuted and killed by Sunni Muslims who insisted they were not real Muslims.

Euzu billah," Mahmud says earnestly. These Arabic words mean "Allah must protect us from the devil." For Mahmud, the Alevites are the devil incarnate. Now he raises his voice again. He does not understand how I can seriously claim that Alevites can also be Muslims. "They did not believe in Muhammad, but in Ali being mightier than him," he says angrily.

I know this is not true, as I am married into an Alevite family. But I choose not to share that information with him. Alevites believe in Muhammad; they merely emphasize that Ali, Muhammad's son-in-law, was Muhammad's first successor, while Sunnis rose from the majority, who believed Muhammad's successor should be chosen by consensus. But no matter how and with what I argue, Mahmud says I am not telling the truth. "Ali is not even mentioned in the Qur'an," he says.

"Of course he is mentioned in the Qur'an," I reply.

Mahmud slams the Qur'an on the table and says angrily, "Show me where!"

I do not know if it is his certainty that provokes uncertainty in me, or whether it is the prospect of the effort it will cost me to convince him. I want to give up trying.

But Mahmud has seen through my uncertainty. "Who told you that? Shouldn't we call them? Shouldn't we ask them?" he insists. "If you say the reverse of the Qur'an, if you lie to the Qur'an, you become a kafir (unbeliever) with the same," he almost shouts as he slams his hand on the table. "If you did not mean it, then you should ask forgiveness from Allah right away. It's very dangerous." Mahmud is angry. I can see I have lost him now. The chasm between us is so deep that it is impossible for me to build a bridge.

"But is your Allah so harsh that if you make a mistake, then Allah punishes the sin?" I ask Mahmud. I want to understand how far his anger could go.

"Allah is the one who punishes the hardest, and the one who is the most merciful," Mahmud replies. He tells me that if a sinner repents, Allah will always forgive the sin. But I also know that the discussion we are having right now is, in fact, at the heart of the entire Middle East war between Muslims. Who can define what it means to be a righteous Muslim? And what do you do with those who fall outside the definition?

There are so many movements within Islam that it is impossible to find head or tail. It only adds to the great frustration I feel that the debate in Denmark is so generalizing in relation to Muslims, because it is by no means a homogeneous group. The Sunni Muslims are divided into four schools, and the Shia Muslims are a completely different branch. I could go on. Many of these groups disagree with each other on interpretations of the Qur'an, who are the right Muslims, and who should be fought. Everything turns into a battle between different interpretations of Islam, and this is most clearly seen when wars occur in the Middle East.

At home, however, everything is reduced to a struggle between different religions. If you spend just one day getting acquainted with the conflicts and differences of opinion that are also internal to a religion, the nuances will become more apparent. I am Muslim and do not advocate violence. I can see good elements in every movement within Islam, but I can also see dark interpretations that send chills up my spine.

I try to hold that my knowledge of the Qur'an is right. I feel confident that I am right, yet uncertainty arises in me. Is this how they convert young people? I realize I feel lost without an imam. I do not have an earthly chance to know all the verses in the Qur'an. Mahmud and I can talk to each other, but we speak from two completely different worldviews. I talk about what I experience, want, feel, believe in, while Mahmud is constantly reading the Qur'an and reading sacred texts. I feel inadequate. What if I had an imam with me? He might be able to answer Mahmud's questions with direct references to the Qur'an. There, at that moment, it seems crystal clear to me that ordinary Muslims like me cannot win a discussion with a person like Mahmud. It's so easy for radical Muslims to label us nonbelievers. They could not do the same to an imam.

My anger is no longer directed at Mahmud, but at the imams who fail to take up the fight against these radical views. Why aren't there more imams who go out with direct references to the Qur'an and explain why people should not resort to violence and murder? Why don't they use the Qur'an to show that ISIL is a terrorist organization? Why don't they all give us some tools so we can protect society from the venom that is poisoning it?

When Mahmud says, "Alevites are worse than Shia, and Shia are worse than Jews," he seriously underscores the war that exists between Muslim groups. For Jews, Mahmud is a clear and indisputable enemy. He doesn't even spend time explaining it; his hatred of Jews is a matter of course. And if Muslim groups, which count millions of people in the world, also become legitimate targets in his worldview, then, yes, he helps to legitimize ISIL's terror against Muslims. I am thinking of Hamza from Hizb ut-Tahrir, who said that it is not Muslims who have destroyed the Middle East. Mahmud's argument follows the same track, but with the marked difference that Mahmud does not direct the anger at the West or the United

States, but instead at other Muslim groups in the Middle East. In his thinking, the West is not the enemy, it is unbelievers who dress up as Muslims that are the biggest threat.

"Then you have to feel that what's happening in the Middle East is justified, because now all those who are not 'the right Muslims' are being purged," I say confrontationally.

"I see what you're up to," Mahmud says, and again he slips out of my hands like a wet piece of soap.

"Is it righteous to be a jihadist?" I ask.

"You're good at talking in headlines," smiles Mahmud. "Is it good to go to hell?" he asks.

"No," I reply.

"So how do you avoid hell?" he asks.

"We have different perceptions of how to travel to Hell or Paradise," I say dryly.

Suddenly I realize that the door is closed and the third man no longer sits in the room with us. The conversation with Mahmud has become so intense that I have not even noticed that he has left the room. Mahmud's nature makes me feel uneasy, and I remark out loud that the door is closed and we sit alone.

"No," Mahmud says, pointing to the third man standing in a corner of the room. "He's still there."

I am overjoyed at the relief I feel knowing that I am not alone with Mahmud.

I am sure there are limits to how many times I can challenge Mahmud's understanding of Islam. I weigh my words before I utter them. I formulate my positions on neutral questions: Can't people misinterpret? Can't humans fail? Can't people have an interest in interpreting religion in a certain way? Why is there such a difference between Muslim countries if interpretation doesn't exist? Could it be that people are abusing religion to justify their attacks on innocents?

He wonders that I could even ask such questions. In his eyes, a true Muslim follows what is in the law, without putting his own thoughts at risk. Mahmud says he is following the Qur'an, word for word. He has a much larger enemy list than the imam from Hizb ut-Tahrir. His list doesn't just count Jews, whether they are Israeli or not. It also contains almost half of the earth's Muslims. I feel like I'm on that list too. For people who are "integrated," who speak of "interpretations of Islam," who call the Alevites and Shia "real Muslims," and who "advocate democracy," they are also the enemy of Muslims in the world of Mahmud. They are unbelievers and they must be fought. We go on at length about this, but never seem to reach accord.

When I push him too much, he says he gets migraines. The more I hold on to my insistence that different people read the Qur'an differently, the more he raises his voice and gets angry. Mahmud is Kurdish like me. I am Muslim, but not like him. The distance between us is too big at the end of our conversation.

I want to find something that we both like. I ask him if he wants to read his favorite verse in the Qur'an. "One that you love a lot and that means a lot to you," I say. Mahmud lights up. His raised eyebrows lower. His voice becomes gentle and kind. His eyes are smiling. He immediately finds his Qur'an, and in a soft voice, he reads it. He has chosen "Ayat al-Kursi," which is of great importance to Muslims. It is one of the longest verses describing and praising God's greatness and divinity. I love the verse myself. Partly because it was one of the first verses I learned as a child. Partly because I have often read it during life crises to find strength and inner peace—when a relative developed a mental illness, when I was left alone to care for my child, when I was afflicted with severe stress, and when I lost my beloved grandmother. Here it is:

Throne Verse (Ayat al-Kursi)

"Allah—there is no deity except Him, the Ever-Living, the Sustainer of [all] existence. Neither drowsiness overtakes Him nor sleep. To Him belongs whatever is in the heavens and whatever is on the earth. Who is it that can intercede with Him except by His permission? He knows what is [presently] before them and what will be after them, and they encompass not a thing of His knowledge except for what He wills. His Kursi extends over the heavens and the earth, and their preservation tires Him not. And He is the Most High, the Most Great."

(Al Baqarah Chapter 2, Verse 255)

I thank Mahmud. There is a calm energy in the room now, and I want to end the conversation here. But I am well aware that we have not achieved cohesion. The Qur'an binds us together, but I know that the same Qur'an is used to tear us apart.

I pack up my stuff to go. Mahmud follows me out through the mosque, all the way to the entrance. I put my hand on his chest and say goodbye since he doesn't extend his hand to shake mine. I'm sad. I always feel great sadness when I meet people I can't reach an understanding with. Mahmud and I both have Kurdish roots from Turkey. We share a language and a cultural story with each other. Our hearts are both breaking over the oppression of people we both feel tied to, the Kurds. But there's a point where our similarities end. There are so many ditches between us that it will take decades to build this bridge.

Patterns

My thoughts are shattered into thousands of fragments as I cycle through Norrebrogade. What should I do now? Should I call the security service and tell them there is a man they should be watching? I spend a lot of time thinking through the scenario. What effect would it have on Mahmud that I take advantage of his openness and desire for dialogue with me and break his confidence? Will he ever trust others, or will I affirm his notion that freedom of expression does not apply to Muslims? And should one be punished for one's opinions and not solely for one's actions, which is otherwise the practice in a democracy like Denmark?

I wonder where my idea of reporting him comes from. Why didn't I feel this same need with Kim, who wants to solve problems with Muslims in front of the mosque with a machine gun? Why is it different with Mahmud?

The sadness fills me. It seems to me that this is not about Mahmud, or Denmark's security. It's about me. I want to be secure from criticism. I am a Muslim and am often told on social media that I cover up for "my own." I would like to be inoculated against that criticism, which is why I am considering reporting Mahmud. I want to avoid being placed with his ilk. To prevent anyone from saying, "You Muslims agree, you are not loyal to Denmark, only to each other."

In the end, I know it's not my job to report Mahmud, nor to protect my reputation. I am writing a book, and so I talk to a number of people, some of whom are semi-criminal, some of whom have very extreme views, others who are just very generalizing. I am not a cop who reports, I am a writer who details conversations I have with these people. I have to treat them fairly.

I feel a great heaviness lift from my heart. But why is all this so complicated?

Before meeting with Mahmud, I was convinced that dialogue was always the path to peace. That we could talk about everything and solve everything via conversation. But after talking to Mahmud, I can see that the solution is not always dialogue on its own. For the first time, I understand why some people call it naïveté when I insist on dialogue coffee with extremists. I have seen many times that conversations have helped, but my meeting with Mahmud reminds me that dialogue cannot stand alone. I still think we should talk to people who have radical views, both leaders and their associates, but when we meet people who are willing to kill themselves and others for the cause they believe in, then dialogue is not enough. Those people are dangerous and should also be treated as such. Claiming the opposite is naïve and irresponsible when there is a threat to public safety.

Some of the solutions must be found outside Denmark, for—as my meetings with the boys at the Red Square, as well as Hizb ut-Tahrir and Mahmud, have shown,—major foreign policy agendas play a role in our domestic problems. The conflicts in Israel and Palestine, the wars in Syria, Afghanistan, and Iraq, the persecution of groups of people in Turkey, all affect the people of Denmark, and it affects Denmark as a nation.

Is it possible to influence young people before they are radicalized? One issue we face is that wars abroad affect people who come here seeking refuge, but many of the problems can be addressed by paying more attention to our youngest citizens. Children are born neither extremist, evil, nor criminal. When they wind up there as young people or adults, it is because something has pushed them to an extreme.

The young people who grow up in poverty may have never seen their parents enjoy the benefits of hard work. They may never have discussed history, read a newspaper, or scrutinized the world situation over dinner. How can young people be expected to be strong democratic ambassadors when they have not entered a democratic society at birth?

That is why schools and educational institutions are so important to enable young people to break the pattern. Social mobility is crucial for young people. Schooling and education can make young people financially independent and equip them with the knowledge that will save them from the dark movements that seek to gain power.

I believe that it is possible to reach people before they become radicalized. No matter how dangerous the terrorists and fundamentalists become as adults, they were all innocent children once. They have kicked a ball, watched television, had a girlfriend, and had dreams for the future. But, at some point, something went wrong—when they didn't get an education, but instead training on how to use a gun.

A crucial part of the solution must come from the religious environments. There is a need for a qualified Islamic counteraction, so that the boys at the Red Square are not easily seduced by extreme religious views such as Mahmud's. If we are to argue against extreme interpretations of religious scriptures, first and foremost, moderate imams must play a far greater role. They need to take on the critical conversation, not only with those who express the extreme interpretations of religion, but also with more silent associates. It is of no use to society that some of the leading imams shake their heads and neglect the problem. Mahmud constantly reads the Qur'an and has memorized verse after verse, which he uses to support his position. So should the moderate imams. They could help ordinary Muslims by supporting our position with their knowledge of the Qur'an that we can use to protect ourselves from the poison being introduced into society by Mahmud and others like him. Unless the imams assume responsibility, I am afraid that Mahmud's views will stand unchallenged. The critical debate against Hizb ut-Tahrir and the Salafists is one we Muslims cannot pursue on our own without the support of religious leaders.

Now that I know Mahmud, I am a little more worried about what I'm doing with these discussions. I see clearly how anger can easily erupt into violence. Is it even worth it to try to continue having these discussions?

My good friend Carsten Jensen quoted words from Turkish author Hakan Gunday's novel *More, More.* "There are two kinds of knowledge: the kind one seeks and the kind that comes to one.

If knowledge comes to anyone, it is with an intent to bargain for something, to make him swallow a political lie or sell him a new phone. Furthermore, knowledge that travels a long way is dirty and reeks of shit. The only knowledge that is worth anything is the kind that one must seek out. Only that deserves trust."

That quote becomes my answer to the question of whether it was worth talking to Mahmud. It is always worth seeking out knowledge.

I have read and heard so much about radicalization and about people who are fundamentalist. But only through sitting down with Mahmud do I clearly understand what religion can do to us humans.

So far, I have only examined this phenomenon in relation to Islam. But what do Christian fundamentalists really think about, for example, being gay?

CHAPTER 7

CONSISTENT CHRISTIANITY

"Do not judge, or you too will be judged. For in the same way you judge others, you will be judged, and with the measure you use, it will be measured to you."

–The Gospel of Matthew, chapter 7, verses 1–2

"**J**esus is there. We can't see him, but he's there. It is your job as parents to tell your son that Jesus is with him. Pray for him. Read the Bible and help him remember to come to church so he is close to Jesus." The priest's gentle but loud voice fills the whole room. It is raining outside, but that was no obstacle for the 350 or so people who have shown up to hear the sermon this first Sunday of Lent. We are not inside the church itself, but in another building. The congregation has grown too big for the church.

Now the priest takes the child from his mother. He steps away from the baptismal font and walks to the center of the room. He raises the child up before the congregation and says with joy in his voice, "Welcome, Sylvester!" Now, the boy is part of the fellowship of Jesus Christ. Sylvester is unaffected by the excitement around him and looks at the assembly with wide eyes. I am not part of Jesus Christ's fellowship, but like everyone else, I can't help but smile. For a brief moment, I feel like getting up and clapping.

We all get up, not to clap, but to pray. Many look at me and smile. I smile back. We sing hymns. Some of them I know, and the rest I get help with from the projector, which shows the text on the large wall at the end of the room.

When the music stops, the priest stands at the pulpit and begins his sermon. Only the sounds of children break the silence of the room. The priest smiles, but raises his hands. This signals that he is ready to get serious, and his voice becomes deep with feeling.

"I hear many say that technology has made it much easier for us to live. Has it? That totally depends on what angle you look at it from... Try looking through the vantage point of a five-year-old Filipino girl sold by her parents to someone who wants to film her and livestream it over the internet to a Danish man. Try seeing this from the angle of a modern Danish hospital, where modern technology is used to remove tiny babies from their mother's womb because they are considered body waste. How about a high-tech hospital in the Netherlands, where there is an incurably sick man in bed, who feels he has no choice but to ask to be killed, as the law allows, because it is so obvious to him that his family wants him to die, even if they won't say it out loud?"

He cites a number of examples. Pretty crazy, I think. I agree with him on everything except abortion. But it is not agreement that has brought me to the East Jutland town of Solution.

After the service, many parishioners greet me. Friendly and smiling, some ask about how I'm doing and what I'm up to now. We laugh together, and I take a picture with Sylvester's family.

Outside, the rain continues at full strength.

Cursed Modernism

It may not be a coincidence that I ended up with Henrik in Solution. Maybe this is where I find out what my mission is really about. Henrik is a pastor and part of the Inner Mission. As I stand in the dining room of his vicarage, the first thing I notice is the large white church, which is framed by the window and leaves no doubt that Christianity is part of the solution.

Henrik offers lunch and, after eating curry with eggs, we settle into the living room. Henrik has lit up the stove. He sits in his rocking chair while I sit in an armchair close to the fire. The only thing I know about Henrik is that he sees homosexuality as something unnatural. I have been made aware of him through people in the Inner Mission, and I have neither Googled him nor further investigated who he is. I don't want any preconceptions about him to alter the direction our conversation will take.

Henrik is fifty-seven years old and has been a priest in Solution for seventeen years. He was born in the Faroe Islands to a Norwegian mother and a Danish father. The father died when Henry was eleven years old. "He got a blood clot on Monday and died on Tuesday," says Henrik. He does not remember much about his father, but is convinced that it mattered later in life that his father was a priest. Henrik grew up in Hirtshals with a mother whom he describes as "solid and cool." She had been a part of the Norwegian resistance movement, just as her father had been active with the Danish. While married, she was homebound, but when Henry's father died, she took an active role in civic society. She had read English and French at universities in Norway, and the local schools inspector offered her a job. She thanked him for the opportunity and took a job, but did not work full-time so she could also mother her seven children.

The Inner Mission played a role in the home, however, which was not characterized by the highly pious faith for which the Inner Mission is known. "I would call it a very consciously believing, church home. Where faith and life followed a natural direction," says Henrik with a smile. Henrik later moved to Aarhus, where he began to read theology and thus followed in his father's footsteps. He quickly became part of the Christian Student Union. "KFS was the place where I found my identity as a Christian," Henrik emphasizes.

Shortly after completing theology studies, Henrik married "the unattainable princess," his childhood crush. Throughout childhood, they had seen each other every two years when their families met, and when he finally got himself together and told her how he felt, it turned out that the feelings were mutual. The two were married four days before Henry's twenty-fourth birthday. For a number of years, he was a priest in Norway, but returned in 2000 to Denmark. Since then he has lived in Solution with his wife and five children.

Henrik wonders why I ask so much about his background. "I didn't know you were writing my biography," he says.

My interest in Henry's life story is deliberate. It's easier for humans to dehumanize when we see each other as groups, rather than as individuals. Henrik is more than just a pastor who has a thriving fellowship with the Inner Mission, just as I am more than simply the Muslim Özlem. It is often through sharing our life stories that we humanize each other.

According to Henrik, the missionary movement is strong in the area, and it started before the Inner Mission was founded. "Around 1800, there was a revival called 'The Strong Jews.' A strange local revival which had a great impact in many ways. Among other things, they have been behind the legislation we have on free schools. The first to form a free school came from here," Henrik continues proudly. "They were on the field long before Grundtvig. Strong believers and strong people. They no longer exist, but I still bury people from their lineage. Some of the elders in the church grew up in their families and attended a free school, where a significant part of their teaching for seven years was *Luther's Small Catechism*," Henrik says. It reminds me of some of the most conservative Qur'anic schools found in Turkey, Pakistan, Iran, and other Muslim countries, where the only thing the children learn is the holy scriptures, but where they do not reflect on or analyze the texts.

"As the Inner Mission emerged in the 1860s, the strong Jews perceived them as overly superficial."

"Are you a pastor of the Inner Mission?" I ask.

"No, no," Henrik rushes to say. "I am a pastor of the Danish National Church." But he understands my confusion, as he has been asked the same question by countless journalists before this. "I am a priest in Solution and Corning. I am employed by the Danish People's Church and live in an official residence. I feel good about Inner Mission and they feel good about me. I think they say and mean sensible things. They invite me into their mission home and to come to church. But I am just as much a priest to Mr. and Mrs. Nielsen, who would not dream of setting foot in the Inner Mission," Henrik says.

I feel a bit stupid and ignorant, but still keep asking my questions. "Why are you not in the Inner Church?" I ask. It turns out to my surprise that the Inner Mission does not have a church at all, but is an ecclesiastical organization that wants to reform the church. The Inner Mission started as a grassroots movement in the National Church around 1850. The leader was a pastor named Vilhelm Beck. Henrik describes him as one of the greatest speakers in Denmark. "He could draw ten to fifteen thousand people to the Inner Mission summer gatherings at Mount Heaven. He was a fabulous orator." Henrik sounds excited, and I feel sorry I don't know anything about Vilhelm Beck.

"What is the Inner Mission in opposition to?" I ask.

"They are in opposition to a kind of indifference to faith, to God, and to the Bible," Henrik says. I can almost touch his enthusiasm. It radiates out from him.

"Is it strict doctrine that you miss in the National Church, or consequences to falling to the wayside?" I ask.

"It's not strictness, but more consistency. There must be much more vibrancy in it. More spirit in it. More joy, it must be more authentic, more filled with spirit." He energetically recounts how the movement spread in the National Church. Around 1910, a large part of the National Church, the priesthood, and the diocesan college had a closer connection to the movement. "Ten percent of the population had close contact with the Inner Mission at the time. So there were a lot of people," Henrik says enthusiastically.

The connection waned during the twentieth century, when, according to Henrik, Inner Mission and Grundtvig were set up as opponents. "But it's not right to put it that way. That's why I usually say I'm the last living twig off the original tree." He pauses and smiles. "Okay, maybe not the last one, there are a couple of us left."

"I am also a fundamentalist," I say.

"Good," Henrik says dryly. According to him, one can be a supporter of Grundtvig in many ways, for example, by adopting his philosophy on people and popular movements. "You can have a warm heart for him. But when I say what I say, it is because I also have a sense of his Christian vision. He had a strong spirit of revival, just like the Inner Mission. Both Inner Mission and Grundtvig were reactions to rationalism which had permeated the Church of the People and made it necessary to adapt the truth of the faith to modern beliefs." The contrast he sees between Christianity and modernism is evident in his voice. There are many who criticize imams for not keeping up with the times. I can't help but think that it could be fun if a couple of them were here with me in Henry's room. At the same time, I am also becoming more and more aware that various movements in the church are constantly trying to leave their imprints on it, change it, interpret it, or perceive it in a completely determined way. Like in my own religion.

In 2016, I sat on a panel organized by the National Church during the cultural and spiritual festival called Heavenly Days. There, I called for a clear voice from the church in the debate over what should be valued by its leadership. In Henry's living room, I realize how naïve my desire was, and how much it illustrates my lack of knowledge about the church. It is the same as when someone demands a common voice from the Muslims—that voice does not exist. The desire is naïve, because both Christianity and Islam are full of diverse voices, movements, and branches. Should they find a definitive opinion, it could only be ambiguous. It is natural for each branch to want to be represented in any official statement, and therefore all the voices must be contained in the words. As I share my thoughts with Henrik, I feel that I'm hitting a sore point. "It is a huge problem for the National Church that it has lost its bite and become indifferent. It accommodates everyone and will say whatever is necessary. It wants everything in the pot at once, but then it tastes like nothing," Henrik says.

Henrik does not believe that the National Church should adapt to the challenges and developments of the time. "Christianity should not be fluid and flexible." He sounds serious. I tell Henrik that the Salafist Mahmud thinks the same, and that many imams share Henry's views. They also want a consequence to falling from the faith.

He refers to a study that Christian Dagblad did several years ago, in which the twenty most visited churches in Denmark were listed. In this top twenty, Henrik could see a clear statement from Christians. "In virtually all the churches on the list, preaching was done in the same way I preach here on Sundays. In the fundamental, classic way, where the message is in line with what the Bible says."

Henrik himself has had good experiences in attracting visitors to his church. In 2008, he was allowed to erect a new building to provide space for more congregants. Henrik preaches every other Sunday, as he shares the pulpit with one of his colleagues. It is quite common that there are between 250 and 400 Christians gathered for services each Sunday, whether or not Henrik preaches. Henrik, however, will not take credit for the impressive attendance. "There was also a large congregation before I came. There is a strong tradition of going to church here. And that's because we have never stooped to modernizing, liberalizing, evasive service."

I ask Henrik what he means more precisely by modernizing service. He has two concrete examples and starts with Thorkild Grosboll, who, in 2003, became known as the priest from Taarbaek who does not believe in God. "Grosboll began to say that God should be spelled with a small *g* because God exists between people and is not the creator. That came as news to me, and I disagree with him," Henrik says. For him, Grosboll is the perfect example of a modernizing, relativizing understanding of Christianity, "where you take something as central as God and say it doesn't suit our time, because we believe in the Big Bang, and evolution, and so on. Now we must make Christianity palatable for modern, civilized human beings, so we shrink God down to something that's very little. I mean, you can talk about both Big Bang and God. The question is, who turned on the bang for the Big Bang?" he says with a serious voice.

Henry's second example is homosexuality, which he says has the same problem at its root. "The Bible makes it very clear that homosexuality is a sin. But then someone says that it was written very long ago, and that after all, we have evolved over the past two thousand years and that the situation is different with gays today than it was back then. It's just not true. In ancient times, homosexuality was a widespread and culturally accepted phenomenon. When you say today that we are somewhere else, it is the same as what Grosboll was doing. A liberalization, which is profoundly unfortunate, because you make Christianity something that you can change and shape and model according to the whims of the time," Henrik says. He claims that there are several places where it is written in the Bible that homosexuality is a sin and that the expression of homosexuality is against God's will.

"What is the punishment?" I ask.

"There is no punishment," Henrik replies.

"But what consequence are you calling for publicly in church?" I challenge him. "And is it no longer your own interpretation that gays are sinful if there is no consequence for being gay in Christianity?"

"Well, there is actually a consequence," he says. "What is the penalty if I beat my children and my wife? What is the consequence for pedophilia? There are social ramifications, yes. I could give another example. What is the consequence if I consistently lie? Or if I'm stingy? There may not be an immediate penalty for these behaviors, but in Christianity there is eternal punishment in the form of hell. You know that from Islam too, I think. Whoever consciously goes against the will of God, who acts and lives against it, regardless of whether he or she takes the name of God and Jesus in his mouth, will be punished forever," Henrik says calmly.

I lean forward in the chair. "So gay people will go to hell?" I ask him.

Henrik exhales and breathes quietly. There is complete silence in the room. Henrik has recently thrown a new piece of wood into the fireplace, and the roar of the fire is the only sound in the room.

"If a person deliberately chooses homosexuality, then that person is at enormous risk. Yes, that person will be judged forever," Henrik says. He sounds almost sorry. He says he would like to add an important nuance, and then begins to talk about people who are gay, but agree with him. They live out their lives in celibacy, fully aware that they can "fall in" and be "tempted."

Henrik emphasizes that it is not sinful to be gay in thought. It is only the action that is punishable. "It may well be that the thought turns to the desire and the action, and then there is a way back. That's the path of forgiveness," he says.

I'm so surprised at how similar Hamza's and Henry's arguments are about gays. For Hamza, sin also lies in the act. "So if you only think of sex with someone of your own gender, yet never perform the act, is it not sinful?" I ask.

"No, it's not," Henrik replies. "Old Luther said: You can't prevent birds from flying over your head, but you can prevent them from building nests in your hair. In a sense, there is a sin in everything we do. When I stand on the pulpit and people think I'm good and I enjoy the admiration, I am sinning. Sin is always my companion, and therefore I cannot go beyond being a sinner," Henrik says. Then he loses some of his calm. "Isn't it interesting that gays identify themselves by their sexuality? Do you go around saying you are heterosexual?" His voice is louder now. "That kind of gay-lesbian militancy...it has become a very strong ideological issue for many gays and lesbians."

"Do you really think it is an ideological matter to be gay?" I ask, shocked.

"It's not something I think. It's something I know. It is not so for everyone, but it is for those who work for their cause. For example, LGBT organizations—it's a big project for them to convince us all that gender identity is not something we are born or created with, but rather something we can switch on and off." Henrik leans back. He seems satisfied and is almost waiting for a reaction from me.

I can't hold back my outrage. I've taken on these debates and conversations so many times, but I still get annoyed at how predictable my reaction is. I know I should keep myself collected, but it's so difficult, because when Henrik talks about homosexuals, I think of my gay friends, of their children and all the stigma they face. It becomes too personal to me, and neither my brain nor my heart can be tactful at the moment. So I raise my voice in outrage. "Henrik, you can't mean that!"

"Then you must not have followed the debates," Henrik says.

But I have. I talk about my collaboration with the LGBT organizations over the past ten years. My personal relationships with friends who are homosexuals. I lay out my argument. "Sexuality or gender are not ideological struggles, nor do they constitute a political standpoint. They're about the way some of us are born," I say insistently.

"It's getting very interesting here," Henrik says, smiling.

There is also a fundamental divide between Henry's and my attitude toward an individual's right to live his or her sexuality or live as the gender he or she identifies as. So long as no researchers have been able to prove that homosexuals have a specific gene, Henrik does not believe that one can be born a homosexual. He adds, "Maybe there is a hormonal predisposition in men, but not in women."

"Do you think so?" I ask.

"Well, that's how it is," he replies.

Henrik is fundamental in his point of view, just as much as I am. Neither he nor I give way to doubt or to a conscience that haunts us. I mean, I think I'm right, and he thinks he is. But why am I so surprised by Henry's attitude? This is not the first time I have heard a priest say what he is saying. I chaired the Social Committee when the Danish Parliament decided that homosexuals should be elected in the National Church. I will never forget the hearing we held on the topic in the Common Room. The venue was filled with detractors of the proposal, including people from the Inner Mission. The Danish People's Party and the Left's Birthe Ronn Hornbech led the debate. At one point, Birthe Ronn said that homosexuals could not reproduce. Back then, I thought she was one of the fools of the parliament—a thought that is terribly generalizing and condescending, and I've changed my mind since then. The difference between then and now is that at that time I never got to know the detractors as people. Now that I am sitting here with Henrik, I'm almost sad that his attitude does not match his smiling face. We disagree on several issues, but Henrik maintains the disagreement without becoming personal or vicious. That is why it becomes even harder for me to put him in his place—also, I think he is basically a good person. As I think about it, I get scared about what would happen if anyone heard what I was thinking. Can you be a good person if you have such strong attitudes about homosexuals?

"Do you really believe that people are born with a gay gene?" Henrik asks.

"I think people are born the way they are," I reply calmly.

Now it is Henrik who breaks the calm in the room. Now it's his turn to flip out. He throws back his head, leans back and exclaims, "Özlem! The general research, the one that is not politically correct, says..." When I interrupt him, he asks me with a twinkle in his eye if he can now cite the kind of research that justifies his position. The mood is by no means unpleasant. It is as if we have known each other for a lifetime and are old high school chums who have stuck it out through many years of debates about life. There will be smiles, and there will be shouting. Henrik says that until the 1970s, in research circles, there was a consensus that homosexuality was a disease. "That was the case until a militant LGBT movement in the United States emerged that changed the law so that homosexuality was no longer a disease. There were no real reasons to change it," Henrik says.

"But there is no scientific proof that homosexuality is a disease," I object.

Henrik takes a deep breath. "Well," he says reluctantly, slapping his thigh, "I'm afraid you've only heard of homosexuality from one side."

"That's why I'm sitting here," I say. "I want to hear your take on it too."

But Henrik doesn't hear what I'm saying. And like many others with whom I have disagreed, he offers me some written material about his position. I've noticed a tendency, among those with whom I disagree, to believe that it all comes down to a matter of ignorance on the topic that can easily be solved with pamphlets and propaganda.

I persist with my question. "So you think the LGBT movement went on a crusade to change the thinking on this issue. And do you mean that, fundamentally, gays are ill? But you're not saying it straight out. Why not just come out and say it?"

Henrik shakes his head. "No, hear me out. The idea of illness is problematic, because we associate something completely different with it, and illness is not the concept I'm trying to convey." Henrik illustrates his point. "Jensen lives in the city and is neurotic. Is he ill? No, but he has a problem that controls his life, and occasionally, his issues make life difficult for his children."

I try again. "Henrik, do you think that there is something in the gay person's brain and body that causes something not to work properly, thereby contributing to the person having some deviant behaviors?"

That phrase works for Henry. "Quite right, it is very accurately described."

"If it's a defect, would you do whatever you could to compensate for it? Or to suppress it?"

Henrik thinks about it. "A large part of psychological research, not to mention ordinary, secular research without any particular Christian agenda, seems to indicate that gay and lesbian tendencies are linked to developmental issues that begin in childhood. There is no certainty about a genetic component, but for men there might also be a genetic link. Something that makes them more likely to develop into homosexuals rather than heterosexuals. In the case of women, nothing has been found to show that genetics have a role in determining sexuality."

Why the insistence on gender distinction? It seems strange, I think, but I choose to leave it at that. He's already made too many wild claims on the subject for me to keep up with him.

Henrik cites several examples of how society cares for people with deviant behavior—including pyromaniacs and kleptomaniacs. But at the same time, he is very conscious that people tend to be less compassionate toward the idea of helping homosexuals. "Still, in the Netherlands and around the world, there are psychiatrists who work with this problem and help those who want to change. There are therapeutic methods of converting these people's tendencies. I know a gay man who's now happily married to a woman. He'll probably always have some sexual desires for men. But through therapy and behavior modification with experts, he has learned to understand how to free himself from this predilection."

Henrik is about to share another example, but I interrupt him. "Isn't that an example of someone who suppresses his sexuality because he has been told that it is sinful?" I ask. At the same time, I can't help but think that many people think Muslim women wear scarves because they have been coerced into submission.

"Yes, and is there anything wrong with that?" he asks pointedly.

For the first time, I sense that his patience is waning. And he's right, I think. If the individual chooses to be "treated" for his or her homosexuality and either marry a partner of the opposite sex or live in celibacy, is it not his own choice? Many people make choices that I do not agree with. Do I want to push my own definition of freedom on them when I resist having others define freedom for me? No, that's not freedom after all. Everyone should have the freedom to make informed choices for themselves. But one person's personal choices should never set a precedent that leads to stigmatizing, suppressing, or empowering an entire group.

According to Henrik, homosexuality is a symptom that results from problems in childhood. Therefore, "it's like taking a painkiller for a concussion. It might ease the hurt in an immediate sense, but it doesn't really heal the injury. Do you understand?" Henrik asks.

I don't agree because I don't believe that homosexuality is a symptom of a disease. I see the high suicide rates and mental disorders among gay and transgender people not as a character defect, but as a sign that a better system of support and understanding is needed. It has to be difficult to forge an identity when you are seen as sick and sinful by the society you live in.

Henrik shakes his head. "I'm not saying they're going to hell. My job is to say, dear friend, God is delighted with you, and you will be much happier with God in your life. You're his child. Live your life according to his commandments." He pauses briefly. "I'm merely giving you the short version. It's a little more difficult to reach them; I try to talk about hell. Hell is a real consequence, but it's a lousy motivator. I believe in Jesus myself. It is not the fear of hell that motivates me."

Although hell is not a motivating factor for Henry, he says he will never offer a blanket welcome for homosexuals into the membership of his church, since he will not "contribute to sin." However, he won't try to prevent gays from attending services, and he's willing to baptize their children because they need all the help they can get. But gays should expect to be challenged on their behavior. "There was a lesbian couple who wanted their child baptized in the church. I told them they were choosing a difficult path. They couldn't just raise their child in the Christian faith and teach the child to live by the word of God, when their own way of living was antithetical to God's word. I offered to baptize their child, but they chose another pastor and another church. They got angry. I haven't seen them in town since," says Henrik.

His advice to congregants who live together but are not married, regardless of sexual orientation, is consistent. If they want to live by the word of God, then they must be married before they have sexual relations. He is also opposed to divorce on the grounds that marriage is an unbreakable covenant with God. It doesn't matter if the woman is being beaten or the man has committed adultery, in Henry's eyes divorce is just not acceptable.

The conversation is getting seriously intense. I try to find some way to agree with his logic, but it appears there's nothing I can accept, and it's because we interpret religion differently. "Is it a matter of interpreting scripture differently that determines whether homosexuals can be admitted to the church? Other ministers have no issues welcoming gay people into their congregations." I ask, "Can a majority of the clergy be mistaken?"

Henrik has had enough. "We live in this damnable time where everything is subject to interpretation. But not everything is subjective!"

I do not know why, but I break into uncontrollable laughter, despite how serious he is. Perhaps it is due to how differently we see the issue, but maybe it's the striking similarity of fundamentalist attitudes in all religions. As I try to get my laughter under control, I think of Mahmud, who also got angry when I started talking about interpretation and thought it was all I wanted to talk about. When I catch my breath, I tell Henrik about Mahmud and how I can see similarities in their thinking. The big difference between Mahmud and Henrik is that, although Henrik strongly disagrees with my opinions, he laughs with me.

Henrik argues from the Bible and says how consistent Jesus was. When he quotes scriptures, he concludes each passage with "Amen."

"In many circumstances you can easily make it a matter of interpretation, but facts need to be taken into consideration. The disciples ask Jesus if it is true that the Law of Moses says you can remarry. Jesus confirms that it is permitted under the law, but says the opportunity was given only for the sake of your hard hearts. What does Jesus really mean by that? Sure, he agrees that sinners are given an opportunity to reform their lives, but divorces are granted at city hall, not in the church."

"There was probably no town hall in Jesus's time," I say jokingly.

"No," Henrik replies, "but the Law of Moses is a law of society."

It is interesting how Henrik sees his interpretation as fact, but criticizes others for interpreting the same text differently. It is a little difficult to argue against him, because when it comes to the Bible, he can easily skew the message to fit his ideology. It's like talking to imams who use the Qur'an to fit their agenda. I choose to argue with what I know. "The majority of the priests in the National Church allow people to worship in their churches even after a divorce."

According to Henrik, this is a new phenomenon. "Grundtvig shook his head at that, but he was persuaded by church leaders and politicians that the priesthood should overlook it."

I don't understand how a religious person can use the power of the pulpit to exclude anyone from fellowship rather than using it to create an inclusive community, and I confront Henry with this. "I believe that God creates everyone equally, and I don't understand how religious leaders like you can say that anyone is not welcome in the house of God. Who gave you that power? It is up to God to judge, and you are neither God nor Jesus!"

It takes Henry some time to answer. In fact, it is the longest pause in our entire conversation. When he speaks, I can clearly hear the hurt in his voice. "God gave us very clear instructions on how to lead our lives, and I don't think we can set his rules aside in the name of inclusion. It is not the role of religion to say yes to everyone, because we are all going to the same place. People make different choices. Some choose the word of God, and others choose to abandon it. It started with the fall of Adam and Eve, which is also found in the Qur'an. Paradise was a place where only good existed; there was nothing evil. But the moment the fall occurred, a necessary boundary between good and evil was drawn. That's why we were given rules to live by. It's also why we must choose to follow God, and why we must turn our backs on those who choose not to move in the same direction. There is a choice, and some people choose the wrong path," Henrik says.

For a while, I consider my views on equality, and question my consistency. I am a believer myself, but can't envision a Paradise that accommodates pedophiles, dictators, and psychopaths. But whether they make it to Paradise or not, I believe that all people in this world should be treated equally and have the same rights protected. So, I wonder again out loud about how Henrik is using the power of his platform. I don't understand it! I see Henrik is struggling to help me understand, explaining that this is not about a power he has taken from God, but on the contrary, a love he feels for his creator.

"Özlem, you told me earlier that you, as a rule, won't lie. But what if you are told you cannot be a member of parliament if you can't play by the rules of their game and lie like all the other politicians do? In that situation, you might feel bound to your own values and rules. Someone might tell you that your rules of life aren't yours, but were dictated by the Qur'an or by some other source. You wouldn't abandon the rule and start lying, because you fundamentally understand it is better to tell the truth."

Henrik's example impresses me. He speaks in a language I understand. I see now why neither of us can just drop our positions.

Henrik continues. "I feel the same in relation to, for example, homosexuals. I believe that man and woman are created for each other. I believe in two sexes. I believe I must follow the rules that are in my Bible. I sincerely believe that we have failed gays by offering them painkillers, knowing that it won't heal their concussions. Mental illness and suicide are very widespread among homosexuals, and some say it's because they are stigmatized. But research shows that, even in the society we have now, where there is openness about homosexuality, they are still more vulnerable. I think it's about not getting the help they need."

We let the matter of homosexuality drop, because it turns out that another topic is more pressing for Henrik. "If anything gets me worked up, even more than the issue with gays, it is abortion," he thunders. Henrik tells me about his sister, who works with the Right to Life movement, which runs a hotline, and how desperately unhappy women call them looking for help because they feel pressured by their boyfriends to have abortions.

I tell Henrik that I know about the problem firsthand. "As a nursing student, I worked in a gynecological department. I learned through my work there that no woman thinks abortion is fun or easy. Emotionally, it is a difficult choice that affects many women. But, despite how difficult it is, I'm glad free abortion is an option."

"Why?" asks Henrik in wonder.

"Because I believe women should have the right to decide what happens to their own bodies, of course," I say.

"But it's not her body. It's another body renting out space in her body," Henrik says.

I disagree with that.

Henrik argues back, "I think we've sacrificed women. We've left the whole burden of the decision on the individual woman. She must decide what goes on in her own body, we say. But what about the man's responsibility for his actions?"

I do not entirely agree with Henrik, but it can be difficult to raise basic ethical and responsibility issues when abortion is the topic. There are too many abortion advocates who have an equally fundamentalist approach as the most averse abortion opponents. I tell Henrik that as a nurse, I assisted with abortions in women who were opposed to using contraception, preferring instead to use the procedure a couple of times a year to end their unwanted pregnancies. Fortunately, this was a very small minority, but I had an extremely hard time understanding those women. More often the women who came for abortions had gotten pregnant at a very young age because they had forgotten to take their birth control or had used a contraceptive that failed to prevent a pregnancy, and they didn't want to raise a child. "It's not an easy decision for any of them, and some feel they have no choice," I say, eagerly waiting for Henry's reaction.

"I think you're right," he says. Henrik is not opposed to preventing unwanted pregnancies through contraception, but he is against the contraceptive pill because, he says, "At that point, the sperm has already merged with the egg." Henrik shares this untrue belief with virtually every imam.

It strikes me that Henrik is the first person I've discussed abortion with in Denmark who is pro-life. It allows me to open up about the dilemmas I faced as a nursing student, which I've rarely felt comfortable discussing. "Do you know what the hardest thing was?" I ask. "I was a nursing student and had to help with a late-term abortion. That is, she had carried the fetus past the legal cutoff, but had been granted an exemption. She was in bad shape, and she didn't want the baby. She went through a pelvic birthing, and like most other women who give birth to a dead fetus, she did not want to see the baby. I can understand that. I had to take the dead baby from the birthing table, put it in a yellow bucket and throw the bucket into a medical waste bag. That child was perfect, although very small. It had delicate skin, ears, ribs, fingers... I lifted one of its legs and saw that he also had a small penis. I started to moan. In the birthing room next door, another woman was wailing because she had started bleeding in the fourth month of her pregnancy. She wanted a child desperately but had miscarried five times in a row. It ended in the same tragic way; she couldn't hold the child. It was so strange, throwing that perfect stillborn baby in the trash and then going to comfort the mother who couldn't host a baby in her womb." When I finished my story, I was completely relieved. I was a little surprised at my own reaction. *Why am I relieved?*

Henry's reaction comes promptly. "It's murder."

I think for a brief moment. "I don't think it is, but at least it's a very difficult ethical dilemma," I say.

"To me, this is not an ethical dilemma at all. It is a perfectly clear and impossible situation," he says firmly.

Suddenly I find Henrik doing the same thing many of his opponents do. He uses my example to legitimize his position and close the debate. Similarly, many abortion rights advocates close the debate by saying that the woman has the right to decide matters about her own body, period. But why was that right given?

We sit quietly in Henry's living room. He is clearly influenced by what I have told him. And I'm happy to have found someone I could unburden my heart to. Although I do not agree with his solution, I don't have a better option than the one our legislation provides.

"If we are to maintain the welfare of our society, we will need a population of workers. We're killing the future," Henrik says.

In my thinking, it's not that simple. I wonder why the number of abortions has remained fairly consistent over the past decade despite increased education efforts and access to contraception. How can supporters of abortion rights be happy with that? Maybe the number of women seeking out abortion would decrease if abortion rights advocates had to fight a little harder by engaging in open-minded debate on the problems. I support abortion rights, but Henrik doesn't. We agree that a critical debate might help us find a way to at least prevent more abortions.

I sigh. "You mentioned that it's difficult to discuss homosexuality, but if you knew just how difficult it is to talk critically about abortion without getting people riled up," I say.

Henrik quickly picks up the thread. "You come from a religious tradition where interpretation of the law is extremely important. Muslims do not speak with one voice; no one in Denmark agrees on everything," he continues.

No, we do not, and neither do Christians. We can at least agree on this point. I tell Henrik about my meeting with the Church of the People, and how I visit the church often and was welcomed by the priest in every place I've lived. I also take my children to the church, so that they have an interfaith education.

I feel like I'm soaring inside as I tell Henrik that we share a community, but Henrik says the one thing that brings me crashing right back down to earth in response. "When I mentioned that you come from a religious congregation where interpretation of the law is important, I didn't mean Christianity. Diversity in the Danish Church doesn't extend to interpretation of the text. The problem with the Danish Church is that it consists of just two groups: one group, like me, who believe in the creed and the words of the Bible, and then a second group who believe that everything is constantly evolving and subject to reinterpretation. Even God is evolving. They seriously think that God is becoming wiser." Henrik shakes his head. Everything is divided so clearly in his logic. There are rarely more than two groups, always firmly pitted against each other. I have a very hard time accepting the simplicity of a binary opposition; everything is not all just black or just white.

"I often find it is easier to find fellowship outside my own church with Catholics, Pentecostal people, and other Free Church congregations than with pastors in the National Church," Henrik says.

"As well as a larger community with the conservative imams," I laugh.

"Yes, especially where homosexuality and moral implications are concerned," he says, while insisting that these are two very different religions.

Bridges are built and torn down many times during our conversation. But I see more clearly now that, even though a bridge can quickly collapse, a new one will soon rise to bridge a gap in our understanding.

Henrik hands me a book to take with me as I head out to drive to Fredericia to meet a man who has spent sixteen years of his life working with members of the gay community.

Helping the Gays

I enter a spectacularly decorated red-brick villa. It could be featured in a modern interior design magazine. Everything is elegantly laid out in bright vibrant colors and natural wood. The bookcase was obviously custom-designed for the space by a carpenter; the craftsmanship is so beautiful that it is impossible to overlook. The black piano is the only dark object contrasting with the light shades of the interior.

I put on a pair of wool slippers as I enter.

Johan lives in the villa with his wife, Ruth. Their two daughters have long since moved away from home. The youngest is twenty-eight years old and works as a graphic designer at HAY, while the oldest, who is thirty, is an actor in Copenhagen. Ruth has returned to college, and can only greet me briefly, as she has a big assignment due on a tight deadline. Cookies are waiting on the table, and we drink coffee and tea in handmade mugs.

Johan is a deacon who received an ecclesiastical degree that focused on both social and theological subjects, and he has spent most of his career in the Danish People's Church and in the Inner Mission. Among other positions, he headed the Inner Mission's film distribution company, where he imported films to prepare church members for confirmation and provide Christian education. But technology has greatly impacted the film industry, and it became more difficult to turn a profit. In 2006, Johan created a website, filmogtro.dk, where films are reviewed from an artistic angle as well as a Christian vantage point. For the first several years, Johan did the editing himself, and although he has now retired, he still writes reviews. In addition, he lectures, preaches, and acts as an assistant to a caretaker when needed.

Johan was born in Skive and left primary school after seventh grade, because he was bored with school. He worked first as an agricultural aide and then started an apprenticeship as a blacksmith. When he became a teacher, he attended Lutheran Mission College in Hillerod. He then studied nursing at the Deaconess Foundation in Frederiksberg before being admitted to the Deaconess College in Aarhus. During six months of study in Copenhagen, he met Ruth. She was eighteen and came from a church family in North Zealand. Johan was twenty-six.

Their time in Copenhagen was characterized by a tight-knit community. Johan visited the Deaconess Foundation with a group that included the Salvation Army, the Church's Cross Army, and coworkers from his former workplace. This led him into an internship at the Church Korsher's Inn in Norrebro. When he completed his education as a deacon in 1977, Johan traveled to the United States for three months to visit social institutions and Lutheran churches. In 1984, he repeated the tour, this time with Ruth, whom he had married in 1981. During his travels, Johan established a tight network with Christians in the United States, whom he relied on later when he began distributing films from the US.

Since returning home in 1984, Johan and Ruth have lived in Fredericia.

Johan grew up in a typical working-class family. "My father did everything. He was unemployed, he was a factory worker, and he had many unskilled jobs. He ended up working as a church servant while my mother stayed at home. As we grew older, she helped him out with cleaning and hosting the church coffee gatherings," Johan says. Johan's family was very religious, and when they moved to Skive, they became part of the Inner Mission. "When I started at Diakon High School, I quickly became part of the community at the Inner Mission in Aarhus."

"The advantage of being a Christian is that, whether you are in Denmark or abroad, you can find a community," Johan continues. "Christian people may be different in many ways, but they share basic values and attitudes. When I first came to the United States, I was welcomed into a local church in New York. During my time there, I became involved with other churches that had different values and beliefs than I did."

Johan never gets drunk. "The Bible says that one should not drink wine to excess," he reasons. But there was a period when, like other young people, he rebelled against his parents' lifestyle, when he partied on weekends and chased girls. But he began to feel that life felt empty and was lacking greater meaning. "The adults around me brought faith into my life. I looked up to them, and today my Christian values are central to everything I do," Johan says.

It is interesting for me to meet people like Johan and Henrik. Within my own religion, I know many observant people, and I have often talked about faith with my friend Bent Melchior, but I rarely meet followers of a faith elsewhere in Denmark. Few Danes talk about their personal beliefs, and the leftist environments that I have been a part of tend to be secular in nature. I have always felt a fellowship with believers, for we often speak a common language. Not because we agree on everything, but there is a basic common understanding that there is something greater than what we can see with the naked eye. Among believers, I find that values such as charity, solidarity, fellowship and humanity are very strong pillars of the community. While the religious faithful make up a big portion of the overall population, in a country like Denmark where science is valued over faith, it has gone through a hard period of adjustment. The prerequisite for any discussion is usually whether you can prove what you say. As a Muslim, I've found that others look down on the notion of a fundamentalist faith, which is why I rarely discuss it. But Christians don't necessarily receive better treatment. I've heard people say that Christians are "strange."

"I pray and meditate every morning, and read a passage from the Bible," Johan says quietly. He is much calmer than Henrik. Not once does he raise his voice, laugh out loud, or show an outburst of emotion. If the questions are difficult, he becomes thoughtful and takes extra time to formulate his answers. He is very precise in his language and carefully chooses his words. But his faith is strong, and it cannot be shaken.

Johan had some eye-opening experiences during his studies in Copenhagen. "I didn't think the church organizations held the bar high." He was not impressed by what he experienced in his internship at the Church Korsher's Inn in Hillerodgade in Norrebro. "The only thing they offered us was a sermon one Sunday a month at nine in the morning." Johan shakes his head.

Johan and a number of others decided they wanted more than the established church social institutions were offering them. They opened Agape (Divine Love) Treatment Ward with the intent to rehabilitate alcoholics and drug addicts. "They live in a collective there, and a Christian understanding of life helps them form basic values. I don't believe in helping people in an ethical vacuum. They must first have a strong faith," Johan emphasizes.

It strikes me that his argument is similar to that of Hizb ut-Tahrir. They also believe that people must have strong faith as a foundation before you can help them reform their lives. They see abuse and other destructive behaviors as an expression of people not being anchored in faith. Developing faith is thus a treatment in itself.

Agape receives many private donations, ensuring financial stability. But they also charge patients for treatment on site. "We don't help them just because they have pretty faces," Johan says.

"I have a younger brother who is gay and Christian. That's just the way he is. Our family has accepted him as he is for many years. He has had a hard time with it, because he grew up at a time when people did not talk about it openly," Johan says. "He was sixteen when he first told my mother about it. At that time, no one else in the family knew. My mother took him to a psychologist and a psychiatrist in Viborg to see if he was really gay. They confirmed that he is," Johan says with confidence in his voice. "My mother was sad. I thought it was strange that he was gay. But, at the same time, he was still my brother, and I knew that I had to treat him with care and respect."

No one in the family condemned Johan's brother, but there was a great deal of disagreement over how to deal with his homosexuality. Was it a disease, or should they "simply" accept it? According to Johan, the brother struggled because no one understood him, no one could identify with his sexuality, and no one wanted to talk to him about it.

"I have worked a lot with gays. I've talked to a lot of people and I've written a lot about it." Johan tells me about Dr. Alfred Kinsey's scale of human sexuality, which puts it on a scale of 0 to 6. "According to Kinsey, people who identify as exclusively heterosexual are at 0 on the scale, while those who identify as exclusively gay are at 6," he says. At Agape, Johan and the therapists and psychologists try to assess each patient individually on the scale so that they can better meet their needs to build a healthy, happy life. "We try to cater to the needs of gay patients in particular. They feel that Christian communities don't accept them or understand them. We provide them with special weekend courses and discussions," Johan says. One of the participants in the program was Johan's brother.

Many of the homosexuals who came to the treatment center share Johan's understanding of the Bible; in their eyes, you cannot partner with someone of the same sex.

"The purpose of the talks is to support them in maintaining their Christian faith, even if it seems incompatible with their homosexuality. But it also helps them determine if they are predominantly heterosexual or gay. For many of them, this is the first time they've talked to anyone about their sexuality. We started this work in 1992, and at that time there was no other church working in that direction. We were pioneers," Johan says.

The conversations did not change anything for Johan's brother. He is still gay today.

In the following years, the program's development did not expand as Johan had hoped. The growing equality movement was pushing for homosexuals to be accepted on an equal footing with everyone else, and for them to be consecrated in the National Church. Johan felt the discussion was heated, and he didn't necessarily agree that the teachings in the Bible accommodated gay married couples. "Even though I have a brother who is gay, I hold fast to what's true and what the Bible says about homosexuality," he says.

During our conversation, Johan repeatedly says a healthy sexuality is important to overall health. Does that mean he considers homosexuality to be an illness? "No. I have become more careful over the years. The more you know about things, the more complicated it gets," he says.

I agree with this view. In my attempt to understand why powerlessness, frustration, and hatred are increasing within various population groups in Denmark, I have also experienced how complex issues really are. The more I immerse myself in a topic, the more complicated it becomes. The world is usually more nuanced than journalists and politicians report. Before I met Henrik and Johan, I had very clear preconceptions about people in the Inner Mission. I did not know anyone from the Inner Mission myself, so it was easy to distance everyone from the movement from what I read and heard about them in the press. My husband has taken an after-school in-service with them, because "there was no room anywhere else." He told me they were no different from other people and that I should get to know some of them before stereotyping the whole group. Now I have met two people from the Inner Mission. And, although Henrik and Johan have opinions I disagree with, our meetings also reveal nuances that challenge my view of them. With both, I have been welcomed openly and kindly. Both want to talk and stand by their opinions without being vicious, personal, or perfidious. At the same time, during our conversations, it has become clear that they believe as much in their causes as I believe in mine. I'm surprised at how much I recognize their attitude toward homosexuality from Jewish and Muslim environments.

"I'm leaning mostly...well, I don't believe in..." Johan says in response to my question about it being an illness, but breaks off again with a long pause. It is clear that he is trying not to offend anyone. "I do not rule out the fact that some people, by virtue of their nature, have an easier time developing a homosexual orientation. But I also believe that there are environmental, cultural, and familial reasons why some develop homosexuality." He takes his time formulating this response.

"Does that mean you can influence children to become gay?" I ask.

"In the community in which we live..." Johan pauses again before continuing. "I think things are going the wrong way now. Children, both boys and girls, need strong role models. For your daughter, it's important that she has you to look to as a feminine ideal. She can mirror herself in your image. The moment she does that, it becomes part of her identity. That is why childhood homes play an important role in healthy gender identity, and why we don't help children by minimizing gender differences—on the contrary," Johan concludes.

Johan is not provoked once during our talk, and he never raises his voice. I'm finding it hard not to be provoked. Does Johan really believe lesbians are any less women or less feminine? Is it his faith that creates prejudice, or is his prejudice a more widespread, common one? He tells me about vulnerable young people who came from homes with a lack of love, lack of resources, or where their parents were ill, and who believed they were gay due to a lack of nurturing. His main argument is that environment has a bearing on whether one develops homosexuality.

Like Henrik, Johan points out that no scientists have found a gene for homosexuality, and that there is thus no evidence that God created them that way. He agrees that they should not be consecrated in the church, "for the church will not give them the blessing that the Bible does not give them. Neither should they be allowed to adopt, because we have to take into account the child's gender identity." When I confront Johan with the findings that no research has shown that having a gay parent makes one more likely to grow into a gay adult, he becomes silent.

"The Bible doesn't say much about homosexuality, but it is presented in a negative light whenever it's mentioned. If you ask gay people, most probably wish they were heterosexual. That's how we are created, we have a need to be with our opposite sex. It is a biological imperative for humans to have intercourse and reproduce. This is how God created us. There is no benefit to the community, the families, nor the children that we are moving away from a natural path. I can't see it making people any happier for the same reason," Johan says, referring again to a study.

As I listen to Johan, I become aware of the importance of free research. There has always been a political struggle to control research and limit the boundaries of scientific inquiry. Johan is conscious of the power of research and how it can be used and abused. We sit in his living room and toss research claims back and forth. But when I show evidence that contradicts what Johan claims, he returns to his starting point, the Bible. "Of course, I listen to science, but Christianity is my foundation," he says calmly.

On the other hand, I do not let myself be disturbed by the results he presents to me.

Johan switches tracks. "Amongst almost all the gays I have been in contact with, there was a broken, imperfect, or downright negative relationship with the same-sex parent," he says.

I can't hold back from asking him if that was the case for his brother as well.

"My brother didn't have a very close relationship with my father, but he had a close—and perhaps too close—relationship with my mother. And when boys are trying to build a gender identity, we have to mirror ourselves in male role models. My father was a very shy person who rarely shared his feelings and thoughts. He had a hard time showing emotion. None of us boys had a close relationship with him. One might ask why I did not become homosexual. I think that's because I got help through my peers. When I did not have enough emotional contact with my father, I reflected my masculinity in them and other men I looked up to."

Johan doesn't judge anyone, but in his own words "guided and advised them to a healthy, Christian life." And he has done this for sixteen years. However, he is no longer convinced that people can suppress their gay natures. "There *are* examples of people who, despite their homosexuality, choose to live a heterosexual life, get married, and have children. But there are very few exceptions."

I have a hard time believing my own ears. "Do you admit that all you have believed—that you can teach gay people to lead a healthy life—is not possible?" I ask.

Then Johan says something that makes a deep impression on me. "But I feel obligated by my Christian view of life to try to help them in their struggles."

Johan is simply fighting for what he believes in. I understand him. We both believe that conversations can move mountains. He just wants to move the mountains somewhere else. His fight is as legitimate as mine. And as long as he doesn't use weapons or coercion, he has as much right to fight for what he believes as I have. That doesn't only apply to Johan and me. It also applies to Hamza from Hizb ut-Tahrir, Kim from Odense, and the boys from the Red Square. Our only acceptable weapons in the democratic struggle are our words.

"We also have regular contact with people who come to us and, despite conversations, stand by their sexuality. I tell them it is their choice and that I cannot live their lives for them. But it is my duty to tell them what the Bible says," Johan concludes.

Is he different from me? Or different from all the other people who believe in a cause? We both make an attempt to understand the other side, but seem to keep reaching the same conclusion. The Peace Guard has been in Christiansborg since October 19, 2001, from morning to evening, seven days a week. Are their actions more or less damaging than Henrik's and Johan's? Or what about Greenpeace activists who, in the wake of a protest at one of Gazprom's oil rigs in the Arctic, risked fifteen years in prison for drawing attention to oil pollution? What about the activists killed when special forces from Israel boarded a ship sailing to Gaza to break a blockade the Israelis had created? Like Johan, they all fought for a cause. Each of these causes had groups locked in opposition for their own side. I should be careful about judging Johan when I can't even understand why others judge my opinions as they do.

"It's okay that people don't understand the things I'm fighting for, but my intention is sincere, to help other people. I'm not hate-filled. I have clear opinions, yes, but I could never vote to ban homosexuals, like we've seen in Africa, or support the persecution of homosexuals, as they do in Russia," Johan says. It is the first time during the conversation that I sense feeling in his voice. He is sad.

No matter how much I disagree with some of his actions and opinions, I, as a human being, have gained an understanding of how they developed. During our conversation, Johan has become more than merely his stance on homosexuals. He is first and foremost a human being.

CHAPTER 8

WHERE DIALOGUE STOPS, VIOLENCE TAKES OVER

"A pessimist sees obstacles in every opportunity, an optimist sees opportunities in every obstacle."

–Winston Churchill

Many of the people I talk to have an issue with one particular group, the Jews. The young men in the Red Square and the imam Hamza from Hizb ut-Tahrir have a broiling hatred for them—at least the population living in Israel, especially those who settled on land that once belonged to the Palestinians. Anti-Semitic hatred runs through many communities beyond just some Muslims. Six million Jews were exterminated in Europe during the Holocaust. Denmark was occupied by Nazi forces during World War II, and the legacy of that war is still echoing in the sharp click of boot heels on pavement worn by swastika-emblazoned young men at demonstrations on our city streets. Nobody hates the Jews more than the Nazis. I decide to seek out some Danish Nazis to find out why.

I make a couple attempts to contact Nazi groups in Denmark. First, I search websites that belong to the modern Nazi movement. There I find not only hateful criticism of Jews, but vitriol directed at Muslims. For the numerous emails I send out requesting a meeting, I receive only one short response: "We don't meet with people from other races." I don't give up that easily and locate the address of a Nazi group in Greve. I drive to the location and find there isn't much there. The house faces a main road and is surrounded by a high fence. The tree in front is ancient and completely green with algae. Barbed wire covers its bark. Cameras point out from every corner of the lot and one is situated above the door. After walking around the house several times and mustering my courage, I knock. After what seems to me a long wait, a young blonde woman opens the door. I tell her why I'm there. She replies, "I have nothing to do with them, I just rent the house. They are no longer active either."

Home from my trip to Greve, I call Redox (a left-wing, anti-fascist research group) for any information they may have about far-right organizations in Denmark. They confirm what I suspected from browsing the web. In their opinion, Nazis are no longer focused on hating the Jews, but have turned their spite toward Muslims. "It might be easier for them, since even more recognized parties share hatred toward Muslims," Redox says.

I sigh. "Yes, unfortunately. I know."

I give up on trying to contact any Nazis. But there must be someone out there who has strong opinions about Jews and is willing to talk to me. Many people on the far left are vocal in expressing anti-Semitic sentiments.

Even I began to form opinions about Jews at an early age. In the beginning, my feelings about the group were linked to stories I heard about a small rural area on the eastern shores of the Mediterranean, which I have never visited. Jews, Muslims, and Christians call it the Holy Land, but it has been pockmarked for centuries by the bullet holes of a bloody conflict between Israel and Palestine. When I was a kid, I saw pictures on television of dead Palestinian children, who had been killed by Israelis. I cried when I saw those pictures and the injustice they represented to me. What harm had those children done? To me, the Jews were all evil. I could not yet distinguish between Jews in Israel and Jews in Denmark. Jews were Jews, and whether it was land, money, or human rights, they just wanted to hoard more for themselves. My family was not politically engaged, so my understanding of the situation came from elsewhere. I don't remember talking to my parents about the pictures of the dead Palestinian children. My growing resentment toward the Jews was one I kept to myself. Then one day a new girl showed up at Ny Carlsberg Road School. A rumor spread among my classmates that she was Jewish. I looked her over for a long time to check her out. She looked pretty much like any other girl in the school. She must have caught me staring at her, because one day she said hello to me. I returned her greeting, and that day we began playing basketball in the school yard. She was cute and we could talk about pretty much anything, but I never told her how I felt about Jews.

One day she invited me to her home. I was unsure if I should accept the invitation, because it felt like I was somehow siding with the Israelis and betraying the Palestinian children. How could I justify a friendship with her? I don't know how long I thought about this, but the friendship won me over. When I visited her, my understanding of what made a Jew was radically altered. She lived with her mother and father, like I did. They didn't eat pork either, and, like me, they observed different holidays than the other children at Ny Carlsberg Road School. I stopped seeing her as a "just a Jew" and, as a result, I gave up my hatred of Jews. She was neither armed nor different from me. She was adorable and, in my child mind, all Jews were like her.

Later, I met several Jews in my early adulthood, after I had become politically active. I got in touch with an academic association that worked for ethnic equality in Denmark. Two of the board members, sisters Maia and Eline Feldman, fought against discrimination in the labor market, and were active at educational institutions. They were the first Jews I met who worked actively for equal treatment across religious and cultural divides. To them I was never just the Muslim Özlem, I was always the human Özlem. And to this day I do not see Maia and Eline as Jews first and foremost, but as simply two beautiful friends.

Later in my life, I met another Jew. I was a newly elected member of parliament and had just published a book, *From Fotex to the Parliament*. At a reception held by my publisher, Gyldenal, a strange man showed up among the guests. Someone whispered in my ear that it was Rabbi Bent Melchior and that the publisher had invited him. When I greeted him, it was as if we had known each other for a lifetime. He was warm, cordial, and outgoing. He wanted to greet my parents, who were very honored that an important rabbi had come to their daughter's reception. Many of those in attendance flocked around him. It was clear that he was a special man.

When I later held the parliament's first Ramadan dinner, Bent Melchior accepted the invitation. Ramadan dinner can best be compared to a Christmas lunch, but without alcohol. The meal marks the end of Ramadan, a month during which Muslims fast every day from sunrise to sunset. There is good food and people gather across religious, ethnic, and political divisions to eat it together. The purpose in holding the event was to create a welcoming space for people to gather in unity. The Ramadan dinner had given rise to some debate in assembly meetings because the Danish People's Party did not think that the Danish people's parliament should be used for Islamization. They saw it as my attempt to slip Islam in through the back door.

I was worried that Bent would cancel at the last minute. But he came, and he stayed throughout the dinner, even after the government, opposition leaders, and the leadership of my own party had left. When TV 2 asked him why he agreed to attend the Ramadan dinner, he replied with a twinkle in his eye, "You don't say no to a free meal." His son, Michael Melchior, who for many years served as a minister in Israel, and as a member of the Israeli Knesset, participated in several Ramadan dinners each year. Bent couldn't see why a dinner should be so problematic.

It became a tradition for Bent to invite me to his home whenever I found myself tossed around by political storms. There, we sat in his kitchen, ate some salmon, and talked about the meaning of life and the political solutions we thought were right for Denmark. During my time in parliament, he served as my mentor and spiritual advisor. He gave me courage when I was in doubt, and peace when everything around me was chaotic. I will never forget the day I said to him, "You know, Bent, my grandfathers died so early that I never got to meet them. Can you adopt me as your granddaughter?" I said it half in fun and half in earnest.

He looked at me with the most loving eyes and said, "From now on, you are my granddaughter and I am your grandfather."

Through Bent, I was also introduced to Jewish culture. We had many discussions about traditions and rules within Judaism, and he helped me network with the Jewish community in Denmark. I went with him to Jewish funerals, holidays, celebrations, and festivals. I also cried with him when things turned tragic. I will never forget the memorial service for volunteer guard Dan Uzan, who was killed in front of the synagogue in Copenhagen by an Islamic terrorist, Omar. I attended that service with a burdened heart, along with many other Muslims. I wasn't guilty, yet I felt an extremely deep guilt. What did the Jews in the synagogue think of us? Did they think Muslims were all alike? Did they make the same generalizations I had made about Jews as a child? Didn't Dan Uzan's father have good reason to hate Muslims? While those thoughts were running through my mind, I was greeted at the entrance with open arms by Alan Melchior, one of Bent's sons. He was glad I had come. And when I met Dan Uzan's dad, he gave me a hug. His mother cried and thanked me several times for attending. That day, a strong bond was established between us. I'm a friend of the Jews, I thought. They had taken me in, and I had become part of them. It felt natural.

Since I've had such a hard time arranging a meeting with anti-Semitic group leaders in Denmark, I begin to toy with the idea of visiting

Israel and Palestine. I still want to understand anti-Semitism, and if there is anyone besides Nazis who doesn't like Jews, then Palestinians seem like a logical choice. But when I talk it over with friends, they don't like my reasoning. My leftist friends tell me that the conflict is not about hatred of Jews, but about Israel violating some of the basic human rights of Palestinians. My Jewish friends emphasize that some Palestinians might be anti-Semitic, but remind me that the conflict is about much more.

The person who makes the greatest impression on me is a Norwegian doctor, whom I come in contact with through a friend from Norway. He sends me an email:

> It sounds like a very exciting project. If you want to analyze the distance between population groups and choose the Israel-Palestine conflict as an example, you navigate an active minefield. Everything is interpreted politically, even a discussion about hummus being a Jewish or Arab dish. When you define the Palestinians' hatred against Occupy Israel as a form of Jewish hatred, you have already taken a political stand. For Israeli authorities, it is important to categorize most of the criticism of the Israeli government's policies as anti-Semitism or Jewish hatred. I'd rather categorize it as hatred of the occupier, not unlike how Norwegians (and probably Danes) looked at Germans during and after World War II. But with an occupation that has lasted more than fifty years, you will also find a more genuine Jewish hatred among Palestinians. But it usually requires more long-term friendship to emerge. Conversely, you will also easily find strong racism prevalent among some Israeli Jews against Palestinians and other Arabs.

I read his email again and again. Am I biased? And what is the purpose of visiting Israel and Palestine if not to get a close understanding of anti-Semitism?

My idea of a trip to Israel becomes a hot topic of discussion with friends and political acquaintances. Some want me to write about how the Jewish settlers oppress Palestinians in the West Bank. Others think I should go to Gaza and write about how the Palestinian organization Hamas oppresses women and kills innocent Jews. No matter who I talk to, they have an attitude about the conflict.

My friends' reactions teach me one important thing: how to easily lose the nuances of a conflict. I decide that I want to go, but not to write about the conflict or anti-Semitism. I do not want to be forced to choose a side. I would rather go to Israel and Palestine to talk to the fiery folks who believe conversation with an adversary is a path to peace in a country where violence has taken over. I want to ask them what happens when the conversation ends. How can one keep hope in a country where the fronts are so sharply drawn? I want to hear the voices that insist on the conversation, because when I say here in Denmark that dialogue is a prerequisite for solutions, those who prefer to remain silent turn their eyes on me. "It's naïve," they say. Am I naïve to think that conversation is the most important weapon of democracy? I want to see to the Holy Land with my own eyes and what the consequences are when the conversation ends and violence takes over.

I decide I want to be subtle in my approach to these conversations. I have to be nuanced. I think of Maia, Eline, Bent, and my other Jewish friends. They will also read this book. Friendship with them forces me to see both sides of the matter objectively. I find it is valuable to have friendly ties to people with whom you do not share religion and culture. Friendship is a powerful vaccine against generalizing prejudice about "others." Most people reconsider their thinking when forced to look at someone as an individual and not what groups they belong to; you know, a Maia, an Eline, a Bent! Friends help balance irrational emotions that crop up when encountering hatred, anger, and powerlessness. This is why it is so important that we talk with each other in Denmark and maintain friendly ties to those who can help maintain dialogue, even when difficult.

I plan to meet with peace workers on both sides of the conflict.
I call a few of people who play an active role in the region to ask
them for help with my trip. Everyone wants to help, and I quickly
establish contact with a number of organizations and people in Israel
and Palestine.

As my journey nears, pressure from my circle of friends increases,
and, on several occasions, I feel trapped by other people's experiences,
knowledge, and attitudes. For example, there are many who ask who
is helping me set up meetings. When I mention Bent's son Michael
Melchior, one of the Palestinians says, "No, not him."

When I mention the chairman of the Danish-Palestinian association,
Fathi El-Abed, several of the Jews shake their heads. "No, not him."

Everyone seems to know so much about that conflict that sometimes I
fear I'll make mistakes or offend someone with my limited knowledge
of the subject. At the same time, I am not part of the conflict myself,
and therefore I can also consider it from an objective stance. It's
a position I wish I could take when the conversation is about the
problems between Turks and Kurds, where my own Kurdish roots are
interwoven in the conflict.

I have mixed feelings about this trip. Will I maintain my friendship
with my Jewish friends when I return? Can I even be a friend of both
Jews and Palestinians? And are the things I've heard Palestinians say
about Israel accurate? Is it even possible to insist on conversation
when such strong feelings are in play? With all these thoughts
pressing, I pack my suitcase. It is a fall holiday, and I have decided to
take Devrim and our two youngest children, Yasmin and Yusuf, on the
trip for a vacation. Once we are seated on the airplane, I realize again
that I have no idea what awaits me. But I know we have to stop in
Istanbul, and that makes me nervous.

I was in Turkey during the military coup attempt in 2016, and
subsequently wrote on Facebook about the conditions in Turkey. I'm
worried that any update that is critical of the Turkish regime will flag

me as a threat and cause me to be detained. I'm prepared for that possibility, and my husband knows to contact the foreign ministry if I'm arrested. My heart is in my throat as I hand my documents to the officer at passport control. He doesn't make eye contact with me and I know there's cause to worry, because Erdogan has used the military coup attempt to crack down on his political opponents and detractors. Between the time of the coup attempt and my trip to Israel, thirty thousand people have been arrested, over 110,000 have been fired or suspended from their positions, and about three hundred thousand Kurds have been displaced internally within Turkey.

"Next," the officer says.

I sigh, relieved. The Holy Land awaits me.

The mood in Tel Aviv is serious. The police officers here are dressed as though they are ready for combat, with large assault rifles and helmets. As we wait in the passport line, we witness the guards removing several people from the line who are escorted to other rooms, where I assume they will be questioned.

Before the trip, Michael, a former Israeli minister, offered to inform the Israeli foreign ministry of our arrival so that we might avoid a comprehensive questioning. I was unsure about whether to accept his offer, because several Palestinians told me about their experiences being interrogated at the airport, and part of me would like to experience that for myself. Was it really as bad as they described? But Bent encouraged me to accept Michael's offer, and he had a good argument. "Don't play any games with them if your children are going with you." I accepted Michael's assistance, and as I stand in the queue and see how people are pulled aside, I'm glad I did.

We make our way through passport control and out of the airport. The warm air feels lovely, and the palms are visible confirmation that we are far away from Denmark. We take a taxi to Tel Aviv. It is my first visit to Israel, and in many ways the country resembles any other country in the Middle East. However, it appears that the

Israelis have more money to dedicate to infrastructure than their neighbors. The cars are newer, the roads smoother, the sidewalks cleaner, and then a mosque pops up on every street corner, as it does in Muslim countries. It's a bit eclectic, because Israel is a hodge-podge of Western countries and the Middle East. The familiarity of the city makes me feel secure.

My parents call to ask if we are okay. "Yes, why wouldn't we be okay?" I ask.

"It's not very far from Gaza," my father says. He's right. It strikes me how easy it is to forget the conflict when the sun is shining.

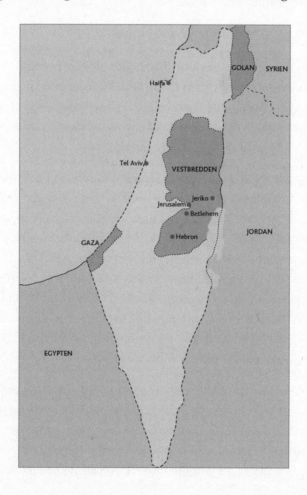

Overcoming Hate Through Dialogue

I talk to an Israeli woman in a store, and when she asks me what I think of Tel Aviv, I reply that it's too bad that I'm just now visiting the country at the age of forty. I'm sincerely polite, because Israel has thus far impressed me, but she hears something else in my answer. "We are not at all what others write and say about us," she says. She is a Jew, and while on the one hand I do not know what to say to her, at the same time I feel a bond with her that's difficult to describe. I sometimes formulate the same kind of reply when I meet with people who are skittish of Muslims. It makes me sad.

Devrim can see I'm getting upset and comes to my rescue. "You have to be careful not to believe everything you read in the newspapers," he says, and the woman nods contentedly.

After a couple of days to relax in Tel Aviv, we drive toward Jerusalem. I have an appointment with Linda Herzberg, whom I know from Denmark, where I am part of a network she organized for Jewish and Muslim women. She is vacationing in Israel with her husband, Bjarne. They have an apartment twelve miles from Jerusalem, and when we arrive, Linda stands on the street corner waiting. We hug each other, and, as I am used to watching Jewish events in Copenhagen, I just have to get used to the fact that Linda now stands as a matter of course on a street corner in Tel Aviv. She has invited us to lunch with her friend, Nomi Raz. Nomi is a Jew and a professional psychologist.

Infectious Hopelessness

Nomi is retired and has worked with children for many years. Her husband is a peace activist and has spent his entire life building bridges between Palestinians and Jews. But he's growing older, his health is failing, and he can no longer be as active in peace work. He's not feeling well enough to join us. I'm a little disappointed by that, because Linda has told us so much about his efforts, and I've prepared questions for him. How do peace workers maintain hope and spirit for their cause? Where do they get the energy? Now I sit and hope that Nomi can answer them. But she starts somewhere different than I expected.

"I don't think dialogue is important. The reality needs to change before we can make peace. We have tried dialogue with the Arabs, but nothing changed," Nomi says, with a hint of anger in her voice. She admits that dialogue may improve relationships between two individual people, but not between groups. "What happens between groups is bigger," she states several times. "For years, we organized football teams for Jews and Arabs, theater nights for Jews and Arabs, and we've taken other initiatives, but that has not changed the reality of the situation here." Her pessimism surprises me. When she sees the expression on my face, she says, "I'm sorry to be pessimistic, but while dialogue sounds like a good idea in theory, it doesn't work."

I tell my own story of how, as a young woman, I had strong feelings toward Jews, and how my encounters with Linda, Maia, Eline, Bent, and many other Jewish friends has changed and nuanced my view.

"Yes, yes... I have Arab friends too, so what?" she says. "My dentist is Arab. Everyone in town goes to him. So what?" She doesn't allow me to interrupt. "My husband has done everything to ensure direct dialogue. He mobilized Jewish support groups when incidents with Arabs occurred. My son has been just as active. But that hasn't changed anything for us!"

I sit back in my chair. Her pessimism is contagious. I sigh deeply. If a Jew who lives just twenty miles from Jerusalem and has all the privileges and rights can think this way, how does a Palestinian living in the West Bank feel about living butted right up against illegal Jewish settlers? Does Nomi see good things happening between Jews and Palestinians at all? Shouldn't she be more grateful for what peace does exist?

"Isn't the situation here better than the war in Syria?" I ask.

Nomi doesn't believe this is a fair comparison. According to her, the Israelis want to be the best at everything. That may be okay. But when the ideology of Israeli leaders is steeped in hatred, democracy is harmed. Human rights are collateral damage. But most urgently, children are hurt, Nomi says. Already, just in kindergarten, they are picking up hateful ideology.

"But what's the solution?" I ask. If Nomi doesn't think dialogue between people helps, if all the fiery folks who work for peace on both sides aren't helping, then what is helping?

Nomi wants a new government in Israel. "The only way we can achieve peace is by changing the leadership in power."

"But doesn't that require you to engage in dialogue with people to encourage them to vote differently?" I ask.

She shakes her head. "I don't trust people. That's why my husband wants to go into politics now."

Now, it's my turn to be a pessimist, I think, and I tell her about my experiences working to strengthen democracy. How, as a newly licensed nurse, I saw the need to reform programs for children with mental disabilities, but found that, if you wanted any say in what happened, you had to get elected to the board of the Danish Nursing Council. In my first run for an open board seat, I was only twenty votes from beating the Vice President, who had been sitting in the post for almost twenty years. But I quickly discovered that only unions fought for better wages and working conditions. That is why I founded 1001 Cups of Coffee, where we sold coffee to raise money for the homeless and tickets to cultural events to raise awareness of the situation of the most impoverished, vulnerable children in Denmark. Volunteering is good, but unfortunately it doesn't change the structure of society. So I became active in a political party. The election fell on the Socialist People's Party (Socialistisk Folkeparti or SF) because Villy Sovndal had done a lot for the homeless. If you really wanted to make a difference, you had to sit on the main board. I was three votes away from beating Villy Sovndal and was the runner-up in that race. But if you really wanted some influence, you need to be an MP. I did not enter the race in 2005. In 2007, I was elected and discovered that, in order to cast a deciding vote, one needed a party seat in parliament. SF came into government in 2011, and it was in every way an unhealthy process, as the party didn't make any decisions and wouldn't stand by its own principles. I was not reelected in 2015, although I was the runner-up again in the party race.

Throughout my political career, I've worked to gain influence, but today I know that I had the most influence as a nurse. I could make a difference immediately with my patients. In 2016, SF offered me a seat in parliament, but I refused. Big changes come, not from the politicians, but from individual people. People have power, and people can build bridges faster than politicians dig trenches.

As I finish my heated recounting, Nomi looks at me. I have a hard time deciphering her gaze. Have I hit a sore point, or does she see me as someone who has written off parliamentarism? She gathers her energy and says angrily, "We have the most racist and most fascist government. If the Left had power, they could really make some changes."

I look at her skeptically. "Which Left are you referring to?" I'm not waiting for her answer. "The left wing is no better than the right wing, their leaders have forgotten where they come from, and too often, they jump at easy solutions because they are popular in public opinion," I say with abandonment. Can she hear my disappointment? I can hear how unreasonable I must sound to her. I started with grassroots work, but quickly saw its limitations. That was why I joined a political party. Yes, I was disappointed in SF, but SF is not representative of the entire left wing.

At least the conviction in Nomi's voice is strong. She believes that change comes first and foremost from parliament. Her phone rings. It's her husband, who needs help. She goes, and I'm left alone, feeling dark and hopeless, in a beautiful garden filled with a whole spectrum of colorful flowers.

What happened to me? I think. Isn't the purpose of grassroots work to get lawmakers to make the world a better place? What alternative is there to parliamentarism if I'm so disappointed in it? Do I want to abolish parliamentarism? No, I don't. Could apartheid have been abolished in South Africa without parliament? Would Blacks have been guaranteed equal rights in the United States if the elected officials had not changed the Constitution? Would homosexuality have been taken off the list of diseases if the Danish Parliament hadn't decided that it isn't an illness? How could we protect people from abuse, war, and persecution if a majority of the world's parliaments hadn't joined the Human Rights Convention? These landmark decisions all came as the result of a convergence of forces involving parliamentary, popular, and charismatic leaders with vision, such as Nelson Mandela, Martin Luther King, and Mahatma Gandhi. The solution is neither grassroots work nor parliamentarism. We need both people and parliament.

Faith Shows the Way

I say goodbye to Linda and Bjarne and begin my trip to meet Michael, who lives in Jerusalem. The mental journey to Jerusalem seems much longer than the twenty-minute drive. The landscape is changing, and it is becoming more and more evident that I am in the land of the Jews. The number of men wearing black clothing and hats is increasing. The curls are longer, and even children have them. Many are carrying long green fronds and small bags. I think it must have something to do with the Sabbath, but I don't know what. I know so little about Judaism that I am ashamed. I know we have a lot in common. For example, Muslims and Jews share some prophets. David, who made a name for the star of the Jews, is also seen as a prophet by the Muslims—we just call him David. Jews also abstain from eating pork, segregate men and women in the synagogue, and circumcise their boys, all things Muslims do.

I don't know much about what sets us apart. It's never interested me enough that I wanted to investigate it. I'm more interested in what brings us together. And Judaism, Christianity, and Islam really have a lot in common. First of all, all three religions can trace their traditions back to the story of Abraham. Therefore, they are also called the Abrahamic religions. I have always loved the idea that the god who appeared to Abraham is known to Jews, Christians, and Muslims.

At the same time, I also know that the differences between the religions have led to numerous wars. People kill each other because they think it brings them closer to Paradise. But how can the road to Paradise be covered with corpses and blood? I've never understood how spiritual devotion to a higher power can create such negative energy that one could practice such evil. There is something terribly wrong with the very idea of killing in God's name.

"Let's go sit in the sukkah," Michael Melchior says. A sukkah is a temporary hut constructed for use during Sukkot, a week-long Jewish festival that falls in autumn. The name refers to the booths the Jews built and lived in when they wandered in the desert after leaving slavery in Egypt. Before we reach Michael's balcony, which literally looks like a booth, we pass several rooms filled with big, old, heavy books, whose worn covers indicate they've been well used. A rabbi and former minister, Michael has been trained to speak slowly and clearly. The natural breaks in his speech indicate that I am facing a man who weighs his words. He's not afraid of saying something wrong, but wants to be clearly understood.

I am fascinated by his calm, because I know he's leaving for Spain the next day to head a large peace conference. Since the late 1980s, Michael has spent hundreds of hours talking to leaders from Hamas and Islamist judges with the goal of bringing together the region's religious leaders for peace. In 2002, together with Sheikh Talal Sider, one of Hamas's founders, he took the initiative of organizing the first interfaith meeting. It took place in the Egyptian city of Alexandria; the participants called for peace and dialogue, and it was sponsored by the Egyptian Mufti, the Archbishop of Canterbury, and Israel's rabbis.

For the conference in Spain, Michael brought together many religious leaders from Israel and Palestine, including those with the most fervent attitudes, many of whom have spearheaded resistance movements. His "coalition," as he calls it, consists of both Hamas and Jewish extremist movements and parties. This conference will be the first in which the participants shake hands and appear in public together. "We take responsibility for the peace process at a time when it otherwise appears to have stalled," he says, referring to the information leaked by WikiLeaks, which included emails from Hillary Clinton, among other political leaders. He was saddened to read that Clinton had spoken of a "fictional peace process," something that resembles a peace process without actually being one, and which aims to quiet detractors who believe everything has stalled.

But why, as he himself asks, has he spent his entire life on a peace process when even the world's leaders no longer believe it? "I hold on to hope because I see that when you work purposefully, you can succeed in getting people to work with you—even if these same people have been an obstacle to peace in the past." I ask Michael if he'll have a chance to talk to everyone, and he replies with a smile. "There are some people I'd like to meet more than others. But the more fervent a leader, the more important it is to meet him."

I have a hard time understanding why Michael meets with people who are intent on killing Jews. What is the purpose of meeting anyone who spits such venom? Does it sway anyone's mind, or is it just a ploy for the photo ops? Michael has no doubt that he's doing the right thing. "I haven't had any meetings yet that have not changed attitudes and given me reason for hope." In his thinking, the problem is that many people believe that they make a difference by speaking to people on the same side of the political spectrum. For example, the extreme Israeli left works together with the extreme Palestinian left; they meet to agree on programs, conferences, and plans. That's something they've been doing for twenty years. But it's not enough on its own, because they are starting to lose steam, and fewer people are participating in fewer events. "Now the Palestinians are also saying they no longer believe it's effective. Why meet with the Israelis who believe in peace when it doesn't bring change, because the Israelis they meet with are not in government and have no power?" Michael continues, "That's why my argument is that, instead of talking to those you already agree with, one should instead talk to skeptical, distrustful opponents of peace."

"How do you talk to people who don't want to move an inch in attitude?" I ask. "How can anyone convince them of something they are opposed to with all their heart?"

"It's about finding the origin of their skepticism and distrust," Michael says. "Afterward, it's important to ask, 'Can we do something about that?' And then, finally, it's about finding a common language—a different lexicon than you may be accustomed to. Most people want peace as their starting point, but they don't want peace that robs them of their beliefs or their identities. If you create a contradiction between peace and identity, then people usually choose identity."

I know the situation in Israel and Palestine doesn't compare to what's happening in Denmark, but what Michael says about identity makes me ponder the reasons people at home have for facing off against each other. Is it because we don't take each other's concerns seriously? Is that why the debate about what is Danish flares up so regularly? Is it because some folks, including myself, don't realize the importance of preserving identity? Will it become a choice between preserving Denmark, Danish roots, and traditions, or helping refugees and immigrants who cause our identity to evolve? The thought of how many times I've supported this false dichotomy makes me sick. Given the choice between being Danish or Muslim, how would I choose? Some pieces fall into place here in the sukkah. The discussion of identity sheds light on some past debates I've found ridiculous. It does, in fact, matter if pork meatballs are served in daycare centers. It does matter if there's a Christmas tree in a community center in Kokkedal. In the past, I thought the discussions about meatballs and Christmas trees were ridiculous, but the lack of common language is digging deeper trenches, and I haven't been understanding enough about those who fear losing their identity. It's important to me, for my cultural identity, that my children don't eat pork meatballs. But I also have to acknowledge that it may be just as important to others that their children not eat halal meatballs. Everyone's right to forge an identity should be equally protected.

Identity is a strange animal. In our day-to-day lives we may not give it much thought, but the moment it's under threat or we risk losing it, our identity suddenly becomes crucial to well-being.

Then Michael mentions something I often encounter when drinking coffee with people. Regardless of who they are, it's the fault of others that the situation is as bad as it's become. It was the others who started it, and the others must stop. Can circular reasoning that vicious ever be brought to a stop? "Yes," Michael says. "It's possible! This is done by guaranteeing that no one has to give up their history, their rights, or their dreams for the future."

Wow, I think. Can I meet any man face-to-face who dreams of having me deported from Denmark, acknowledge his dream, and still cross a bridge to meet him somewhere near the middle? How can you argue for that rationally? Michael leans now on his religious background, and the argument changes in character. "We who believe in God also believe that it's no coincidence that the two of us are here together in this place. It's obviously something God ordained. Just as we believe that God has granted us our homeland, we also must have faith that it's not due to a divine misunderstanding that other people live here as well. The Palestinians believe as much as the Israelis that this is their holy land. And their religion also tells them to respect the people who live here with them," Michael explains. "So, we need to seek a solution within a framework of religious understanding."

He talks about how he seeks out one venomous leader after another in the hopes of finding a common language—a language of peace that doesn't require secularization but recognizes the importance of religious identity. Religion, so often blamed for conflict, may, in Michael's view, be the key to peace. I think of the imams in Denmark and my conversation with Hizb ut-Tahrir's imam, Hamza: Imagine if they could hand out leaflets that didn't say they were against democracy, but instead that they were against violence, crime, and the root causes of those problems. What a difference it would make if young people who spoke a religious language were met with a religious language that led them in a common direction. It's not religion, but people who pose the danger. Michael is both a religious man and a man of peace.

I like Michael. I don't know whether it's his unshakeable belief in peace, whether it's his calm and long-standing experience, or whether it's his "right" religious approach, but I feel prepared to endorse his work. Not once did he blow me off when the discussion got tough. He speaks about his opponents with respect. He's been clear that he understands only one part of the truth and that his opponents understand other parts.

I think of Nomi and her criticism of politicians. Why aren't political leaders more like Michael? Why don't they have the same courage? Michael has apparently always been brave. He, a religious man, has always fought for the separation of politics and religion. For example, in the Israeli parliament, he went against his own party and voted for civil marriage.

"Why?" I ask him.

"Because it's not my place to impose religion on people who don't want it. I think religion is a voluntary matter, and one does not serve religion by force," he argues.

I can agree with Michael's arguments about the roles of religion and faith. I fast during Ramadan. I believe in Allah and in life after death. I eat halal meat. I've circumcised my eldest boy, and my youngest will also be circumcised. I didn't have to search in different religions to find the truth like some do; I found the answers I needed in Islam. I've remained in the faith I was raised in. Though, as a teenager, I was looking for tangible answers in the Qur'an, today I am looking for solutions in the community. That shift happened as I became more politically active. At the same time, my religion became more personal to me. But it still guides me.

I would call my relationship with faith pragmatic. It's something that enriches me—not something that restricts me. I was raised to see Islam as a projection of love, and so I always call for meaningful discussions that seek understanding. I believe that Allah forgives us, and so we must also forgive each other and dare to believe in the good of other human beings. And because I am a believer, I know that faith really can move mountains. So yes, religion can be part of the solution as well as part of the problem.

It's hard not to get excited about Michael. When you sit in his sukkah, you feel that anything is possible. He tells me his father always says, "When you cannot see the light at the end of the tunnel, it is not because there is no light at the end; it's because the tunnel isn't straight." It's important that we, as human beings, even when we differ, learn how to bend together in the right places so that we can reach the light.

"How close are we to peace?" I ask Michael.

"It's just around the corner." He smiles.

Later in the day, together with Devrim and the children, I visit the ancient city of East Jerusalem. Our first stop is Graedemu; it's clean. Originally it was part of a large temple. The temple was destroyed by the Romans, and today the Wailing Wall is considered the holiest place in Judaism. Here people are teeming, and you can clearly see that Jerusalem is a holy city for all three Abrahamic religions. Orthodox Jews stand in front of the Wailing Wall, praying, as more people hurry toward the shrine while trying to avoid hitting women crossing the road. Muslims are moving fast in another direction, the women with their scarves and the men with their small white embroidered hats. A bit further from us, a priest walks with a cross around his neck. The whole place looks like an ant colony. No one shouts or speaks loudly, yet the constant murmur creates a powerful sound that is difficult to find distinction in. As I look at the assembly, I can see the meeting of three great religions. Seriousness lies like a heavy quilt over the square; strong forces are at play here, and I feel a thrill go through my body. Here faith is strong, but also scary. For the first time, I feel an atheistic critic bubble up through my consciousness. Is religion really opium for the masses? Would some of these people really sacrifice everything, including their lives, to go to Paradise?

The atmosphere is very somber. On the street corners, there are soldiers with large machine guns, and the distance between people seems wider. After visiting the Wailing Wall, I first ask some soldiers and then a group of civilian Jews if they can show me the way to the Rock Mosque, which is also in the old town. It is the oldest building of Islam and one of the most important shrines of the Muslims, since we believe it was here that Prophet Muhammad rose to heaven to speak to God before returning to earth to spread Islam. Nobody wants to show me the way. At first, I think they may not know where the mosque is or have never heard of it. But that doesn't seem likely. Jews and Muslims have fought so much over that particular mosque, and Orthodox Jews must know its story. It must be because they will not show the way to a Muslim. They must be so hateful that they won't even tell where a mosque is located, I think. Suddenly, an anger rises inside me that I recognize from childhood. I'm a little frightened at how quickly I return to generalization and prejudice. A voice inside me says that they really might not know the place or that they were busy going to prayer. I feel divided in ambivalence. It is as if bridge-builder Özlem is looking on at ditch-digger Özlem.

When we find the mosque, which is not very far from the Wailing Wall, we are greeted by a Muslim guard who wants to know if I am a Muslim. I confirm that I am, but it is obviously not enough. I also have to read him passages from the Qur'an. When I'm done, the guard looks over my husband. "What about you?" he asks.

"I'm a follower of Allah," Devrim replies. Alevism is the most pragmatic and cultural branch of Islam, and for many years the Alevites have been persecuted, especially in Turkey, but also in the rest of the world, because Sunni Muslims regard them as unbelievers.

The guard widens his eyes: "Alevite? They're not Muslims."

One of the guard's colleagues has also been listening. Now he turns to me. "You know that as a Muslim you are not allowed to marry a non-Muslim."

I am furious. Who has given the guard the right to judge my marriage and to judge what Muslims may or may not do? "It's not your job," I say firmly.

But that doesn't change the conclusion. My husband has to stay outside as the kids and I go enter the mosque. Why are people so exclusive? The children are obviously not happy that their father has been left behind.

"Why?" they ask. It is hard to explain to them the conflict that has caused Muslims to fight each other for centuries. As I turn around and see Devrim standing back, I'm reminded of how religion also divides— and that conflicts can exist, not only between religions, but also within the same religion. It stabs right into my heart.

I will be stopped again on my way to the mosque. Now it's my clothes that the guards are picking over. One guard points his machine gun at my dress, which I wear over my pants and which reaches my knees. It's too short, he says. I'm asked to go back to the first guard and get a skirt I can put over my pants and dress.

"I've been to mosques for forty years, so I know what you wear in a mosque," I say angrily. "What's the problem? Aren't men and women separated in there?" When he confirms that's the case, I argue irritably, "Then it doesn't matter if my dress goes to my knee or to my ankle, I still have pants on inside."

He maintains that the dress is too short. He grabs his machine gun tighter, and I feel I need to stop. I return to the first guard and get an ugly skirt to throw over my dress.

As I sit in the Rock Mosque, I forget all my worries. It is serene and I enjoy the beautiful decorations, the religious hymns, and the fellowship with strangers. I sit in the mosque for a long time, even after the children have run out to be with their father again. When I reach them, they are having a good time talking to some Israeli soldiers. Devrim tells me that he quickly fell into conversation with the soldiers, and that he has taken pictures of them with the children. Who is an ally and who is an enemy can be hard to determine in Israel and Palestine, I think.

I can hardly sleep that night. Michael's hope feels like adrenaline. I am confident I can talk to anyone, that it's all about having an open mind. But I get a reality check when I meet Bassam in Jericho in northeastern Palestine the next day.

Surrounded by Enemies

Palestine covers two territories, Gaza in the west and the West Bank in the east. The two areas are separated by Israel, but they are also separated politically. The West Bank is led by the Fatah Party, while Gaza is controlled by Hamas. The two parties have tried on several occasions to establish a Palestinian unity government, but it has proved very difficult to bridge the gap between secular Fatah and Islamic Hamas. Jerusalem is located in the border between Israel and the West Bank. You can compare it to Berlin before the fall of the wall, when the German capital was divided between West Germany and East Germany. But in Jerusalem there is no agreement on the division. The Palestinians claim East Jerusalem, while the Israelis claim the entire city. The border is a deeply integral part of the conflict in the Holy Land, and it's the one I cross today.

Several people have warned me not to drive into Palestine. According to the Jews, my Israeli car will be at risk of being stoned by Palestinians. The Palestinians have told me that I must count on extra transport time, as I will be constantly stopped at checkpoints established by Israeli soldiers controlling traffic in and out of Palestinian areas. The children and Devrim have stayed in Jerusalem, as I don't want to expose them to danger or to anything traumatizing.

As I drive through the desolate Palestinian landscape, I do not feel insecure, but extremely free. I'm a little proud of myself. My mother has called several times to make sure I am well. "How dare you go there, a woman alone?" she asks. Her understanding of the world isn't the same as mine. She left school after third grade, and her upbringing was marked by chronic insecurity. I haven't inherited that from her. What should I be afraid of? If anyone wanted to kill me—and I have a hard time imagining why they would—it would just as likely happen in Copenhagen on a late night. There are also traffic accidents all over the world. I believe in destiny, that is, what is meant to happen will happen. But I don't believe in the new version of destiny—the one where you passively wait for what will happen to pan out. Fate or not, we all have a responsibility to think and act for ourselves.

Unlike what my mother thinks, for me, being a woman doesn't mean I don't have liberty. I make my own decisions in every situation I face. That doesn't mean I never consult my husband. I do this all the time. But for him, it's also important that I make my own choices. He supports my choices, although sometimes I can tell that he's worried. He was worried when I left for Palestine alone.

Bassam is chairman of an organization for Israeli and Palestinian parents who have lost their children in the conflict and are now working together for peace. An acquaintance from Denmark established contact between us, and I'm confident it will be fine. I emailed Bassam ahead of the visit, and we agreed on all the details. At ten o'clock, we will meet in front of the Hotel Intercontinental, Jericho's tallest building, located on the outskirts of the city on the main road from Jerusalem. Bassam will drive over to meet me in a black Kia. The evening before, we talked on the phone and confirmed the agenda. It takes longer than I expected to get out of Jerusalem. I send him the first text at 8:48, to let him know that I will be delayed.

"How long do you think?" he asks.

"Thirty minutes," I write.

However, I'm not stopped on the way by angry Palestinians or Israeli soldiers, so I arrive earlier than planned. "I'm here already," I write to Bassam.

"Five minutes," the answer reads.

In the driveway at the hotel, I'm stopped by a guard who wants to know what my errand is before he lets me park. I tell him I have a meeting and give Bassam's name. As I park my car and walk up to the hotel, the guard yells at me that my contact has arrived. Bassam drives up in a black Kia as planned. He talks on the phone and signals to me that he will be there in two minutes. I nod to him and walk into the hotel lobby.

Bassam comes in shortly after and extends his hand. If I were to guess, he's in his early fifties. He's bald, clean-shaven, wearing bright velvet pants, and a white shirt with blue and brown stripes. He pours a coffee for himself and gets me a Coke. I turn off my phone and turn on my recorder. I'd like to start the interview and learn about him and his organization, but Bassam is more interested in learning something about me. I excitedly tell him about my bridge-building work and my interest in peace-making, but I'm a little disappointed that Bassam isn't as gregarious as I am. He says he has three daughters, and one of them is dead due to illness. He wants peace because it's the only path to stability. He repeats this a couple of times and I don't really feel like we're moving anywhere in the conversation. In all, we talk for forty-five minutes, and I'm annoyed at how little I get out of him. He insists on paying the bill, and we say goodbye to each other.

As I settle into my car, I turn on my cell phone. There are three messages from Bassam. One says, "Where are you?" In the next, "I'm looking for you on the main road." In the third, there is a text that I simply have to read several times, because it doesn't make sense. "I'm very sorry, dear. I waited for you from 9:40 to 10:56. I'm sorry we didn't get to talk. It's urgent that I contact my sister, who is in very critical condition at the hospital, and our family has to be there. I'm sorry, but I have to drive to Hebron now." It runs a chill down my spine.

After sunning myself for a few minutes, I write back, "I don't understand. I just sat with Bassam in the hotel in Jericho for forty-five minutes."

I receive a text that reads, "The message cannot be sent." I try sending it again. The message is rejected again. I call him several times, but the number is unreachable.

I try sending a new message, "Dear Bassam. I was at the hotel at 10:10. I met a man who came in a black Kia and introduced himself as Bassam. I talked to him for forty-five minutes. When I said goodbye to him, I went back in my car and turned on my cell and saw messages from you. I tried to call you back, but I'm not getting through. Who was that man if it wasn't you?"

"The message cannot be sent."

None of this makes any sense. If the man in the lobby is not Bassam, then who is he? Why did he present himself as Bassam? Why was he driving a black car, exactly as we agreed he would? Why can't I get hold of the real Bassam? For a brief moment, I consider going back to the hotel and confronting the man I met to find out who he really is. But something is off about the situation, and I decide to get in the car and drive away. I can feel the paranoia sticking to me. Was it an agent of some sort? And would he think of doing something to harm me? Was it the Israeli intelligence service? Who else knew we were meeting?

On the way back, my husband calls me. I choose not to say anything about the false Bassam. I am shaken, and since I've put my phone away, I sing to distract me from reliving the experience. I sing through "Circles of Enemies," "In the Middle of the Night," and a series of Turkish songs. I realize how off-key I sing. I remember my uncle's wife once told me, "Sing alone, preferably in a forest!" I can't help but laugh. I'm not in a forest, but a desert is probably close enough.

Soon after, my phone rings again. It is Fathi El-Abed, calling from Denmark. Fathi is chairman of the Danish-Palestinian Friendship Association and has helped me set up a series of meetings in Palestine. Now he acts as my guide, as the GPS doesn't work in Palestine. According to Fathi, this is because the Israelis are blocking the signals. He also warns me to look out for Israeli checkpoints along the way. I tell him that the drive to Jericho was fine, but he's distrustful. "Don't believe everything the Israelis say," he says.

When I tell him I had a good conversation with Michael Melchior, he replies, "The Israeli lobby is powerful." I can sense that trying to convince him of the opposite will be a waste of international phone time when his distrust is based on the experiences and abuses of a lifetime. But I also feel that the experience at Hotel Intercontinental has made me more alert. It's very difficult to see who is an enemy and who is a friend in a country where people have been fighting each other for years. I follow Fathi's directions and they take me back to Jerusalem.

My next destination is Bethlehem, located a few miles south of Jerusalem, where I will pick up Firaz. Fathi has arranged a meeting with Firaz's mother, Nadia, who is the leader of a Palestinian women's organization. Nadia works in Ramallah, north of Jerusalem, so I can meet her later in the evening. Before then, Firaz and I will be visiting Hebron in the southernmost part of the West Bank.

One cannot easily drive from Jericho to Bethlehem, even though both cities are on the West Bank. I have to drive out of the West Bank and cross Jerusalem to get to Bethlehem. The GPS behaves as Fathi predicted it would. As soon as I am on the Israeli side, it works, and as I cross the border again, this time to the West Bank, it goes out again. It is difficult to find my way navigating with Hebrew and Arabic signs, so instead I drive along the wall—gigantic, fierce, tall, and unusually ugly. It cuts a long, crooked divide between Israel and the West Bank and is visible evidence that the conversation between the people on each side of the wall has ended.

Many of my Jewish friends also claim that the wall was erected to cut off a violent wave of terror from Hamas. One of them told me, "It's hard to see if you're standing there looking at it, but it works and has saved many lives." My Palestinian friends, on the other hand, maintain that the violent attacks by Hamas came as the result of an

Israeli government-sponsored terrorist attack. I understand this debate well from the conflict between the Kurds and Turks, and I've found it too easily leads to a chicken-or-egg discussion. It's difficult to find an answer that can bring together people from both sides of the conflict. Whatever the answer, the wall is a reality. The wall curves around Bethlehem, which is surrounded by it on three sides, to the south, west, and north. I drive in from the north and am quick to wave my red passport at the Israeli soldiers guarding the checkpoint to Bethlehem. Fathi has warned me about Israeli soldiers. "You risk being shot if they have any doubt about who you are."

When I look at Firaz, I feel that my trust in other people has been shaken by the experience in Jericho. I don't know if I can trust him, and I'm more vigilant than usual. He meets me outside the house, where he lives with Nadia. It is a huge three-story building that is half-finished. Only the top floor has walls; everything else is raw concrete. Firaz is a young man of thirty years. He's a musician, speaks fluent English, and is very friendly. When he meets me at the car, I look out the window and up at the house. There are bullet holes on the walls. "Is that really your home?" I ask Firaz. He nods. I start the car and continue south, in the direction of Hebron.

Hebron is another point of contention in the conflict between Israel and Palestine. The city is home to the Abraham Mosque, which is sacred to both Muslims and Jews. In 1994, an Israeli settler attacked the mosque and killed twenty-nine Palestinians during prayer. As a result of the massacre, the mosque was split in two. Today, Hebron is a popular city for Jewish settlers, many of whom immigrated there from the United States.

"You have to see the settlement with your own eyes," Firaz says as we drive to Hebron.

"Yes, show me," I answer. The road to Hebron is beautiful, if we disregard all the military vehicles that stand along the main road, manned by combat-fatigued, machine-gun-toting Israeli soldiers. "Why are they here in the West Bank?" I ask, thinking right away that

I must sound stupid to him. But Firaz takes the time to explain. The main road goes through almost the entire West Bank and connects a number of large cities, and a wealth of small villages. The road is owned by the Israelis, which explains the soldiers, and sometimes, according to Firaz, the Israelis choose to close the road without warning. "What if you have to go to the hospital, or if an ambulance has to get through?" I ask.

"There's not much we can do," Firaz says.

We talk further and I start to let my guard down. Firaz is a confident man, and we laugh several times on the way. But as we stand under the barbed wire in the old city of Hebron, there is nothing left to laugh about. Palestinians have set nets across the pedestrian zone so as not to be hit by the bricks the Israeli settlers above throw down on them. I don't believe my own eyes. It can't be true! Can people be so evil that, by daylight, they throw bricks at people who've done nothing to them?

"They also throw garbage at us," my guide tells me. I look around and only then notice the many piles of garbage lying next to the bricks. It's so bizarre and grotesque that it's hard to conceive.

I'm thinking of Michael. Peace is not just around the corner in Hebron. And there is absolutely no light to see at the end of the tunnel. I have a hard time breathing. Is this really true? Or is it just another conspiracy theory against the state of Israel? I'm most likely to believe the last thing I see. Reality is so hard to hold onto that I try to get through the moment by relying on denial. A text message chimes on my cell phone. It's Fathi. "Remember, it's okay to cry when you're in Hebron. It does that to everyone who sees what you are going to experience."

Already, I have a lump in my throat.

Firaz has hired a guide to show me through the settlement. His name is Ghassan and he is twenty years old. "There are five hundred Israeli settlers living here. They're all from America. They have two thousand soldiers looking after them. They carry machine guns, and they're violent. They've either taken our houses or built right on top of them. They throw rocks and garbage down on us. See?" he says, as he points to the netting. Together, we enter the old town. According to my guide, the street was once filled with small shops and teeming life. It's very hard to imagine. Virtually all the small shops are closed, and the few that are open seem completely out of place. The street is empty, and an eerie silence makes the mood in the city even more somber. Even the few children I meet aren't noisy. They aren't running or shouting out in play. No one is moving to the distant music faintly heard in the background.

"Where is that music coming from?" I ask.

My guide tells me that it is a Jewish holiday and that is why they have blocked off the old town. He points to a closed gate. Unfortunately,

Overcoming Hate Through Dialogue

this also means that the Palestinian immigrants who live in settlement areas cannot get in or out of the area. Neither do they have water. "The Israelis decide when they want to let us have water." Ghassan speaks as if he is reading. Obviously, this isn't the first time he's told this story. His white shirt is freshly ironed, and he has a sharp haircut. He could be one of the young people I met back in Norrebro, but the difference is that he doesn't smile once. He was an exchange student at a Danish college in Viborg but returned home after a year. His facial expressions are either serious or rather sad. When he talks, it seems as if the energy is being sucked out of him, as if he is imprisoned. Is his guide work a chore? Does it feel as painful as it looks? My head is full of questions.

"Why?" I ask. "Why would you live in Hebron if it's so awful?"

Without hesitation, he replies, "Because this is my home. I was born here. My family is here. My friends are here. This is my homeland. I can't go anywhere else." His voice is brittle, but he continues speaking without shame. "We can't do anything. When one of the Jewish settlers is in the street, six to seven Israeli soldiers walk with them. The settlers aren't like any of the other Jews who lived in the city before they arrived. These settlers are insane and create problems. For example, they throw alcohol at us when we fast during Ramadan, and they know we don't touch alcohol," says Ghassan.

But why don't they talk with one another? Why doesn't Ghassan tell them that their behavior is so upsetting? Why can't they sit down and figure it all out together? My questions give rise to a puzzling look from Ghassan. Did I say something wrong? I wonder.

Ghassan's eyes are full of fear. "We can't," he says very seriously. "They shoot if we get too close. If we're out of range, then the soldiers who man the booms shoot at us."

Can that really be right? I think. Who would point a gun at someone who just wants to talk?

We're standing on the roof of one of the Palestinian houses. The building next door belongs to some settlers, as revealed by the facade, whose bricks are brighter and newer than the others. "Look," Ghassan says. From the roof we can see soldiers on the settlers' rooftops. They're ready to shoot. Suddenly I realize that they're on many of rooftops. As I look down on the street, I can see that some of the settlers also carry large machine guns. Israeli flags hang on the buildings.

"But we can't hang Palestinian flags. Then they take them down." Ghassan says that the family in the house beneath us lost both of their sons when the settlers threw a grenade through the window one evening. Now they've offered the family a million dollars to move out, but the family won't go, because they're afraid that would start a domino effect. "If we leave, they win," Ghassan repeats time and time again.

I'm finding it difficult to breathe. I wear sunglasses and am glad that
Ghassan doesn't see me crying. There isn't a single cloud in the sky,
and the sun is beating down on us. Still, everything seems so dark.
I feel completely drained of energy. How could it end so wrong?
And why is it so difficult to pick the conversation back up? I don't
know, but I think of those in Denmark who call me naïve when I
insist that there is no alternative to conversation. They should come
down here and see what happens when you give up conversation and
breathe hatred.

I'm sorry as I say my good-byes to the children who tried to sell me
a Palestine bracelet. Everything feels unreal and extreme. On my
return trip, I see women shopping in markets, men sitting on street
corners playing backgammon, kids kicking a ball. Everything seems
so normal, but then the wall catches my eye each time I almost forget
it's standing there, reminding one of the seriousness of it all. I think
of Michael who told me that as long as you can't talk with each other,
there will be walls.

There's an eerie quiet as all the trees, flowers, and buildings lose their
colors. Darkness falls over the landscape. There are no streetlights
illuminating the main road as we drive. Blue siren lights blink through
the darkness along the way. There are more soldiers in the evening
than were here during the day. I'm glad Firaz is with me now, though
I don't know him well. He tells me about his dreams for the future.
He's a musician and talks about his band, girlfriend, and prospects.
We talk about our families, our educations, our countries. Firaz tells
me that he's a Christian, and we also talk about the similarities that
exist between Christianity and Islam. And so our drive becomes a
journey into one another's lives, and we stick to things we can agree
on. We curse anyone who doesn't want peace, and rage at Hamas, and
the settlers, and soldiers who use violence.

The Star of Bethlehem

"Are you hungry?" Firaz asks me. I am reminded that I haven't eaten since breakfast. He calls his mother, Nadia, and tells her that we're on our way to Bethlehem. "I made some dinner before we met," he says.

"Did you?" I'm surprised.

"Yes, my mother works," he says, and I reconsider my assumptions about my hosts and the division of labor within their family.

The traffic heading into Bethlehem is thick. I ask Firaz why he and Ghassan don't turn to violence when their human rights are violated daily.

"When we throw stones, they shoot back at us with machine guns. They are much, much stronger," he says. But he also says he doesn't believe in violence as a solution. "Just look at Hamas. Violence makes it all worse." He shakes his head. He is disappointed with Hamas's actions in Gaza, and he is disappointed with Fatah in the West Bank. He's disappointed with the whole world. But he still believes in peace. "Sooner or later it will come."

Firaz, his father, and his mother live in part of the half-finished building right next to the wall. It was supposed to have been a hotel, but because of the wall, the area is considered high-risk and the bank won't loan the money necessary to fix up the building. The family lives on the top floor, which has been transformed into a huge apartment. The other floors are still bare concrete, without walls, doors, or windows. The air in Nadia's living room is stuffy. She apologizes and explains that she can't open the windows because the Israeli soldiers have just thrown tear gas. They abut a refugee camp, where there are daily confrontations between Palestinians and soldiers.

Nadia's black hair is cut short. She is wearing black pants and a green striped blouse. Her silver jewelry and well-groomed face indicate a proud woman. She is the head of a women's organization that she has spent twenty-seven years of her life building. She is fighting for equality and against the regime in Palestine, both for the government of Gaza and for the government of the West Bank. Men, according to Nadia, are the greatest obstacle to equality. As she tells me this, I feel myself spacing out. Evidently, there is a limit to how much misery one can accommodate in one day. I am tired and have none of the energy left that filled me when I talked to Michael.

But Nadia smiles and laughs, and once in a while, she finds just the right opportunity to tease her husband. She works in Ramallah and mentions off-handedly that on her way home she received chemotherapy. She has breast cancer. I'd like to ask her more about it, but it's clear that she finds it immaterial. She would rather talk about the Jews and Palestinians she works with to make peace. All the fiery folks she has daily contact with who contribute to a dialogue of understanding. She tries to teach the women to be stronger and more independent. "I believe in peace. It will benefit both Palestinians and Israelis. Women, men, children, and soldiers—all of us—will benefit from making peace," Nadia says. She is a mother herself and doesn't want her children to die in the conflict. "Why should Jewish mothers want anything else?" she asks rhetorically.

I tell her everything I've seen in Hebron and that I marvel at her optimism.

Nadia notes dryly, "You're in shock, because this is the first time you've seen it."

The idea of getting used to what I've seen today gives me goosebumps. Is that what happens to us at home in Denmark when we look at each other every day? Is that why we become desensitized to the harsh rhetoric we use about each other? Does the passage of time not only create the patience that I sense in Nadia and in Michael, but also make us immune to the hatred and resentment of others? Does it push us past the boundaries of what we should tolerate?

All day long, I swing between hope and pessimism. With Nomi, I was drained of energy, then, while visiting Michael, I felt I'd been given a shot of adrenaline. My confidence was shaken by the incident with the Bassam imposter. I was in shock in Hebron, and now I'm back with someone who's full of optimism. This is what it's like to be human— we let ourselves be influenced by what we experience; we feel the emotions of those around us, and sometimes our emotions betray us. Perhaps this is why it's especially important to socialize with people who can pick you back up when you feel like you're in the basement.

The role of the fiery folks in Israel and Palestine is not just to work for peace, but also to be lighthouses whose fire lights the way for people who periodically swing between despair and hope. It takes time to get fired up, I think. You have to go through the rollercoaster of emotions many times before you can find with certainty what you believe in most. I think of my own reaction when I get hate email. How I have become thick-skinned because I have read it all so many times now. I have gradually learned that, when someone calls me a bigoted slur, the term is rarely addressed to me as a person. More often, it expresses a feeling of powerlessness toward immigrants or Muslims in general. If we are to go on with life and do what we really want to accomplish, we mustn't take the outcries of people who feel disempowered as personal, but should instead insist on having tough conversations. But in Nadia's kitchen, I can't see how that could be possible in Hebron. After all, there is no opportunity for conversation here.

Overcoming Hate Through Dialogue

"Who will win?" Nadia asks, and immediately answers herself, "No one!" I joke about how she seems to be so positive about the peace process when nothing in her environment signals hope. "Why not?" She replies. Then she says that if you have to change anything, you have to start by meeting with the people you disagree with. "Participation and civic duty are important. People need to feel like they are part of the community. They need to feel it first, so they can believe it too."

For Nadia, the conversations should happen everywhere, and she engages in dialogue with everyone, whether on the street, at the doctor, or at work. She is a great woman. Not only physically, but in her personality. She has spoken about this topic thousands of times, but I don't detect any kind of talking-head points at all in her arguments. She is committed and passionate. "Conversation works. Dialogue is the only way to peace," Nadia emphasizes.

We have dinner together, drink tea, and eat cake. Afterward, Nadia gives me fruit to take back with me in a plastic bag. It is a fruit I have never seen before. The scent of it is so sweet that it's impossible to describe. Like the wall outside Nadia's kitchen, but in reverse. I get a hug and leave infected with Nadia's optimism. If, amid all this hopelessness, she can still retain her enthusiasm, then there is definitely hope for the rest of us.

Soon I'm stuck in the line of cars waiting to pass the checkpoint in Bethlehem. Everybody is checked over meticulously. Cars are scanned; trunks are opened, and bodies are searched. As I drive out of Bethlehem and back toward the hotel in Jerusalem, I am completely worn out. It's late now, and the sun has long since set. The darkness, the wall, and the silence fill a good part of the road, but they disappear as I approach the center of Jerusalem. When I enter our hotel room and see Devrim, it's almost midnight and our children are sleeping peacefully. I find it difficult to put my experiences that day into words, because I have so many mixed feelings. But I try to say them quietly; my words are spoken softly so I can tell my husband about the amazing, cruel things I experienced in Jericho, Hebron, and Bethlehem without waking the children.

I send Bassam an email explaining what happened. "Who was the other Bassam?" I ask. To which he writes back, "I don't know."

Devrim, on the other hand, has no doubt. "It has to be either the Palestinian Liberation Organization or the Israeli Mossad. The intelligence services in this country are some of the best in the world," he says.

"I'm a little brave." I smile.

"A little brave, yes—and maybe a little too dumb, too," he teases.

That night, I dream of the quiet children in Hebron, bricks falling from the sky, and the wall moving closer and closer. Several times I wake up and kiss my children. How lucky we are.

Achinoam's Song

On November 4, 1995, Achinoam Nini sings at a peace concert in Tel Aviv, held for the occasion of the peace agreement signed in Oslo by Israeli Prime Minister Yitzhak Rabin and Palestinian leader Yasser Arafat. The optimism and hope have returned to the region. Achinoam is twenty-six years old, and she is proud to be on that stage. Tel Aviv sings with her, and she feels like part of something bigger than herself that will be recorded in history books. Both Rabin and Arafat give her a hug on stage, and on her exit from the stage she notices an Orthodox Jewish man sitting in one of the front rows. She wonders, as his clothing, and especially the long curls, indicate that he belongs to the most devout communities within Judaism. Something is not right. From that day on, the man's face will be burned into Achinoam's memory, because ten minutes later he begins shooting at the prime minister. Rabin dies, and hope and peace seem to die along with him.

It's Thursday, and I'm sitting with Achinoam at a café in Tel Aviv. Michael has set up the meeting so I can speak to one of the strongest cultural forces fighting for peace in Israel and Palestine. She wears a long multicolored dress, and her long, brown, curly hair covers her back. Achinoam's English is flawless, but that's not the only reason she is so easy to understand. Above all, she seems ready to spit fire when she talks about her strong attitudes toward the conflict and the prospect of peace.

Achinoam is a Jew who has roots in Yemen. Her family first settled in Israel, but later immigrated to the United States. Her parents, afraid she might lose her connection to her Jewish roots, sent Achinoam to a very religious school in the hopes it would bring her closer to God. "For my parents, religion was also a source of security," she says. Achinoam did not look like the other girls in her school. She was the only girl with dark skin, and she was neither religious, nor rich, nor born in Israel. But no one could top her academically. She quickly identified herself as the school's most accomplished student and ranked highest in English, math, and religion.

As a sixteen-year-old, Achinoam went on a trip to Israel with other schoolchildren. For their safety, they were joined by Israeli soldiers for part of the tour, and strong chemistry quickly developed between Achinoam and one of the soldiers. The chemistry turned into a crush, and one night when they were together, she decided to marry him. He was ten years older than she was, but the feelings were mutual, and they exchanged contact information. Achinoam returned to the United States, but she and the Israeli soldier continued to call and write to each other. When she was old enough, she applied for admission to a university in Israel. When the application was accepted, her parents were both proud and happy that their daughter planned to return to the Holy Land. Achinoam told them nothing about the real reason.

After university, military service (which is mandatory in Israel) was expected of her. Achinoam's high class ranking allowed her to choose what function to serve in the military. When she chose the music department, everyone thought she was raving mad. Why didn't she select a field as an officer that would pave the way for a successful career? But Achinoam chose to follow her heart. The same thing happened when she married the soldier she met as a sixteen-year-old. They are still married.

After Rabin's assassination, several weeks went by where Achinoam could neither work nor sing. "All the energy expressed with my voice came from what I felt in my heart," she says. She decided to throw herself into peace work. Today she sings for peace and spends all her spare time building bridges between groups. Among other events, she performed in the Meloday Grand Prix with a Palestinian; together, they sang "There Must Be Another Way."

Achinoam tells me about the organizations she is involved in, about the many conferences, films, and debates. She keeps such a fast pace, hell can't catch up with her. I hear what she's saying, but beyond the actual words, I notice anger in her voice, not joy. I have a hard time deciding whether the anger stems from her frustration at the lack of results from her efforts, or if it is that she knows peace is further away than she hopes. But above the anger, her voice rises, powerful and fast. "I won't give up!" Is she trying to convince herself?

"I get so many hate emails," she says. Most come from Orthodox Jews who oppose the division within Israel around the peace efforts. They think she agrees with the Palestinians and criticize her for singing for peace-making organizations. Or they rage against her criticism of the illegal Israeli settlements in Palestine. "But I always try to talk with those who send me hate mail and call me a traitor. I never answer them in the same language they write to me. I respectfully respond to them, and I suggest that we meet for discussion and debate. Many times they just stop writing to me." Her voice is full of wonder. When I ask her why she thinks that happens, she says, "They're confused when I respond and they can't just rely on a kneejerk reaction."

As an example, Achinoam talks about footage she shot for a documentary produced by the German-French television station Arte. While she and the TV crew were walking through Tel Aviv, some men on the street began to shout, "National traitor!" and, "Why do you hate your country?" Achinoam didn't turn away from them, she did the exact opposite. She approached the men and tried to speak to them. "They were angry, and I asked them directly why they were angry. I began to talk about my understanding of the conflict. After a few minutes, they gave up completely," Achinoam says. She ended up taking pictures with the men that day.

But Achinoam also has examples where dialogue does not work. She tells me about an event that was held for families to commemorate all those who had died in the conflict. The event was for both Israelis and Palestinians. "I said yes to singing, precisely because it was about letting both sides share their grief." After the concert, however, Achinoam was attacked on social media, by people who thought she should be deprived of her Israeli citizenship because she had sung for terrorists.

"The thing is that the vast majority of victims of the conflict are Palestinians. It's primarily Palestinian children, young people, and women we lose, who have been trapped in the struggle between Israel and Palestine for many years. But the Israeli government believes that anyone who works for an independent Palestine is a terrorist. The government doesn't understand that if you have been under occupation for so many years, it is a natural urge for people to fight for their freedom. Of course, there are also real terrorists, but not everyone fighting against the soldiers is a terrorist," Achinoam says.

"It sounds like it might be the same strategy all repressive regimes use," I say, mentioning how in Turkey they often refer to Kurds as terrorists in response to their demand for equal rights. Achinoam nods. According to her, it's black-and-white propaganda that tries to prevent one population group from seeing the other side's grief and pain, because if they can prevent people from walking in the other people's shoes, they also prevent empathy from bridging the gap between people. And Achinoam emphasizes that empathy can bridge great divides. She cites, for example, the reaction of imprisoned Palestinians the first time they were shown films about the Holocaust, and how they cried over the situation of the Jews. "Of course, it also affects Palestinians. If you are able to see another's grief, you can't help but begin to see the other as human. That's what propaganda prevents when it turns anyone who works for a free Palestine into a terrorist."

Moving on from the conflict, according to Achinoam, requires three things: acknowledgment, apologies, and sharing. "We have to start by recognizing each other as people who have dreams, rights, hopes, pains, frustrations, consciences, and a whole range of emotions. We need to recognize each other's history, religion, and standing in general. Next, we need to apologize to each other. Wherever and however it happened, we created great suffering for each other jointly. Everyone is an accomplice in the pain, both Israelis and Palestinians. And in the end, we have to share the burden of that grief. We must share land and resources so that we can live together in dignity. That's my philosophy," Achinoam says with confidence.

"You're speaking what's true to your heart, but what does that tell you about right now? How close are you to making peace?" I ask.

She looks away and gathers her thoughts for a moment. "We need a new government. I believe that the people are ready for it. The people can see that we're not getting anywhere, that we are destroying our relationships with the rest of the world, and that many people are suffering from this conflict. Israel is no longer the most popular member in the club," she says, explaining how, for example, Scandinavian countries completely changed their views on Israel and are now significantly more critical. "I'm also critical of the Israeli government, but I love my country. One has to distinguish between the government and the people." She sighs, and at that moment it dawns on me that we are sharing something. The experience of being held accountable for something for which you are not responsible, that you have criticized and acted in direct opposition to. It is similar to the way I and other Muslims are held accountable for actions committed by Islamist terrorists such as ISIL or Islamist regimes.

Achinoam barely breathes as she speaks. Her energy and drive are impressive. She touches on all the difficult topics. She is critical about her government's role in the conflict but is still able to see the pain that people on both sides suffer. I feel hope bubble up inside me, imagining peace might be just around the corner. And then a military plane flies just above our heads. It flies very low, and the engine noise overpowers the conversation. I lift my head to see the monster. Achinoam hardly notices it. She continues to speak, undisturbed, and I wonder whether the sound has become such a mundane experience that she's immune to it. Or is she just so focused that it's nothing but noise for her?

She talks relentlessly. She tells me that she's a realist, but also an idealist. She wants to see more interconnections between the two sides. Otherwise peace won't be made. I admire her ability to focus on what's essential.

"Where do you get your energy?" I ask.

She smiles and says that her mother asks her the same thing. "I take responsibility for myself. I've been given a gift with my speaking skills and my voice. It must be used for something good," she says with a steady gaze.

"But how do you remain optimistic when you talk about politicians, organizations, and movements that sabotage peace work?" I ask further.

Achinoam's response is very human—and liberating. "I constantly switch between optimism and pessimism. But I never use my pessimism as an excuse to do nothing. At times, I feel the depression pressing itself on me, but I make my way out of it by doing something positive. It's important to keep going, because action always leads to more action."

She is now planning one of the largest peace concerts in Israel's history, with many international performers. Initially, many of the people she contacted wouldn't stand up for Israel. "Solve your problems first, then we'll come," many of them told her. But she persuaded them, one at a time, with the argument that they shouldn't come to entertain, but to inspire people. "Even people who believe in peace are almost in a coma over the situation here," Achinoam says. "We need inspiration. Only by waking people up can we start to live again." She does not pretend these are easy conversations. "It's a very uphill climb. The worst are my Arab artist friends abroad. In their eyes, the very act of coming to Israel signals an endorsement of the conditions," she says, shaking her head. I know this premise well, because I encounter it often in my own work to encourage discussion.

We continue to talk about the hard parts of peace work. I feel the subject draining Achinoam of her energy. She leans back, and her expression becomes sad. "The hardest thing is all the hatred. I have two choices: Either I can give up my citizenship, put Israel and being a Jew behind me, and leave with my children to live far away from this conflict. Or I can fight to make this country a better place."

Imagine if everyone had that set of options, I think. This place requires commitment and activism, community and solidarity.

"If I don't act, then others will act. Everyone has an agenda. I have to fight for my peace agenda, otherwise others will be left to set the agenda." She continues, "The biggest problem is when you allow yourself to become a victim by saying that the others don't want us, they'll kill us, they'll take over our country. It becomes self-reinforcing and helps to justify abuse. Violence triggers more violence." She mentions some former Palestinian leaders who were involved in major actions against Israel—the Intifada—but who no longer believe violence is a tool for peace. According to Achinoam, Hamas is violent and has at least some responsibility for Israel's violent responses.

"But even among the people of Hamas, some people want peace and nonviolent solutions. We need to talk to them," she says. She believes that if someone is violent during a period in life, it doesn't mean their whole life has to be marked by violence.

"Another problem is that Palestinians and Israelis think peace is coming from outside our shared borders. But it is hard work that requires something of ourselves. The outside world can help, but they cannot solve our problems," Achinoam emphasizes. "Our leaders must begin to acknowledge other people's pain, and they've got to stop sweeping all the criticism from Palestinians off the table with the same two aces they've already played: anti-Semitism and the Holocaust."

When she says this, I can't help but think of a debate we had in Denmark some years ago. It centered on buses from the transportation company Movia. A Danish-Palestinian friendship association, chaired by Fathi, bought advertising space on some of Movia's buses and covered them with banners urging Danish citizens to boycott imports from the settlements in Palestine. The Danish Zionist Association attacked the campaign, which they called anti-Semitic, and Movia chose to pull the ads. The banners flew off the buses. I was the media spokesman for SF back then, and I called Bent Melchior to ask him how I should handle the case. Bent asked, "Would you think it was weird if Movia censored statements by Lars Lokke and Helle Thorning?"

"Yes," I replied, "there shouldn't be censorship of legal statements."

"That's exactly why Movia is in the wrong," Bent concluded. "This has nothing to do with anti-Semitism. It's about freedom of speech."

I will never forget my relief. Being accused of anti-Semitism is one of the worst feelings I know. It is often one of the first terms of derision that gets lobbed at Muslims like me.

But Achinoam's words also make me consider my own behavior on another topic, namely the debate over a proposed prohibition on circumcision, which flares up about every two years.

There are approximately 280,000 Muslims and six thousand Jews in Denmark, for whom circumcision of males is a crucial religious, cultural, and historical ritual. That's also the case in my family, and for me, which is why I want to discuss it. It has often been characterized by demonization and accusations, both from supporters of a ban and from those of us who believe that circumcision should continue to be allowed. I have often seen prohibitionists refer to anecdotes and very imprecise investigations, but never to medical evidence, of the negative consequences of circumcision. One very large scientific study has been made of the consequences, and it concludes that in only 0.2 percent of cases, i.e. two in a thousand, are there any complications, which aren't usually chronic. No one has proven that circumcision is harmful to health, and that's the main reason no country in the world has banned it. There remains a more principled argument, namely that circumcision of a boy is an abuse on the physical integrity of the child and leaves a lasting mark on the body without his consent. On the contrary, it can be said that parents make many decisions on their children's behalf with lasting significance. We choose our children's schools, we raise them in a determined way, give them healthy or unhealthy food, and we raise them in the culture and worldview that they carry with them throughout their lives.

This is how the arguments are currently posed, and this is how it should be in a democratic society. Something about what Achinoam said sent me off on this tangent. Something deeper than concrete arguments. It is about how, along the way, I've often thought that the resistance to circumcision is somehow caused by Islamophobia and anti-Semitism. As I sit with Achinoam, I doubt I've ever used the anti-Semitism card myself to demonize those I disagree with. After all, when people are opposed to circumcising boys, it doesn't have to be because they are anti-Semitic. Their resistance may also be simply because they find it wrong to cut into healthy boys. It is a recognition that is slowly unfolding, and part of me is resistant. But I sense that recognizing it is important. I feel that there's room for it.

As Achinoam continues to talk, the thoughts race through my head. She's seven years older than I am, beautiful as a goddess, sharp as a razor blade, and energetic as a Duracell rabbit.

Suddenly, I'm filled with optimism on behalf of the children in Hebron. They have Michael and Achinoam and thousands of other fiery folks fighting for a better future for them.

"I'm the mother of three children." Achinoam smiles. "And I would do anything to see them grow up in peace."

We take a selfie together, hug each other, and agree that I need to consider holding a peace concert in Denmark with Achinoam, so that we can bring Jewish and Palestinian citizens together.

My remaining time in Israel goes to visiting other organizations that work for peace. For example, Hand-in-Hand School, in Haifa, where Jewish and Palestinian children attend school together. I talk to more Jews and Palestinians who are either hopeful or pessimistic for the future of the region. I've learned that one should hold fast to those who are hopeful, and not cling too tightly to those with pessimistic visions of the future.

On the way back to Denmark, I'm filled with mixed feelings: Joy over my meetings with all peace workers from both sides of the conflict; frustration over the illegal settlements in the West Bank and the lack of dialogue between Jews and Palestinians. I'm filled with hope when I think of Michael's work, but darkness quickly surrounds me when I see the children in Hebron. A powerful voice inside me insists I remain optimistic and believe that peace is possible. But at the same time, there is a gentle stream of pessimism trickling in from my memory of the wall that is quietly poisoning me. I notice an inner war growing within me between optimism and pessimism.

There are roughly two thousand miles between the Holy Land and Denmark. But in the plane, it feels like the distance we travel should be measured in light-years. We seem to be far from a conflict of that magnitude in Denmark. But then I think of how quickly we were embroiled in World War II, and how far hatred took us when it was allowed to gallop with no one strong enough to pull back the reins. The Jews were made scapegoats for unemployment, crime, lack of welfare. Everything! The result of that passivity was twelve million people killed in concentration camps and communities, of which six million were Jews. In total, the Second World War cost the world more than fifty million people.

There is a paradox in the fact that the Israeli government can suppress another people so inhumanely when many of its own citizens went through such cruel treatment themselves. Of all the groups of people in the world, how can Jews justify the illegal settlements in Palestine? On the surface it can be difficult to understand. But I know that this kind of paradoxical behavior is not limited to the Israeli government. Just look at Mahmud, who has been in prison for ten years because he belonged to a minority, and now has the same hatred toward other Muslims because they are not "real." In my work with vulnerable citizens, I have also met many people who have been completely devastated by abuse. Some end up becoming abusers themselves. People who have experienced so much evil rarely become gentle and compassionate; they get scared, fearful, and they want to protect themselves first and foremost. Something has happened to people, organizations, and nations that abandon dialogue. They have often been through terrible things, and this has given them a democratic disadvantage. They suppress others, deprive them of their liberties, and justify violence with arguments like, "We have to look after our people" or "An eye for an eye." The problem with that approach is, as Gandhi said, that we all end up going blind. Paranoia takes over, as I myself experienced it in Jericho after sitting and talking with the wrong Bassam.

My trip to Israel and Palestine has also taught me that dialogue is the most difficult thing to maintain in a democracy. Dialogue requires time, patience, and trust. The easiest thing would be to ban unpopular opinions and actions, but to me that's just laziness. Yes, dialogue requires patience and trust, but it's also the strength of democracy, that we do not kill or judge our opponents, but instead struggle with them to find a point of consensus.

At Kastrup Airport, I am filled with deep gratitude. I am lucky and proud to be a citizen of a country with freedom of speech and democracy. Where one is innocent until proven otherwise. Where the parliament is the supreme authority and where it is the people who elect and fire their politicians. My stomach cramps up once more in Istanbul, and my experiences in Hebron remind me once again how important it is that we Danes do not take our liberty for granted. That we jointly work to protect democratic conversations and speak out at the injustice when someone uses violence to make their point. I could kiss the police officer who sits at the counter and examines my passport, because I know he is not corrupt, that our courts are independent, and that our press is free.

When I get home, I plan to roll up my sleeves and continue to build bridges between population groups, so we never give up conversations that can create peace.

CHAPTER 9

IS THERE A POINT?

"The ultimate tragedy is not the oppression and cruelty done by evil people, but that good people remain silent."

–Martin Luther King

Back in 2010, I wanted to find out why the neo-Nazi who emailed me hated me so much when he didn't know anything about me. He rejected the offer of a mediation meeting with the police, but I pursued the idea, and it became the starting point for me to seek out people who sent me hate mail. Since then, I have met with many for dialogue over coffee. But the more I search for answers, the more questions emerge. One of the questions I encounter more often than others is: Is it useful at all?

At first, I thought that, if people who hated Muslims met me, then they might become "good" again. Today, however, I can see how impossible that form of savior-complex mission is. I no longer meet with people to convince them that what I think is right, but more to hear what they have to say. But the more I listen, the more complicated everything becomes. There is not one answer or solution to how to fight powerlessness, frustration, social problems, and hate.

I spent a long time defining the purpose of my mission. Was it my place to convert those I meet so that they think the same way I do, or should I, as a fly on the wall, observe what they say and do? Do I have to report people who resort to hate speech, or do I have to acknowledge that their commitment to a cause, no matter how venomous it may be, is as legitimate as mine—as long as they do not use or encourage violence? Kim in the colonial garden house, the boys from the Red Square, Mee in North Zealand, and all the others I've met, each has their own piece of the truth.

One of my meetings in particular challenged me. Never in the nine years that I have spent drinking coffee with people have I felt the need to double-check information from someone I have met. But I did, after I had spoken to Mahmud. His story was so unbelievable, and his movement from Communist to Islamist so extreme, that I had to investigate whether it could really happen as he said it did. Was there a story behind his story, or was he just mentally ill? Just posing those questions made me dislike my own reasoning. Just sick! It is convenient and simplistic to reduce extremism to illness. It's nobody's fault that Mahmud has ended up where he is. And what if I actually received confirmation that Mahmud is mentally ill? Is my mission then successful? Is it about showing that extremists are only sick humans?

Despite my objections, I contact my friend Serhat, who knows Mahmud and would like to tell his version of the story. Serhat first met Mahmud in the high school in Diyarbakir, where they attended together until Mahmud was arrested because he was allegedly involved in the killings of five police officers and five soldiers. Mahmud denied that he had killed the soldiers, but confessed to the killings of the police officers, and was sentenced to the death penalty. In prison he stood by the fact that he was Kurdish and a communist. No matter what kind of torture he was subjected to, he never renounced his Kurdish identity. But even though he didn't break in prison, the torture destroyed him mentally. It was clear to his friends when he was released, and they urged him to flee; otherwise, there was great risk that he would be imprisoned again. The Kurdish movement helped him escape, and he was granted asylum in Denmark. Here he became part of the far left and continued his activities for their cause. He often participated in demonstrations and ended up fighting several times. The torture left deep marks in him. Once, he was admitted to the psychiatric ward. Since then he has come into conflict with communist Kurds, and over time he could not be included in the Kurdish rebel movement, PKK. He got help for his trauma, but too late. And along the way, he became more and more religious.

Today Mahmud is a Salafist. Much of Serhat's information confirms what Mahmud has already told me. But knowing Mahmud has killed five policemen has me shaken. It underlines how much Mahmud put into his fight for communism and the Kurdish cause. At the same time, I am still amazed over the evolution Mahmud has made from communism and nationalism to Salafism. Since our meeting, I often think of Mahmud when I hear claims that some people cannot be educated away from their stances. Mahmud has changed his stance.

Overcoming Hate Through Dialogue

In fact, he went from one extreme to the other. He is one of many examples of people who changed their opinions, political views, and ideology. Others might say Mahmud is an extremist who has just switched the causes he uses to cultivate his extremism. But that's not true either. For me, Mahmud is an example that shows that people cannot be reduced to merely extremists. That he has extreme attitudes in one area does not mean his attitudes are extreme in relation to everything. I sometimes still text with Mahmud, and each time I catch glimpses of new, usually hurting, but human sides of him that I haven't seen before. He is interested in politics, he listens to P1, he is on Facebook. And when, at one point, he read in the media that I'd received hate emails, he wrote me a text hoping that Allah would protect me. Mahmud's attitudes haven't become less extreme after our meeting, and I am still nervous that he may one day go too far for his cause. The fear of extremism also exists in me.

After my visit to the Hizb ut-Tahrir Mosque, it was revealed in the media that their second imam, Mundhir Abdallah, called for the killing of Jews. He has been reported to the police by the Jewish community. I hope he gets the punishment he deserves. But I'm worried about how effective the hate speech is in recruiting the boys from the Red Square.

One of them I think about most is Hasan, the angry young man with the gun under his t-shirt. Will Hizb ut-Tahrir get him in its clutches, or will the student, Naveed, succeed in getting him onto a path toward democracy? I'm worried about those boys. Will the young people end up on welfare, like many of their parents? Will they find success in a band? Are they lost because no one in their communities offered them a friendly hand, or will they fail because they won't take personal responsibility and seize the opportunity when it comes? Or will they put my worry to rest and succeed in creating their own lives for the benefit of both themselves and society?

Hasan is also on my mind as I ride my bike past the Red Square one day. Like many times before, I scour the square looking for him and the other boys. They are not there. I drive past the square, further along Mimersgade, and then turn right down Bragesgade. Suddenly, someone yells, "Özlem!"

As I turn around, I see a young man behind the wheel of a small car. His eyes are smiling, and before I can reach him, he parks his car on the sidewalk. It's Hasan. Several months have passed since our meeting at the Red Square, but I was just thinking of him. I smile back, jump off my bicycle, and walk briskly toward him. Hasan opens the door and exits the car. He's wearing a pair of dark jeans and a light gray sweater. He looks more like a young man from Hellerup than one from Norrebro. We hug each other as though we are family.

Just as I'm about to ask how he's doing, he starts talking. "I've completed my education, and now I'm a bricklayer. I've signed a contract with a company and have been given the responsibility of tearing down a building with a crew."

I don't know what's going on in my head, but I follow a sudden urge and start patting him down to look for the gun he carried the last time we met. Hasan laughs and raises both of his arms so I can more easily frisk him. "I'm done with that, Özlem," he says with a big smile.

I want him to swear it. "Say 'Wallah!' " I say in my thickest Norrebro accent.

"Wallah!" he replies.

Then we hug again as I praise him. I know from my work with vulnerable minority children that many of them have great love for their mothers. Therefore, a mother is often the motivator in troubled homes, while the fathers are more often associated with violence, quarrels, and discomfort.

"Your mother must be proud of you," I say.

Hasan is clearly not used to praise. He blushes and has difficulty keeping eye contact. "Have you finished writing your book?" he asks.

"Almost," I reply, inviting him to visit my office with the boys.

We exchange phone numbers and hug one more time before saying goodbye.

A few days later, a text message comes from Hasan, asking when he can read the book. Immediately my concern sets in, because it is three o'clock in the morning, and why is he not sleeping? Has he fallen back into the criminal career? The explanation brings me down to earth. Hasan has just been to a party. "I'm going to sleep too," he writes, adding, "but hey, if you need anything, I'm here."

Why Hasan has been so much on my mind is perhaps because we both come from a lower level of society. My experience in social work tells me that Hasan could easily fall back on his old ways a time or two. Whether he gets back on track will largely depend on his family, his friends, and his work situation. If a healthy community can lure him there, and then hold onto him and invest in building a trusting relationship with him, the democratic community might win him over. But if he loiters around on the street for too long without work, money, and positive role models, others will be happy to give him the identity and confidence he craves. As Carsten Jensen says, "No man is an island, so his motives and inspiration can come from many places." I don't know how it ends for Hasan or the other boys from the square, but our meeting reminds me that there is always hope.

The boys are not only inspired by those they meet in Norrebro. Like everyone else, they are also influenced by the world we are a part of. Hasan has roots in the Middle East, as I do. What happens several thousand miles away can be instrumental in whether bridges are built or burned in Denmark. For me, the bridge to Turkey was burned on the virtue that I'm a democrat with Kurdish roots. Turkey has just been through a referendum that gave the Turkish President Tayyip Erdogan the power to decide over the parliament, judiciary, and police. In other words, a narrow number of votes has given Erdogan unequal power. More than five hundred thousand Kurds are internally displaced, nearly 250,000 have been arrested, and

Turkey tops the statistics as the country that imprisons the most journalists from around the world. I have criticized the obvious human rights violations that have taken place in Turkey, both because I am a democrat and because I have Kurdish roots. Since my trip to Israel, I've been reported by resident supporters of Erdogan to the Turkish authorities for terrorism. I know that there is actually an open line to Erdogan's front office where you can call and report people. So, for the time being, I cannot travel to Turkey to visit family and friends, nor intermediaries in the country, as I did on the way to the Holy Land, because I risk being detained or imprisoned. The saddest thing is that the vote in Turkey has created distance between me and people here in Denmark with Turkish roots, with whom I have worked and forged relationships over the years. We don't visit or talk anymore. Erdogan has managed to divide us. It is just one of many examples of why we must never underestimate how important political leaders are to dialogue between population groups and to strengthening democracy.

As Bent Melchior says, there is always light at the end of the tunnel. When we have a hard time seeing it, it's because the tunnel isn't always straight. It's also important that we, as human beings, can bend toward each other at the right times so that both parties can benefit from the closeness. Since my visit to the Holy Land, more turns of the tracks seem to be blocking the light around the world and fewer people seem to be leaning toward each other.

One day, shortly after the presidential election, I sat down with Bent Melchior for salmon, and felt hopelessness surrounding me at the thought that the work of Michael and other peacemakers had now been wasted. But then Bent reminded me that Michael's work is needed now more than ever. Michael succeeded with the conference "Religious Leaders for Peace in the Middle East" in Spain in bringing Islamist imams who helped organize the Hamas movement to stand side by side with rabbis from Israeli settlements and representatives from the Christian churches in the Holy Land. I was sent a picture of the religious leaders gathered together by Michael, who wrote that they all signed a statement at the conference: "All three monotheistic religions regard human life as sacred... The violence that claimed to be done in the name of God is a defilement of His name, a crime against those who are created in His image, and a debasement of faith." The Israeli and Palestinian politicians were encouraged to return to the negotiating table. Work has been done in individual communities and congregations, where the aim is for young rabbis and imams to learn new ways of speaking and new methods of teaching young people. The hope is that a joint vision of religious peace will inspire many, and that peace will become inevitable. A few months after the conference, Michael received a British Peace Prize for his work in creating interfaith peace.

When darkness surrounds me, I spend extra energy remembering that there is light at the end of the tunnel—even if it is difficult at times to free oneself from pessimism. The best inoculation from darkness is to surround yourself with people who are all fired up like lighthouses, who can share their courage, their responsibility in building bridges, and their hope of a peaceful future. When darkness sets in, the lighthouses show the way.

Credit: Media Department of the Spanish Ministry of Foreign Affairs

Speaking of lighthouses, I am still trying to get Achinoam to Denmark so she can hold a peace concert for Palestinians and Jews. I don't know who'd come to such a concert. Will it be only those who are already convinced, or will skeptics also show up? I have to believe that every little step makes a difference.

Thinking back to my conversations with Ahmed and Hamza from Hizb ut-Tahrir, I can understand why it might seem tempting and easy to ban attitudes, because the conversations are some of the most difficult things to follow in a democracy. It requires time, trust, and patience. When I was at Hizb ut-Tahrir's mosque, I didn't feel like we both had an equal share in finding a solution that was fair. I had a difficult time accepting Ahmed and Hamza's criticisms of democracy, even though it is their democratic right to disagree with me. And when Hamza thundered against democracy and against Jews, I most wanted to restrict his freedom of expression. I thought their attitudes were way out there, and I still think so. In my eyes, some people take nonsense much too seriously.

At times, I am also gripped by my powerlessness in the face of extremist views, and I am tempted to believe that I can't make myself try to change my thinking. But Carsten Jensen always reminds me that the fundamental difference between democracy and dictatorship is that in democracy, everyone—including the nonsensical, the extremists, and the fundamentalists—has the right to speak out, as long as they do not call for violence. Whenever I fall in and want to limit extremist attitudes, he tells me that democracy cannot protect itself with censorship and prohibition. Those things do not make democracy stronger but, on the contrary, weaker. Sometimes it is hard to live up to the democratic principles that Carsten lives by. But the truth in his words make sense to me when I look through the vantage point of a radical right-wing extremist who thinks that I am the nonsensical one whose freedoms he would like to restrict. Or when supporters of Erdogan want to restrict my rights, because I am Kurdish, which they think is enough to label me a terrorist.

In Europe and the United States, extremism is marching forward. The Middle East is at war, and religious and political violence is taking too many lives. Every time the terror hits Europe, my mailbox fills up with hate mail. While reading the messages about how awful I am, and how I should just go home, I might on occasion feel hatred bubble up inside me—hatred for those who send the messages and for those who carry out terror. I sense the hatred in ordinary Muslims who walk quickly past and don't leave flowers at the embassies of terrorist countries. And I feel the hatred of the elderly lady who came to me smiling on the street to whisper, "You are unwanted here."

As I take days off my calendar to respond to "go home" messages, I feel in my body how much our democracy is under pressure from extremists. Political leaders repeat the compulsive phrase, "We must protect our freedoms." Sometimes, you can see that they don't even believe what they say. Freedom is weakened, not only by terrorists, but also by politicians who weaken it, one bill at a time. For example, since I met with Hizb ut-Tahrir, a large majority in the parliament has decided to limit the freedom of speech of imams, priests, and rabbis. I recently spoke with an editor from the *Jutland Post*, who said that much of what the newspaper defended during the Mohammedan crisis, politicians have since let slip away. I had to give him that. The majority in the parliament gives the extremists exactly what they want: a weaker democracy. I know that anti-democratic actions are usually defended with arguments that democracy must be vigilantly protected. But the boys at the Red Square, the fundamentalists at Hizb ut-Tahrir, and the extremist Mahmud believe that makes us hypocrites. And I agree with them. I don't believe that we can fight extreme and fundamentalist positions by reserving democratic rights for those who agree with us. Instead, we should argue against extremist viewpoints so loudly that young people can't help but hear more rational arguments.

We all use media to get to know what's happening around us. Danes like Jimmy, Kim, and Angelo do not have much contact with ethnic minorities, and the stories they read in the media become their primary source of information about immigrants. This is why I also believe that the media fail in the responsibility they have been entrusted with when they choose to cover ethnic minority news without any nuance in their coverage. There is a large group of well-educated Danes with minority roots whose voices journalists are rarely interested in hearing when integration and immigration are debated. The media talks about them, but rarely with them. Ethnic minorities like Muslims are often depicted in stereotyped language, such as tiny little women wrapped in scarves.

All of the media is not guilty of this all the time, but as a whole, the media are not conscious of their responsibilities as "the fourth state power." The stigma and generalization they broadcast through mainstream society helps to dig ditches deeper than planets. The reactions to the media are different. Some people can no longer bother with Denmark and leave for some other place that's more welcoming. Others stay here but are never invited into a community. At the same time, I believe that the overall focus of the media helps contribute to the production and dissemination of fake news, the sole purpose of which is to dig deeper trenches between demographic groups. We demonize each other, not only on social media, but also in our social relationships. I worry that it may ultimately weaken the democratic conversation.

An even greater responsibility lies with politicians. I think that the generalizations from politicians alienate large segments of the constituency. That only threatens the cohesiveness of society and our perception of democratic values.

Shortly after my visit with Kim, he sent me an email with a challenge. If I could showcase a Muslim family with five to seven children, all of whom are well-integrated into society, he would donate five thousand dollars to charity. "A family where everyone does what they can to become a part of my beloved Denmark." I wrote back knowing that, if I found that family, he would want to see another family, preferably with ten children. I sincerely doubt he needs an example to become convinced, or a lack of one to confirm his suspicions about Muslim families. I am willing to find the family, but at the same time I know it will be pointless. I know I'm correct in this assumption when Kim, in the same email where he challenges me to prove him wrong, also writes that Muslims are "violent and impossible to integrate." The ditch is too deep there.

We texted, emailed, and met—but without agreeing on very much. However, Kim has always kept a warm tone and has been kind when delivering "rush home" messages to me. I remember one time when he visited me in Copenhagen. We had an hour-long conversation where Kim repeatedly said, "I don't mind you, but I don't think you should be in my country." In the end, I couldn't accommodate his viewpoint anymore. I no longer wanted to build any bridge with Kim, because he wasn't doing any building in my direction.

"You are hateful," I told him. "Hate-filled, nationalistic, and extremely discriminatory." I didn't give him any space to defend himself. He should understand exactly how I felt listening to him. And I wanted it to hurt him as much as it hurt me. I had spent so many hours and days on him, but no matter how much I tried to listen, understand, and accommodate him, he did not once give an inch. He was suspicious and judgmental, and continued to generalize. He took up the right to speak on behalf of Denmark and all the Danes. That day we left each other in anger, and I promised myself that I would never have contact with him again. That night, I had a hard time falling asleep, and at midnight a text message chimed on my phone. It was from Kim, who wrote, "Özlem. For the first time in my life, I go to bed feeling hated/unwanted. I don't understand why. Maybe I'm stupid. Maybe I don't understand the purpose of our meeting. But dear Özlem, I have no hatred toward you. Sleep well."

Although I sometimes feel I can't take it, the dialogue with Kim has never really ended. He wrote before going to a job interview with a trucking company, and I called him up to give him some support. When he got the job, we exchanged smiles with each other. When spring came, he sent pictures of the flowers in his garden, and one day, when he saw that too many people were calling me names, he sent me sunrises. He was also one of the first people to send a sweet email when I was in Ankara in the summer of 2016 during the Turkish military coup attempt. However, these are bright spots that pale in comparison to the numerous emails, videos, and articles he sends about conflicts that Muslims and terrorists create for the Danes. We deeply disagree about the credibility of the news sources he uses to try to add credibility to his claims. What we can agree on is that we will never agree. Kim's contact is never threatening, and he doesn't use foul language, but it hurts my heart sometimes to even lend an ear to it.

In Nyborg, Angelo reads some of the same news, but unlike Kim, he is often so furious that he sends me inflamed texts. Initially, I try to keep the dialogue going, but it's hard to talk to someone who threatens violence as a solution, and, in my eyes, he chose to stop the dialogue. Still, he surprises me when he's the first to send me a sweet text message wishing my mother a speedy recovery from cancer when he reads about it on my Facebook page.

Sometimes I do a little thought experiment: What if I had met Angelo ten years ago? What was he like back then? Would it have been possible to reach him? But then, I think of myself ten years ago, and, unfortunately, I was one of the biggest trench diggers. It was thanks to Jacob Holdt that I brought my inner racist to the forefront and realized how much I was demonizing people who had not been fair with me. Demonization works both ways. It is not just the right wing that is demonizing by calling Muslims potential terrorists. It also happens on the left toward people who vote right-wing and are called village idiots and fools. Here too, a pattern emerges again that crosses cultural and ethnic boundaries: our prejudices and generalizations about one another are similar in their reduction of humanity to less than equal.

This is not to say that there is nothing wrong with prejudice. First, people have a natural tendency to be insecure about the unknown, and, secondly, prejudice can be practical when making decisions with little knowledge. The problem arises when we don't examine our prejudices to see if they are based in reality. When curiosity ceases to lead us, prejudice and generalizations step in to dominate, and it is difficult to find a common language once prejudice is in command.

It is when we listen to each other with curiosity and struggle to find a common language that we find ways to build a bridge we might not have ever believed was possible. I saw that in Odense when I met Jimmy and his wife, Lone. Jimmy sent me an email with the results of the MRI. It showed that he had a collapsed disk, and he was going to a spinal center to find out whether he needed an operation. He was nervous about the possibility of surgery, and we emailed back and forth about it. The news I received from him in the following days was not good. He'd suffered an aortic aneurysm, and it was uncertain if the doctors could operate on him. He was sad and scared. "I cry like a baby," he wrote. It saddens me that the doctors have been unable to relieve his pain. He gets morphine, but it doesn't seem to help.

He keeps writing to me. He hasn't had any surgeries, as it would be too risky. He needs to find a nursing home where he can receive rehabilitation therapy. And in the midst of all that chaos and stress, he has to worry about medical expenses. The medication alone has cost him several thousand kroner, and his pension is only ten thousand kroner (or 1,480 US dollars). He is frustrated and deeply disappointed by politicians that he feels don't care about people who cannot afford medicine. People who have been struggling all their lives and do not feel secure that the money they have paid in taxes will come back to help them when it's needed. But then, even in the midst of telling me about his hopeless situation, he asks me how I'm doing. "Now take care of yourself," he writes.

Jimmy's frustration is primarily due to a welfare system that wasn't there for him when he needed it. His worn-out body has trouble keeping up with the rest of him. He feels let down by the system, by the politicians, and by the parties he supported with his vote. At times, he has also turned his anger toward Muslims and immigrants.

But Jimmy is not a racist. First of all, he is deeply frustrated with the current situation, and, secondly, he is angry with those who make it harder for the majority—especially when they are immigrants. Personally, while I recognize concrete examples of times when people from minority backgrounds have behaved poorly, I also listen when "New Danes" and immigrants talk about their negative experiences with Danes. We get nowhere by ignoring problems.

If inequality grows and our welfare system continues to deteriorate, the distance dividing people like Jimmy from the boys from the Red Square will continue to grow. Individually, they believe that the other group gets more than they receive, and what results is an unfair fight based on erroneous prejudice between groups who are just trying not to be at the very bottom level of our society—all while the top tier of society reaps benefits from their high incomes and tax cuts, and a general surplus of resources.

Although Kim, Jimmy, Angelo, and the boys from the Red Square could reasonably direct their criticism upward, they often do the opposite—they kick down. This is linked to the fact that the leaders of these groups are skilled at channeling anger in a destructive direction, such as when it is alleged that welfare is not offered to refugees. That kind of reasoning foments hatred between population groups that are struggling under the same neglect from those who have the power to make life less difficult all around. "But isn't that true?" some ask. "Money for welfare can't be spent on refugees?" Yes, but it's only part of the truth. A wider view of the issue reveals there's a lot of fat elsewhere that we're not trimming. For example, tax cuts to the richest in Denmark, the purchase of fighter jets that cost thirty billion kroner (four billion US dollars), corporate relief to the wealthiest companies, a lack of efforts against tax havens that the wealthiest use to avoid paying their share, excessive benefits to property owners—all those things and more are part of the reason why the welfare budget is so tight. There is always a choice! I worry that inequality is growing.

For the greater inequality there is in a society, the deeper the trenches are between us.

One day I received an email from Jimmy. It was shortly after a majority in the parliament passed an opinion that descendants of immigrants, i.e., some, like me, were not considered true Danes.

> To Lone and me, you are and will always be one of the most beautiful, most beautiful Danish people in the country. There are many Danes who could learn from you, by God. And whatever they adopt in parliament, there are not many left who sympathize with them. They're going to have to work very hard to regain my confidence in them.

The intent behind passing the opinion was probably not to strengthen the shared national sentiment between Jimmy and me. But nevertheless, it inspired us and hundreds of thousands of people to come closer together. Danes of all colors posted pictures on social media. I saw them everywhere. The mission is a success, I thought. We've become a strong community! But is the mission to gather under the Danish flag or under the rainbow flag? Should we be homogeneous, or should our diversity make us strong? Or I am I just drawing false contradictions?

Henrik from the Inner Mission is one of the people I'm certain I will remain in contact with for many years, even though we will never gather under a rainbow flag. He and I fundamentally disagree about gays and his fundamentalist approach to religion. But he is also Henrik, the man with the great personality and a great wealth of knowledge. He is fun to debate, because he never makes it personal, but instead laughs when the discussions become heated and we both can see that it is time to breathe. Recently I had lunch with Henrik, his wife, and his father-in-law. Before we ate, Henrik asked us to pray with him, and to my great surprise, I was mentioned in the prayer. I was so moved I could barely hold back my tears. What kind of power makes it possible for us, despite disagreements and fundamental differences in faith and political views, to end up in each other's prayers? Henrik said "Amen," and I said "Amin," because that's what Muslims say. After the prayer, we touch our faces and then our hearts. The purpose is for the good words we've spoken to go directly into our brains and into our hearts. So I did at Henrik. We agreed that it was beautiful.

But as beautiful as faith can be, it can also be used as a devastating weapon that kills and excludes and abuses. My faith means a lot to me, but when I stood in front of the Wailing Wall in Jerusalem, watching the crowd of Jews, Muslims, and Christians swarm past one another seeming not to see each other with clear sight of their humanity, I could understand, for the first time in my life, why some like Karl Marx refer to religion as an opiate for the masses.

In recent years, I have reflected more often on the influence of religion on society. I often feel divided when discussing religion with strongly believing people like Hamza, Mahmud, Henrik, and Johan. Part of me is, like them, a believer in my faith, but another part of me does not like them, nor their ideas about faith. For me, faith is not exclusive, but inclusive. I feel most secure in my own faith when it's private and I'm alone with it. It is a part of me, and I understand people who become more faithful to their beliefs, the more they are told not to believe. I was quite extreme myself during my teenage years. My experience has taught me that religion can certainly be part of the problem, but it can also be at least as much a part of the solution.

Believers or not, we all have something that matters to us. Something we each struggle for. That's why Johan has spent sixteen years of his life trying to cure homosexuals. For decades, Nadia has stood up to the Israeli soldiers in Bethlehem and the oppressive Palestinian men of Fatah and Hamas. Nomi is fighting a continuing battle for human rights. Kim is convinced that one day he will succeed in ridding Denmark of immigrants.

I'm also fighting for something I feel is important, something that is not merely self-evident. To me, democracy, open dialogue, and freedom are worth fighting for and protecting. Not just for me, my family, and my friends, but also for those who think the opposite of me, and especially for my enemies.

I want to welcome more people in our democratic community. And this can only be done with debate, critical conversation, and insistence on a fair and rational dialogue. That's my mission!

I went into politics when I was a nurse at Bispebjerg Hospital. When I started my career in the medical field, I wanted to improve conditions for children and adolescents with mental disabilities. Those kids were the reason I became politically active. First in the Danish Nursing Council, later in association life, afterward in party politics and then in the parliament for almost eight years. I am deeply disappointed by how many bridges were burned by the parliament in Christiansborg, and how deep the trenches many of our politicians are digging are growing. Every day, I wish that Christiansborg would stop pitting population groups against each other, and that some elements of the press would try to be more balanced in their coverage. My fourteen years in party politics in SF taught me that, even on the left, there are strong forces that want to speak to the right-wing nationalists and populists by resuscitating the hatred between population groups. The strategy is to draw more Muslim-critical voters, and by doing so, get closer to power, which is why I opted out of SF. I could not stand for an agenda that digs deeper trenches between population groups instead of building stronger bridges.

For too many years of my political life, I thought power was located elsewhere, beyond my reach. As a nurse, as a union woman, as a party member, and as a member of parliament, I thought other groups decided more. I don't think so anymore. Now, I believe that we each have the power to make decisions, where we are right now, and that is why we each have a responsibility to do something. I'm back where I began, in grassroots work. Now I put my trust in the people, because I believe that the people also have the power. All the major movements—the women's movement, the cooperative movement, the environmental movement, the peace movement, the labor movement, the student movement, and many others—all started among ordinary people whose personal commitment to a cause was the driving force. These movements have all grown from the bottom up, all created lasting changes, and each strengthened the cohesiveness of our society. The people have risen and pushed the elected representatives in parliament to find solid, humanistic, and sustainable solutions. Big movements also often go hand-in-hand with strong leaders. An obvious example is the civil rights movement and Martin Luther King, Jr., and here, in Denmark, you can look to the high school movement and Grundtvig, or the labor movement and Anker Jorgensen.

When I was a kid, I dreamed of saving the world. My parents dreamed of forty sheep and a house in a village in Turkey. Today, my parents can afford to realize their dream, while I find it difficult to speak with any optimism about mine. For while the child's dream is liberating in its naïveté, an adult dreamer runs the risk of ridicule. My dream has evolved, but one point is the same: When I am old, seated in my rocking chair in my colony garden, surrounded by my grandchildren, I would like to say that I did everything I could to make the world a better place. Not to prove anything to others. Not to get a medal. I want to be able to say in good conscience at the end of my life that I took my personal responsibility to make a difference seriously.

I've already broken the mold in some critical ways. I came from a working-class home, hated population groups I didn't understand, and at times I've been very extreme in my religious interpretations. My friendships with Turks, racists, Jews, and Danes have inoculated me against generalizations and prejudices. Along the way, I have been helped by fiery folks who carried the weight of their personal responsibility on their own shoulders, and who have extended their hands to me and invited me into the democratic community. They have spent time arguing with me and talking to me. Those people have shaped me into a democrat and a bridge-builder. Had it not been for those fiery folks, for the lighthouses, and the safety net of the welfare society, I would never have reached as far as I have made it so far. No one abandoned me! And that's why I don't want to give up on others who find themselves in the same situations I've been in.

It is possible to move people away from the edge of a precipice. And every time we save one human, we also save a part of the world.

You, me—*we*—have that power—together!

The Ten Commandments of the Bridge-Builder

1. **Speak kindly**—The more we disagree, the more important it becomes to keep the kind tone in your voice and shoot the ball straight with the other guy. Then everyone in the conversation gets smarter.

2. **Praise the other**—Conversation requires two parties. Praise your counterpart for having the courage to enter into the conversation. The more positive expressions we exchange, the more confidence we build in each other.

3. **Recognize emotions**—You and your counterpart may both be frustrated, feeling powerless, or fearing the loss of identity, values, or principles. Recognize the other person's feelings, even if you do not agree with their arguments.

4. **Find common starting points**—We have far more that binds us together than that which separates us. First, find something you agree on. Then it is easier to talk about the disagreements.

5. **See humanity**—It is legitimate to distance yourself when you disagree, but distance yourself from the attitude, never the human. A human being is very different and much more than merely their opinions.

6. **Listen and search for a common language**—Listen for words and examples that the other person uses to tell you about what they value. Seek to understand and open up to them about what you can identify with.

7. **Eat together**—Where there is food, there is peace. Invite yourself inside politely and remember to bring something you can eat together.

8. **Laugh together**—Humor is one of the fastest, most direct, and most effective ways to bridge divisions between people. When we can laugh together, we can also cry together.

9. **Keep hope**—It takes time and patience to build trust in each other. It may look dark on the journey to understanding, but that's simply because the tunnel isn't straight—there is always light at the end.

10. **Friendship is a vaccine**—When you succeed in bridging a division, you establish a friendship that is resistant to the disease of prejudice and will help you remember that other people are dynamic and complex.

Good luck building!

ACKNOWLEDGMENTS

This book allows you to meet with individuals most people don't want to talk to and whose arguments many choose to overlook, because in many ways they have attitudes that are difficult to accommodate and are, in some cases, hurtful.

First, thank you to the people who contributed to the book. Without their honesty, courage, and willingness to talk, there would be no book. I am grateful to have been welcomed into your world and to have had the opportunity to explore your points of view. I would also like to thank Michael Melchior, Fathi El-Abed, Maia Feldman, Marie Holen, and Linda Herzberg, who have been helpful in making contact with the people I have met and conversed with in Israel and Palestine.

Then a big thank you to my three "lighthouses," photographer Jacob Holdt, Chief Rabbi Bent Melchior, and author Carsten Jensen.

I'll never forget the day I sat in my good friend Jacob's kitchen, crying over the neo-Nazi who threatened me, and Jacob advised me to seek out the people who send me hate emails. Jacob has continued to be a good friend, and he's never more than a phone call away. With his help and support, I can hope, one day, to be as open-minded as he is.

Bent welcomed me within the Jewish community in Denmark. He is also my confidante and the "adopted grandfather" with whom I share my insecurities and inadequacies. When I am most engrossed by pessimism and strongly doubt that dialogue makes a difference, he illuminates my path and gives me the courage to swim against the flow. Bent was kind enough to review the sections in this book about Israel and Palestine so that I could remain focused on the dialogue and not the conflict.

As I traveled to Maribo in 2009, I did not in my wildest imagination believe that Carsten, whom I met on the train, would later become my good friend and a fellow democrat. With him, I learned to fight for freedom of speech, especially for those I deeply disagreed with. Every time I am challenged on my understanding of democracy, Carsten is the lifeline that helps me gain perspective and engage in dialogue. I am deeply honored and grateful that Carsten has read this book with a critical eye and has generously, lovingly, and pedagogically shared his knowledge.

Thanks to my wonderfully talented editor for the Danish edition of this book, Anne Weinkouff, who has helped me critically and faithfully throughout the book. Thanks to her reflections, advice, and guidance, the book has been completed.

A special thank you to my other editor, Simon Lund-Jensen, whose talent is exceptional. He has been a tireless sparring partner and faithful contributor to the making of this book. He has relentlessly edited my work, and he has been an indispensable support when I have at times doubted my own abilities as a writer.

Thanks to my agent Jason Bartholomew, and to editors Shawn Hoult and MJ Fievre at Mango Publishing.

Thanks to photographer Robin Skjoldborg and makeup artist Carina Rehmeier for the great cover photo.

To Devrim, my beloved husband: Without your support and confidence, I would never have dared to throw myself into the bridge-building work. Although I know you may be worried when I seek out people who hate someone like me, you are the firm rock that always gives me strength and courage. Thank you for reading the book, for the critical conversations, and for always being deeply involved and interested in my #dialoguecoffee meetings.

Dear Furkan, you are the coolest and most adventurous son anyone could wish for. Thank you for being so enthusiastic and interested in the people who contributed to the book throughout the writing process. Your questioning and ability to turn things upside down has forced me to see a case from both sides.

Sweet Yasmin and Yusuf, I look forward to the day when you can understand this book. I thought of you as I wrote it, and I hope the book can help make the Denmark you grow up in a better place.

Oo

ABOUT THE AUTHOR

Özlem Sara Cekic was born in Turkey in 1976. She lived in Finland for two years while her parents worked as caretakers and cleaners at the Turkish Embassy in Helsinki. Her family then moved to Denmark at the start of the 1980s.

Özlem was the first in her family to go to high school, after which she completed her education in nursing. She worked in the psychiatric department from 2000 to 2007 with children and youths with mental illnesses, traumatized refugees, and individuals with a drug addiction. In 2003, she was elected to the board of the Danish Nurses Organization as the first woman with an ethnic minority background. For several years, she represented all healthcare workers with an ethnic minority background and was the chairwoman for the network, which put tackling discrimination on the agenda. She is an honorary member of the Schizophrenia Association.

She was elected to the Danish parliament and served from 2007 to 2015 as one of the first female politicians with a Muslim immigrant background. Since 2015, Özlem has been giving talks and providing advice in Denmark, and internationally, on how to build bridges between ethnic minorities, companies, organizations, and local government. She devised the "dialogue coffee" concept, which involves her regularly holding conversations over coffee with people who have sent her hate mail—usually at their home. This is based on her belief that what binds us together is far greater than what separates us. The BBC made a documentary about Özlem and her work with the hashtag #dialoguecoffee, which was shown around the world to an audience of approximately five million.

In 2018, she became the second Dane in history to give a TED Talk, opening up about her experiences with dialogue coffee. At present, the talk has been viewed by two million people. You can learn more by visiting dialoguecoffee.org.

Özlem is also the founder and chairwoman of a non-profit organization called Bridgebuilders—Denmark´s first Centre for Dialogue Coffee, which aims to prevent hate and violence. The Association teaches children about building bridges between different population groups, builds bridges between Jewish, Muslim and Christian schools, and seeks out religious extremists to invite them to open dialogue arrangements, which are hosted by the Association. Learn more about the organization at www.brobyggerne.dk.

Özlem has written several books, including books for children. She has received four prizes for democracy in Denmark for her work with dialogue. She was also awarded the friendship prize from SOS-Racism in 2007 and the same year the Kurdish President Masoud Barzani gave her the "Kurds of the Year" award. In 2016, she received "the year's political fiery soul" prize. She and her husband, Devrim, have three children, Furkan, Yasmin Aze, and Yusuf.

Connect with Özlem on social media:
Facebook: Ozlem Sara Cekic
Twitter: @cekicozlem
Instagram: ozlemsaracekic

Mango Publishing, established in 2014, publishes an eclectic list of books by diverse authors—both new and established voices—on topics ranging from business, personal growth, women's empowerment, LGBTQ studies, health, and spirituality to history, popular culture, time management, decluttering, lifestyle, mental wellness, aging, and sustainable living. We were recently named 2019 *and* 2020's #1 fastest growing independent publisher by *Publishers Weekly*. Our success is driven by our main goal, which is to publish high quality books that will entertain readers as well as make a positive difference in their lives

Our readers are our most important resource; we value your input, suggestions, and ideas. We'd love to hear from you—after all, we are publishing books for you!

Please stay in touch with us and follow us at:

Facebook: Mango Publishing
Twitter: @MangoPublishing
Instagram: @MangoPublishing
LinkedIn: Mango Publishing
Pinterest: Mango Publishing

Newsletter: mangopublishinggroup.com/newsletter

Join us on Mango's journey to reinvent publishing, one book at a time.